THE INDIANA VOTER

Melvyn Hammarberg

THE INDIANA VOTER

The Historical Dynamics of Party Allegiance During the 1870s

THE UNIVERSITY OF CHICAGO PRESS
Chicago and London

MELVYN HAMMARBERG is associate professor of American Civilization at the University of Pennsylvania. He is the author of several articles in professional journals.

THE UNIVERSITY OF CHICAGO PRESS, CHICAGO 60637
THE UNIVERSITY OF CHICAGO PRESS, LTD., LONDON

© 1977 by The University of Chicago
All rights reserved. Published 1977
Printed in the United States of America
82 81 80 79 78 77   9 8 7 6 5 4 3 2 1

Library of Congress Cataloging in Publication Data

Hammarberg, Melvyn
 The Indiana voter.

 Bibliography: p.
 Includes index.
 1. Elections—Indiana. 2. Voting—Indiana.
 3. Voting research—Indiana. I. Title.
 JK5695.H35   324'.2   76-17700
 ISBN 0-226-31516-9

For Carol

Contents

Acknowledgments
xi

Introduction
1

1
Social and Political Issues of Late Nineteenth-Century Midwestern Politics
5

2
Indiana's Electorate in Midwestern Politics, 1860–1900
18

3
The *People's Guide* Counties: A "Grass Roots" Sample of Individual Voters
51

Contents

4
Probing the Social and Economic Structure of
Indiana's Rural Electorate
62

5
Assessing the Ethnic and Religious Composition of Indiana's
Rural Electorate
90

6
Party Allegiance among Indiana's Farmers and Townsmen
118

7
Indiana's Election Dynamics and the Power of
Party Allegiance, 1868-1880
142

Conclusion
177

Appendix A
Voter Transitions between Parties for Indiana's
National Elections, 1868-1880
181

Appendix B
Designing a Sample from Incomplete Historical Lists
193

Appendix C
The Federal Census of 1870 and Measurement of Error on Age
210

Contents

Notes
219

Bibliography
239

Index
247

Acknowledgments

It is a pleasure to thank publicly the many persons who helped make this book possible. Murray G. Murphey guided my initial research and served as a consistent and supportive advisor. Robert M. Zemsky read, criticized, and stimulated my thinking and presentation from the initial draft to the final one. Richard Jensen first suggested to me the importance of the *People's Guide* directories, from which much of the data of this work are derived, and encouraged my use of them in a way distinct from his own.

I was especially privileged to work and study for a year at the Center for Political Studies, Institute for Social Research, The University of Michigan, and am indebted to Leslie Kish, Jerome M. Clubb, and Philip E. Converse for making that period an intellectually exciting and rewarding one. It substantially expanded the horizons of this book and sharpened its analysis. Allan G. Bogue, both then and after, further encouraged me and commented at several points on drafts of the manuscript. Rosie M. Smith and Una L. Deutsch produced the typed manuscript and aided its form.

My wife, Carol, our children, and my parents, each in their own way, supported and encouraged my efforts with love and affection, and followed this task to its completion. To each I say, thank you.

Introduction

Several distinct lines of cleavage cut through Indiana's electorate during the 1870s. Some of these lines were social, separating farmers and villages, laborers and shopkeepers; others were cultural, marking foreigners, native Americans, Protestants and Catholics. Some lines of cleavage followed gradients of class, occupational status, and religious involvement; others had a geographic basis, distinguishing voters by their places of birth and county of settlement. But above all, boundaries in this electorate were political, marking Democrats, Republicans, and Independents. No single cutting of Indiana's electorate was sharp and precise, nor did any one fault line alone determine the winning candidates from among those who fought election battles from 1868 to 1880. But taken together, these lines of cleavage formed the several breaks in the body politic along which civic participation and partisan voting ran. They marked, directed, and constrained Indiana's electoral dynamics in the Granger and Greenback era.

It will be our task to describe these lines of cleavage among Indiana's ordinary citizens and to measure the impact on voting returns during the 1870s of the subgroups distinguished by them. Our description will rest on new data, much like the social information gathered in a Gallup poll of public opinion. These

Introduction

new data are supplied by the *People's Guide*s, a set of business, political, and religious directories for nine central Indiana counties, located in the area surrounding Indianapolis.[1] In all, nearly 40,000 persons lived in those counties, and many supplied information in 1873 or 1874 about their place and year of birth, their settlement and residence in Indiana, their occupation, religious preference, and party allegiance. These *People's Guide* directories provide a basis for the first sample of mass party attachments among individual voters in any nineteenth-century electorate. They will allow us to paint a picture of Indiana's electorate during the 1870s that in many ways is comparable to the kind of picture obtained from present-day voter surveys.

One hundred years ago the sampling and interview techniques for conducting a mass survey were unknown, of course.[2] Population coverage by compilers of the *People's Guide* directories was partial at best; many persons were not included in those compilations. And while information about the individuals who were included was relatively rich, not all of the questions we might have asked were included by the original compilers; answers in the directories were simple and direct, lacking the further probes that might more fully flesh out their meaning. These limits of coverage and information mean that the *People's Guide*s alone will not suffice to establish our sample or to capture a full understanding of voting behavior among Hoosiers during the 1870s. We must become detectives and combine other sources with the *People's Guide*s in order to understand and use for our purposes the information they contain. The federal census manuscript returns are one such source. Their use will help guarantee coverage of the voting-age population in the nine central counties and will supply additional information about the individual voters drawn as a sample from those counties.

But our understanding of Indiana, its social structure, and the voting behavior of Hoosiers will have to range wider than even these two rich sources, especially as we seek to measure election dynamics. The direct evidence for individuals and their party attachments must be compared with their voting behavior indirectly, using aggregate data drawn from county census and election returns. In particular, the county census and election

Introduction

returns will allow us to measure the impact on voting behavior during the 1870s of the subgroups distinguished in our sample of individual voters; they will enable us to develop a quantitative model of election dynamics during the 1870s. We can, I believe, by insight, by inductive theory, by drawing on previous research, by hypothesis formation, and by special recovery techniques—using the *People's Guide* directories and the federal manuscript census returns to characterize individual voters, and using aggregate census data and election returns to characterize county electorates—seek to confirm old insights and frame new ones. Guided by theory and testing our hypotheses against these kinds of data, we will seek to offer a fresh picture of Indiana as a past midwestern political battleground.[3]

The picture of Indiana we will paint will be an analysis of the mass electorate itself, not a narrative history of the parties, their leaders, or special political events. We will proceed in a series of steps. First, we set down the main lines of argument that have informed previous discussions of late nineteenth-century midwestern political history. These arguments are, if you will, the theoretical views of prior researchers about voting behavior in this period and area. The second chapter introduces quantitative evidence at the state level about party competition in Indiana from the Civil War to the turn of the century and then isolates the nine *People's Guide* counties within the state for a detailed view of their internal structure during the 1870s.

Chapter 3 introduces the *People's Guide* directories themselves, which listed individuals who lived in the nine *People's Guide* counties. It describes, briefly, how those individuals were sampled in relation to the federal census manuscript returns and offers our view of how party attachments among individual voters may be understood. Chapters 4, 5, and 6 each show how the social composition of the nine *People's Guide* counties was related to the composition of all counties in the state. Each chapter then describes major lines of cleavage among individual voters within those counties, and the nature of economic, cultural, and social cleavages in relation to the party system and major party support. The final chapter develops our model of election dynamics during the decade of the 1870s, generalized

3

Introduction

from the nine sample counties to all counties of the state, and shows how those dynamics were a function of party allegiance. It shows as well the special role that rural farmers played in giving those dynamics their particular character. Finally, three appendixes detailing technical concerns of this research, but of more general import as well, are included.

1

Social and Political Issues of Late Nineteenth-Century Midwestern Politics

Seeking to describe and account for late nineteenth-century midwestern mass politics, including those of Indiana, historians and political scientists have advanced several different lines of argument. The older, standard, historical accounts traced the origins of successive third-party movements in the electorate, whether Greenback or Populist, and showed their relationship to rural uprisings and the development of farmers' organizations.[1] More recently, revisionists have quarreled with this focus, noting that third parties rarely had a large political impact on voting results and arguing instead that ethnoreligious groups served as primary vehicles for interparty conflict.[2] These historical studies have been augmented by the work of political scientists who now urge attention to legal and institutional factors in their effect on turnout and party loyalty as revealed by the vote in successive elections.[3] Together, the standard accounts of farm organization, the revisionist emphasis on cultural group structure, and the new political studies of turnout and partisanship define the problems which must be faced in understanding Indiana's vote during the 1870s.

Solon Buck, herald of the standard historical view, largely accepted nineteenth-century rural reform rhetoric as the farmer's view of himself and his situation.[4] Buck attributed to most

Chapter One

midwestern farmers the characteristics of a highly self-conscious class bent on altering its economic position by collective organization, independent third-party action, and agitation for political and economic reform. In Buck's view, economic stress on farmers stemmed from industrialization following the Civil War. Their discontent and their political response to economic stress became most serious in the great prairie states of the upper Mississippi Valley, from Ohio and Indiana on the east to the frontier's edge in Kansas and Nebraska, areas where the staple cereal crops of wheat and corn were produced; only later did this discontent arise in the South of tobacco and cotton.

Initially, Buck held that the farmer's problem in the Midwest was one of distribution, with the cost of transporting grain to market and the cost exacted by various middlemen continually constraining group prosperity. While new railroads crisscrossed the prairies, their promise to the farmer of cheap transportation was undercut by the methods used to finance their operations. Railroad promoters secured their capital funds not only from private individuals but also from local, county, and state governments and from the federal government. This capital debt, incurred, so the farmer thought, to enhance cheap transportation for agricultural products, was instead laid back on him in the form of taxes on his land if not in worthless bonds. Discriminatory freight rates, free passes, bribes, and special point-to-point charges similarly conspired to keep the farmer's costs high. In Buck's view, the farmer felt he paid dearly.

> The farmer who had invested [in railroad promotions] with a view to the development of the country ... found himself with a mortgage on his land, his railroad stock worthless, and the expected advantages from the road a chimera. His taxes, moreover, were increased by the investment or donation which his town or county had made for the same purpose. This was one of the principal causes which operated to produce a somewhat blind antagonism among the agricultural population towards the railroads and everything connected with them.[5]

Further, in accord with physiocratic doctrine, Buck argued that farmers viewed society as two great classes, the producers and the nonproducers, the latter including all middlemen engaged in the distribution of services and products between the producing classes.[6] The middlemen faced most directly by farmers were the commission merchants, the grain dealers, and the buyers through whom they disposed of their produce on the one hand, and the various agents and retailers from whom they bought their supplies on the other. Farmers often purchased on credit, both for land and supplies, and at rates of interest which they viewed as high and exorbitant. Caught in a credit system based on liens for subsequent crops, many farmers were chronic debtors, standing in a competitively dependent situation against merchants, real estate agents, bankers, and those they viewed as "monopolistic" manufacturers.

If farmers believed that interest on their debts often ran high, along with their taxes, Buck also argued that an unstable currency added to farm costs. And cheap lands opening westward for other settlers, coupled with new commercial fertilizers and farming methods, increased crop production while driving crop prices down. The farmers' economic life became one depression cycle after another, punctuated most dramatically in 1873, again in the mid-1880s, and then again in 1893. Thus, Buck found it quite reasonable to view farmers as a depressed economic class, consciously bent on altering its relative position by collective organization into Grange cooperatives through the Patrons of Husbandry, by local independent action, and by agitation for political and economic reform through the National Greenback party.[7]

John Hicks extended a similar economic analysis of farmers' grievances from the Midwest to the Far West and the South from the 1870s through the 1890s.[8] In the 1880s new farmers' organizations arose—the National Farmers' Alliance of the northwest and the National Farmers' Alliance and Industrial Union, shadowed by the Colored Farmers' Alliance in the South, each as a congeries of smaller local "wheels" and clubs. In the Midwest, in Hicks's terms, the power of these farm organizations lay "in the complete and thoroughgoing awakening of class consciousness," culminating politically in the Populist movement of the 1890s.[9] More recently, Stanley Parsons extended and modified this view. Examining the balance of political power between rural farmers and small-town cliques in Nebraska, he showed the political awakening of farmers and their attack on village political leaders.[10] For Indiana, however, the older account still stands, applied by Emma Lou Thornbrough to monetary and economic discontent among Hoosier farmers during the 1870s.[11]

Two problems are posed by these studies: a view of rural class structure and a view of farmers as political actors. Recall that most economic and social data for the nineteenth century have been aggregated to the county or state level so that lines of cleavage based on wealth or occupation have been drawn between urban and rural areas rather than within them. Yet, a class structure and wealth or occupational differences are internal to both areas, and the roots of these differences must be laid bare before an adequate account of their aggregate import for politics can be seen. The relation between wealth gradients or status differences by occupation and the parties is a question that must first be viewed among individuals.

The primary problem, however, is not whether there was a rural class structure but, if there was, what it meant for the political behavior of farmers and villagers alike, and whether farmers as political actors were as cohesive, highly informed, and strongly motivated a group as the standard accounts imply. Neither Buck nor Hicks made any attempt to measure the effect of this assumption, to account for more than the gross appearance of third parties in the party system, or to gauge party support among farmers as compared to other kinds of social groups. Nor has this been done for Indiana in the 1870s.

Largely sweeping aside the economic and class framework of these standard accounts, the new revisionists have focused on ethnoreligious groups as the basis for understanding late nineteenth-century midwestern electoral behavior. While a number of younger scholars, armed with skill in quantitative analysis, have offered studies along these lines, the basic premises and directions were laid out by Lee Benson nearly two decades ago.[12] Full interpretations of the Midwest have appeared in major monographs by Paul Kleppner and Richard Jensen.[13]

To these revisionists, previous historians have described past politics largely from the top down. That is, the revisionists claim that the way in which particular elites—newspaper editors, major businessmen, or party leaders—pictured mass events cannot be taken as a description of the way the masses themselves acted. For among such elites economic events and class conflicts often received more weight than among the mass of voters, where group, rather than wealth or occupational, identity had greater strength. Elite views, then, may prove quite illusory with respect to actual political support, which often arose from sources quite different from those presumed by high-placed observers. The only adequate account of party support, the revisionists argue, comes through an examination of the actual mass voting patterns themselves, together with their social and economic correlates.[14] Samuel Hays, making use of Benson's insights, asked historians to look at "grass roots" voting patterns, at the lowest levels of aggregation, as one way to pinpoint sources of party support in the mass electorate. As his example he used precinct returns for gubernatorial elections in Iowa between 1887 and 1918, observing that "economic issues, such as corporation control, seem to have been almost irrelevant in the face of a range of social and cultural differences involving nationality and religion, which centered primarily on prohibition and Sunday observance."[15]

Both Kleppner and Jensen broadened the insights of Benson and Hays by considering the local ethnocultural "structure of human action" in the Midwest from the 1870s through the 1890s. Turning their attention to voting outcomes at regional, state, county, township, and ward levels, and, in Jensen's case, using individual-level information as well, both authors showed that only a small fraction of voters ever aligned themselves with any third-party movement.[16] While numerous Independent, Greenback, Prohibition, Populist, and other third-party candidates entered electoral contests, the major political battle was invariably waged between Republicans and Democrats. Consequently, Jensen and Kleppner argued, the behavior of the electorate in its varying division between the major parties was the element that required primary explanation, not the rise of third parties.

More important, rather than focusing on farmers as the primary political actors in the late nineteenth century, both authors urged that past electoral behavior makes most sense when seen as the effect of cultural issues playing on the ethnoreligious group

Chapter One

identities of the mass electorate. Without denying the effect of gross economic events, such as the major depressions, or of urban and rural differences, both described the major party alignment in the 1870s and 1880s by means of an underlying ethnoreligious continuum composed of Republican-pietists on one end and Democratic-liturgicals (Jensen) or Democratic-ritualists (Kleppner) on the other.[17] In Kleppner's words:

> Divergent values within one structure of society, the religious order, had their parallel in conflicting partisan identifications in society's political structure. As they pursued their particular political goals, the pietists entered into an alliance with the party espousing positive governmental action, the party of "great moral ideas," the Republicans. In defense of their values, ritualists turned to the major opposition party, the party which opposed an expansion of the coercive power of the state, the Democrats.[18]

Both authors then argued that the ordering of party strength by a continuum of ethnoreligious groups was relatively constant through the 1870s and 1880s, giving most elections their fundamental dynamics. Each suggested that the depression beginning in 1893 had the effect of loosening these old ethnoreligious party loyalties and that diametrically opposed changes in the leadership and appeals of the two national parties by 1896 caused a radical shift in party strength and composition, giving the Republicans a long-term hegemony.[19] Thus, the views of Kleppner and Jensen offer an interest theory of voting based on general, but fundamental, cultural groups.

Pieces of the ethnoreligious-group view are readily apparent in earlier work on Indiana. William G. Carleton, on whom Thornbrough's work largely rested, pointed to the small pockets of ethnics in Indiana—mainly German and Irish—and to its clusters of Roman Catholics, and showed that the Democratic vote tended to be higher in such ethnic and religious areas.[20] As an early work using county-level data, Carleton's study is penetrating, though unencumbered by the full ethnoreligious determinism of the later revisionists; and Carleton held basically to an economic viewpoint. Nonetheless, lines of cultural cleavage among individual

Social and Political Issues

voters must be recognized in Indiana if we are to fully explore the meaning of these cleavages for county-level voting patterns during the 1870s.[21] Whether Indiana's ethnoreligious groups formed a continuum of basic political coalitions, having an organizational basis in local denominational and ethnic institutions whose members responded to political issues that were salient to their different values, remains a basic issue for the revisionists' argument.

Finally, a third set of studies poses significant problems for understanding Indiana's vote during the 1870s. These studies deal with party allegiance and turnout—past and present—and with the legal framework of elections. Properly political subjects, these issues have received their most extended discussion in the work of several prominent political scientists and have generated a lively controversy in the recent literature.

The basic stance among most political scientists is that party allegiance is itself a primary means by which the electorate is structured, having its own dynamics quite apart from those induced by social, economic, religious, or other population groupings, or by the way an individual has cast his ballot in the past. This view of party allegiance as a fundamental cleavage in the electorate was stated most forcefully for the mid-twentieth century in *The American Voter,* whose authors wrote:

> The fact that [great numbers of voters have party attachments that persist through time] is confirmed by survey data on individual people. In a survey interview most of our citizens freely classify themselves as Republicans or Democrats and indicate that these loyalties have persisted through a number of elections. Few factors are of greater importance for our national elections than the lasting attachments of tens of millions of Americans to one of the parties. These loyalties establish a basic division of electoral strength within which the competition of particular campaigns takes place. And they are an important factor in assuring the stability of the party system itself.[22]

Among the several kinds of events ordered by party allegiance are perceptions and evaluations of both issues and candidates,

Chapter One

and associated with this allegiance in the mid-twentieth century as well has been the degree of political involvement among citizens, ranging higher among those most strongly attached to one or the other party and lower among those who have considered themselves Independents. But most important, party allegiance has served to anchor in prior commitments the shifts in voting behavior of the mass citizenry.

If party allegiance anchors voting behavior, these political scientists also argue that voter turnout has had important effects on the same shifts in the total vote.[23] For as turnout has varied across population groups—and thereby across the parties—an additional dynamic has been given to the changes registered in the results of successive elections. Both voter partisanship and voter participation, then, have entered as primary determinants of election results.

Part of the historical import of these views arises from an illuminating essay offered several years ago by W. Dean Burnham, who developed a number of indicators of dramatic change in voting at the turn of the twentieth century.[24] Like Kleppner's and Jensen's recent work, Burnham's paper focused on electoral realignment in the 1890s, suggesting something of a "watershed" in electoral behavior between the late nineteenth-century American voting universe and its twentieth-century counterpart. Using V. O. Key's idea of "critical elections," Burnham suggested that temporal boundaries as well as spatial ones could be placed around voter partisanship and voter participation. Thereafter, he expressed an informed skepticism toward any easy extension of present-day survey research findings on individual voters to the period before 1896.[25]

Burnham's five indicators all dealt with the aggregate effects of voter participation and voter partisanship over a series of elections. The best known of these indicators is voter turnout itself, which provides a direct measure of mass participation in elections. From a high and steady rate approaching 80 percent participation over five presidential elections before 1896 this measure dropped precipitously to about 65 percent over the succeeding five elections, and then to a low rate approaching 50 percent in the elections of the 1920s. Two additional measures of participation indicated equally dramatic shifts. One of them termed "roll-off," was taken as the difference in voting rates between the most and least important offices on the ballot; this measure barely registered any magnitude before the 1890s but became increasingly visible after the turn of the century. The other, termed "drop-off," was taken as the difference in turnout between presidential and succeeding off-year congressional elections; it also showed an increasing mean difference beginning in the 1890s. Thus, these three measures, giving quite parallel results, suggested a dramatic secular decay in mass levels of electoral participation from the late nineteenth to the early twentieth century.[26]

Two further measures tapped aspects of party allegiance and voting loyalty. Split-ticket voting, indexed by the absolute difference between the highest and lowest partisan percentage among state-wide offices, appeared to be dwindling to the point of extinction prior to the 1890s but increased rapidly toward the 1930s. And the final indicator, the mean partisan swing, measured by the absolute change in a party's proportion of the vote from one on-year election to the next off-year election, also showed an increased amplitude during the first decades of the twentieth century. Burnham observed that these transformations flowing from the 1890s pointed to "a dissociation from politics ... among a growing segment of the eligible electorate and an apparent deterioration of the bonds of party linkage between electorate and government."[27] Jensen makes a similar point for the Midwest from his assessment of voter upheavals in the 1890s;

> the underlying conditions which produced [a long-run realignment], loosened the party loyalties of millions of voters and stimulated a revival of antipartyism.... An unexpected consequence of the decline in party loyalty, however, was a sharp decline in turnout and other modes of popular participation between 1900 and 1920, together with a decay in the level and sophistication of information about public affairs among the people, as evidenced by the increasing superficiality and sensationalism of the press.[28]

While few scholars have quarreled with the changes registered by Burnham's indicators, a continuing controversy has followed

Chapter One

his suggested explanation of them, revolving partly around whether legal and institutional factors can account for the shifts and partly around whether current survey relationships measuring party loyalty in a mass electorate can be extended to simulate similar unmeasured relationships in the historical past.

These issues are interrelated, and both are important for Indiana in the 1870s. First, survey results in the mid-twentieth century show regular, if moderate, positive relationships between levels of political interest and involvement and two prime demographic variables, levels of education and age.[29] In these two respects, the current electorate clearly stands as better educated and with an age composition of increasing longitude when compared to Indiana's or the nation's in the 1870s. Yet Burnham's data show that political interest, to the extent measured by his participation indicators, dropped off dramatically from nineteenth-century levels, a finding quite at odds with the survey relationships. Further, present measures of political interest and involvement also show rural populations, like that of Indiana in the 1870s, to be less interested and involved in elections than their urban counterparts, while Burnham's measures would indicate just the opposite for rural America in the late nineteenth century. Rural turnout rates then showed consistently the highest magnitudes.[30] Hence, Burnham has suggested that it is impossible to extrapolate current survey relationships backward in time and that in temporal terms scholars must deal with pre-1896 electorates as if they arose from a totally foreign political system.

Philip Converse has been most prominent among those tackling the Burnham work.[31] A willing advocate of the temporal extension of survey findings, Converse reexamined Burnham's contention that partisanship fell away and voter apathy grew after 1896. Two clusters of various counterhypotheses were offered, dealing with the legal framework of voting on the one hand and with institutional practices in the conduct of elections on the other. Both clusters center on election reforms in the late nineteenth and early twentieth century.

Among legal changes associated with election reforms two appear general and striking in their political consequences. One was associated with the introduction of the secret, government-prepared Australian ballot. The effect of this legal change on split-ticket voting has been fully treated by Jerrold Rusk, cited by Converse.[32] Initially introduced to the American arena in 1889, the Australian ballot diffused rapidly during the 1890s in two forms. The original, pure form employed a ballot organized by office blocs without party labels to identify the affiliation of candidates. Massachusetts adopted this form but added the identifying labels. Indiana, however, initiated a variant, in keeping with prior practice, that was organized by party columns. While both were secret ballots, entailing additional provisions for the maintenance of secrecy, the Indiana form clearly emphasized straight-party choice while the Massachusetts form forced a pattern of party search on the voter. Rusk showed that the timing of introduction among the states and variation in shifts from one form of the Australian ballot to the other both correlated with the magnitudes of increased split-ticket voting, patterned by the particular form adopted.[33] Thus, while the goal of this reform was the preservation of secrecy in the act of voting, it had the unintended consequence of increasing split-ticket voting just at the time Burnham's measures register declines in party loyalty.

The second legal change noted by Converse involved the development of voter registration systems. Using work done by Harris in 1929, Converse was able to distinguish between "weak" and "strong" forms of these laws, the temporal variation and regional diffusion of their adoption, and their urban and rural application.[34] While the identity of voters was the primary issue in all such systems, the "weak" laws called for little more than the compilation of official lists of voters' names, often controlled by local political officials. The diffusion of this minimal control appears to have been spotty before the 1890s. The "strong" systems, involving forms of preelection registration—sometimes repetitive before each election—and the use of identifying signatures, came into prominence between 1890 and 1910. Some of these systems required a designation of partisanship and were associated with the institution of party primaries; others did not.

Converse suggested that the adoption of these registration systems across the states and regions had an urban-versus-rural dimension. Urban reformers, who had previously had "weak"

Chapter One

registration laws imposed on them in their efforts to curb city political machines, themselves worked for "strong" systems that would cover rural areas as well. It is readily apparent that the "strong" laws would inhibit the voting participation of the less motivated citizens and those sufficiently uninvolved in politics not to plan ahead by registering to vote. Consequently, the precipitous drop in turnout rates, even more dramatic in rural areas than in urban ones after the turn of the century, would be accounted for by the introduction of "strong" voter registration systems.

Certain institutional practices surrounding elections may have been involved in these shifts as well. One hypothesis is of large-scale rural fraud through the use of "repeat voters" and other methods of adding to a party's vote total, artificially inflating earlier turnout rates in rural areas. Urban instances of election fraud—the voting of fictitious names, of the dead, of the migrant—have been commented on so widely that the major question is only the relative magnitude. The rural aspect of these practices, however, remains largely hidden but at least accords with the rapid drop in rural turnout on the advent of full registration.[35]

If legal and institutional changes can account for the major shifts in voting participation between the late nineteenth and early twentieth century, and the ease with which party defection was expressed, then it is possible that present survey relationships in the mass electorate may also hold in earlier periods. While we cannot take for granted that party allegiance and voter participation were the same a century ago as they appear in survey research today, their positive and negative relationships to other demographic and social variables can serve as useful hypotheses for viewing election dynamics in the earlier period, once the particular legal and institutional circumstances are clearly understood. Perhaps Indiana will not be a foreign land in the 1870s after all.

Not many years ago most historians believed they knew what midwestern politics were all about, namely, the farmers and whether they would raise corn or raise hell. It was claimed that the farmers, hit harder by the depression in the 1870s and 1890s

Social and Political Issues

than others, arose as a class conscious of its need for power. The revisionists sought to demolish this class-conscious economic view. Possessed of a sense of destiny and armed with social-science theories of group behavior, the revisionists saw ethnocultural values as the inner springs of political action, perhaps manipulated at the turn of the century by party professionals, elite reformers, or robber barons. The revision of the revisionists remains in the making. But the new questions being asked, and the need for new data to resolve partially some of the old issues while new ones are still being wrestled with, provide a pressing concern. A systematic treatment of election data is sorely needed. Informed attention to legal and institutional constraints (or their lack) for voting participation is required. And for particular electorates, like that of Indiana in the 1870s, a detailed picture of interior cleavages among individual voters is a kind of richness by which all may profit.

2

Indiana's Electorate in Midwestern Politics, 1860-1900

A main crossroads leading Americans to new homes in the West, Indiana was bounded at statehood in 1816 by Kentucky and Ohio to the south and east, and by Michigan and Illinois territories on the north and west. By the Civil War, Indiana had drawn its people from a wide variety of states to the northeast and south and had made them its own. These people brought the political parties to Indiana and supported them across the counties of the state. In turn, Hoosiers sent some of their own settlers onward to the newer states opening farther west.[1] Perhaps in part because Indiana stood on the axis of regional population movements, its party competition reflected election dynamics that were close to the nation's at large, ones that made politicians very wary.

Indiana was a crucible of the nation's party competition. Elections were nowhere more closely fought after the Civil War than among Hoosiers. And nowhere was civic participation higher. Somehow, Hoosiers showed the uncanny knack (or luck) to cast their majority vote with the national winner in every presidential contest until 1900. They were no better national prognosticators than other voters, of course, contrary to what some politicians believed. But Indiana's winning way was not lost on party leaders either. As one Republican professional wrote in 1876: "A bloody shirt campaign, with money, and Indiana is safe; a financial campaign and no money, and we are beaten."[2]

To see just how politically competitive the Hoosier state was during the late nineteenth century, party competition and citizen participation must be viewed not only in their temporal variation but in comparison to those of the neighboring states of the surrounding region as well. And to see the state-wide meaning of individual reports of party allegiance from the *People's Guide* counties, election results in those counties must be viewed against results across all counties of the state.

The contours of Indiana's presidential vote during the whole nineteenth century are shown in figure 2.1. This figure is constructed so that the percentage division between the major parties is graphed on the top and bottom, running horizontally, separated through the center by the smaller third party proportions. Prior to 1860, fairly wide swings in the party division of the vote occurred, rising upward for Jackson and then falling sharply in the 1830s. This period was one of strong in-migration, a period when the identities of the competing parties changed. After 1830, the Democratic party was successively arrayed against the National Republican party, the Whigs, and then the modern Republicans.[3] As population increased, new settlers had proportionally less impact on the vote, and, in succeeding elections, with one party's nominal identity fixed, the wider fluctuations tended toward a generally even-balanced division. From the mid-1840s onward, then, the two major parties stood opposed to each other, separated in varying degrees only by the intrusion of successive third-party movements, most notably during the 1850s, the late 1870s, and the 1890s. By any account, in the late nineteenth century Indiana was a strong, well-balanced, relatively stable, and continuously competitive two-party battleground.

This long-term stability in levels of competition for geographic communities has been observed before. V. O. Key, Jr., for one, pointed to it as something of a "standing decision," whether among townships, counties or states.[4] He saw clearly that such geographic communities, in spite of election-to-election variation, showed characteristic partisan "centers of gravity" that fixed levels of competition over rather extended spans of time. He characterized this long-term stability as a basic stance of the

Chapter Two

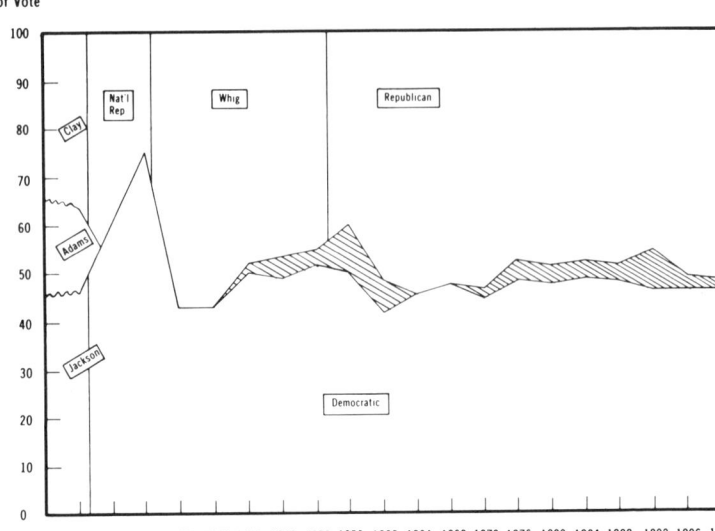

Fig. 2.1 Nineteenth-century party competition in Indiana

community which "fixed a [partisan] line of siege" and as a "benchmark for the identification and analysis of particular electoral shifts."[5] Only occasionally did he find that such centers of gravity exhibited a "critical" readjustment to a new level or show a sustained trend in one partisan direction only.

Key's insights and the nature of Indiana's party competition can be given direct numerical measurement. His "standing decision" is readily viewed as the mean in a broad time-series of elections, with election-to-election variation measured by departures from that mean and their squares averaged as a standard deviation. Table 2.1 arrays Indiana's presidential vote for the two major parties from 1860 to 1900 and carries out these measurements. These data show that the total size of Indiana's voting universe expanded about two and a half times over this forty-year span, from roughly 250,000 to almost 650,000 voters. Nonetheless, the Republican percentage of the two-party vote remained very near the fifty-fifty point of division between victory and defeat (in column 5), characterized by a Republican mean of 51.4

Table 2.1. Indiana: Presidential Vote, 1860–1900

	(1) Presidential Election Year	(2) Republican Vote	(3) Democratic Vote	(4) Total Two-party Vote	(5) Republican %	(6) Election Deviation	(7) Deviation Squared
1.	1860	139,033	115,509	254,542	54.62	3.23	10.4329
2.	1864	150,422	130,223	280,645	53.60	2.21	4.8841
3.	1868	176,552	166,980	343,532	51.39	0.0	0.0
4.	1872	186,147	163,632	349,779	53.22	1.83	3.3489
5.	1876	208,111	213,526	421,637	49.36	−2.03	4.1209
6.	1880	232,164	225,522	457,686	50.73	−0.66	0.4356
7.	1884	238,480	244,992	483,472	49.33	−2.06	4.2436
8.	1888	263,361	261,013	524,374	50.22	−1.17	1.3689
9.	1892	255,615	262,740	518,355	49.31	−2.08	4.3264
10.	1896	323,754	305,573	629,327	51.44	0.05	0.0025
11.	1900	336,063	309,584	645,647	52.05	0.66	0.4356
					565.27		33.5994
					$\bar{X} = 51.39$		$S^2 = 3.3599$
							$S = 1.83$

SOURCE: Svend Petersen, *A Statistical History of the American Presidential Elections* (New York: Frederick Ungar, 1963) is the source for these figures.

percent. Taking this mean as a baseline for Indiana's competitive "standing decision," the shifts in the Republican percentage for each particular election (in column 6) show three "runs" where the results advantaged one of the parties, moving toward added Republican strength from 1860 through 1872, toward the Democrats from 1876 through 1892, and then toward the Republicans again at the turn of the century. Within these periods of party favor, both the election of 1868 and the widely recognized "critical" election of 1896 barely registered any net party change at all, seen most clearly by the zero-to-small squared election deviations (in column 7).[6] Thus, Indiana's "standing decision" was not only a competitive one, near the fifty-fifty point of division, but was also a "tightly" bounded one, on average moving less than two percentage points in either direction from the Republican mean (the standard deviation is 1.8).

These observations provoke two questions: how likely were the Democrats to win in Indiana, given this close balance between the parties, and how did the competition in Indiana compare to that in other states? These questions, too, can be given fairly direct numerical answers. Arriving at answers, however, requires as a mathematical model the standard normal curve. Donald Stokes argued that, for the national electorate, election-by-election shifts in the vote from the grand mean over time might be viewed as relatively independent "samplings" of the direction and magnitude of short-term forces favoring first one party and then the other; so may those for Indiana or any other state.[7] He further assumed that such shifts are distributed in roughly normal fashion, which also does the Indiana data no harm. Then, by fitting the empirical estimates of a mean and standard deviation to the standard normal curve, it is possible to calculate just how far away from the empirical time-series mean was the fifty-fifty division point, on the other side of which Democratic victory would be obtained, and to find the probability of an election result falling in that Democratic region.[8]

Figure 2.2 shows a diagram of the displacement of the fifty-fifty division point from Indiana's Republican mean during the period between 1860 and 1900, fitted to the standard normal curve in terms of the empirical estimate of election-to-election varia-

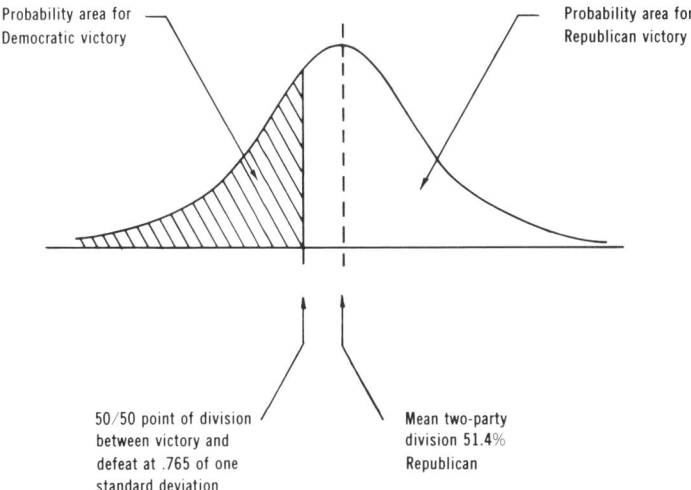

Fig. 2.2 Time-series mean and standard deviation fitted to the normal curve for Indiana elections, 1860–1900

tion. The two main areas under the curve represent the probabilities of Republican and Democratic victory, centered about the fifty-fifty division point. Thus, given the estimate of election-to-election shifts (measured by the standard deviation) and the fixed Republican mean, the probability of a Democratic victory was about .22, encompassed by the Democratic region under the normal curve. In fact, the Democratic party carried the state in 1876, 1884, and 1892, that is, in three out of eleven, or 27 percent, of the presidential elections from the Civil War to 1900.

This way of calculating a probability estimate for victory by the opposition party sharpens the meaning of the term "party competition," for it includes as empirical conditions not only the mean displacement of the majority party from the fifty-fifty division but also the average variation in election results. It also allows a direct comparison of one state's temporal distribution to others by fitting the different state means and standard deviations to the standard normal curve. When this fitting is done, a scale of levels of party competition results that ranges from zero at the lowest level of competition to .50 at the highest level. Values in

Chapter Two

the .20 to .40 range, then, indicate relatively competitive two-party states, in which short-term shifts offered sufficient opportunity for opposition party victory.

The Democrats had nearly a one-in-four chance to win in Indiana during the late nineteenth century. How did this level of competition measure up against that of other states in the Midwest? How did it compare to Democratic chances in the nation as a whole? Table 2.2 displays the mean percent Republican of the two-party vote for a wide range of states surrounding Indiana, their standard deviations, and the probability estimates for opposition victory. Consider first those states to the east and south of Indiana—Ohio, Pennsylvania, Kentucky, and Tennessee —from which Hoosier settlers were most heavily drawn. Of those states, both Kentucky and Tennessee were Democratic strongholds with Republican means in the low 40 percent range; the others were Republican. Of all four, however, only Kentucky had sufficient election-to-election variation to register party competition at the .15 level. Pennsylvania, Ohio, and Tennessee were even less competitive over time than Kentucky. States to the north and west of Indiana—from Michigan, Wisconsin, and Minnesota to Illinois, Iowa, Missouri, Kansas, and Nebraska—showed even less interparty competition, with probability estimates for opposition victory in presidential contests all below the .11 level. Compared to all of these states, Indiana had a high level of party competition. This level matched closely the Democrats' one-in-four chance for the nation as a whole during this same period, as shown by the final entry in this table.

Reflect for a moment on the meaning of these results. W. Dean Burnham, for one, has contended that the presidential election of 1896 signaled a dramatic shift from competitive to noncompetitive state political systems as part of a more general "dissociation" from politics by Americans after the turn of the century.[9] When "party competition" is taken to include election-to-election variation as well as the mean displacement from the margin of victory, then these data largely show noncompetitive pre-1896 state party systems throughout the Midwest. Except in Indiana, national competition rested on compensating but noncompetitive opposition in the midwestern states even before the turn of the century. Burnham's contention, therefore, is not supported.

Indiana's Electorate, 1860-1900

Table 2.2. State-level Measures, 1860-1900

State	Mean % Republican	Standard Deviation	Probability of a Deviating Election
Indiana	51.39	1.83	.22
Ohio	52.84	1.90	.07
Pennsylvania	55.89	4.68	.11
Kentucky	41.43	8.12	.15
Tennessee	45.40	2.65	.04
Michigan	56.67	3.31	.02
Illinois	53.09	2.30	.09
Wisconsin	55.44	3.90	.08
Iowa	58.77	4.37	.02
Minnesota	60.46	2.78	.00
Missouri	45.04	1.96	.01
Kansas	63.17	6.71	.02
Nebraska	58.94	7.36	.11
The nation	52.09	3.11	.25

Further, many views of 1896 as a critical turning point overestimate the partisan aspect of change in this election. Table 2.3 shows the election-by-election departures from Republican mean levels in all presidential elections between 1860 and 1900 for Ohio, Illinois, Michigan, Wisconsin, Minnesota, Iowa, Indiana, and the nation at large. In this midwestern region, the net partisan forces measured by the deviations in 1896 hardly register the overwhelming Republican direction so readily attributed to them by those who have used only the preceding presidential election as a baseline.[10] By taking the election of 1892 as a base (as interelection correlations or election-to-election differences do), every one of these states showed a dramatic Republican "swing." But 1892 was itself *deviantly* Democratic. Hence, using that election as a baseline grossly overestimates the net pro-Republican shift, for nearly half of the shift must be attributed to a "relaxation" of the advantage gained by Democrats in the previous contest. In fact, the net partisan advantage gained by the Republicans in 1896 was well within the range of average variation over the forty-year period for each of these states. Just how "critical" 1896 was may well depend on the baseline from which change is measured.

Table 2.3. Selected State Percentage Deviations from the State Mean Percentage Republican, 1860–1900

Presidential Election Year	Nation	Ind.	Ohio	Pa.	Mich.	Ill.	Ken.	Wis.	Tenn.	Iowa	Kan.	Minn.	Mo.	Neb.
1860	5.42	3.23	2.45	1.91	0.95	−1.29		1.53		−2.68				
1864	3.06	2.21	3.49	−4.14	−0.78	1.32	−11.26	0.44		5.46		4.47		
1868	0.62	0.00	1.13	−3.69	0.31	2.60	−15.98	0.80		3.15	5.72	−1.39		5.20
1872	3.84	1.83	0.72	6.46	7.19	1.05	5.59	−0.61	2.17	6.11	3.86	0.35	−0.98	11.18
1876	−3.60	−2.03	−2.27	−4.70	−2.54	−1.27	−3.42	−4.24	−5.19	1.67	4.22	1.10	−3.38	5.57
1880	−2.04	−0.66	−0.45	−3.71	1.80	0.32	0.19	0.30	0.25	4.70	3.85	−0.53	−2.64	6.90
1884	−2.21	−2.06	−0.78	−1.26	−0.42	−1.16	2.14	−3.06	2.81	−6.13	0.86	3.33	1.19	−0.36
1888	−2.52	−1.17	−1.64	−1.82	−4.13	−1.56	4.34	−2.23	1.37	−4.72	−0.03	1.02	2.37	−1.57
1892	−3.79	−2.08	−2.78	−2.60	−4.27	−4.73	2.13	−6.38	−3.46	−5.96	−14.09[a]	−2.74	0.79	−7.74[a]
1896	0.10	0.05	−0.43	6.81	−1.37	3.50	8.60	6.39	1.59	−2.39	5.42	−5.56	0.56	−11.90
1900	1.08	0.66	0.54	6.79	3.23	1.22	7.69	7.08	0.47	0.75	−9.82	−2.39	2.11	−7.29
												2.33		

SOURCE: Petersen, *Statistical History of the American Presidential Elections*, recomputed.
[a]Opposition vote is that for Weaver, Populist candidate.

From these observations on party competition and the pattern of presidential elections between midwestern states, it is little wonder that close observers in the late nineteenth century took Indiana as a barometer of the larger, national electoral scene.[11] Its average interelection variation around a Republican mean that was close to the fifty-fifty division made the state a relatively competitive two-party arena. Its election returns matched the direction and magnitude of national party advantages at only slightly lower levels. And unlike in other states, Indiana's Democratic party had nearly the same chance of victory as did the national Democratic party itself.

These relationships were disturbed, of course, by the levels of third-party voting in each state. As table 2.4 shows, the highest levels of all third-party voting occurred in the newer states of Kansas and Nebraska, and the lowest levels were registered in the older states of Pennsylvania, Ohio, and Indiana. Partisan stability was therefore least affected in these older states. Their level of competition was less subject to the more violent shifts that occurred elsewhere.[12]

Indiana was not only a well-balanced theater of party competition in the late nineteenth century, it was also an arena of action that called forth high citizen participation. The parade of people going to the polls each election day was long. For presidential elections after 1868 this parade included virtually all classes and groups of men, from those of high station to low, whether native-born or foreign-born. Off-year congressional elections were less exciting affairs than the presidential ones, and turnout declined accordingly. But compared to other states, Indiana even then remained very active. In any election Hoosiers were as prone to arrive at the polls as they were to divide their state-wide support between the major parties. Party competition and citizen participation went hand-in-hand.

Figure 2.3 graphs the variation in turnout for presidential elections from 1860 to 1900. On average, 92 percent of Indiana's total eligible electorate regularly joined the voting parade at presidential contests. This mean level of participation centers the graph, and turnout at each succeeding election is measured as a deviation from this mean level. What this picture of civic duty

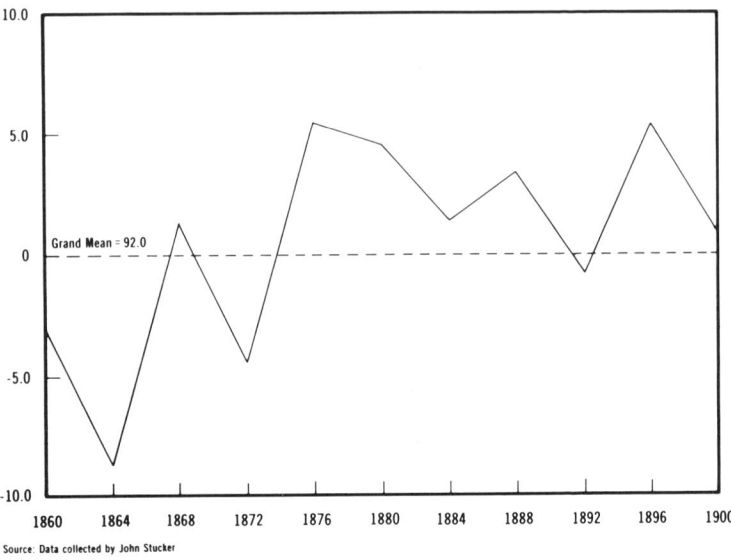

Fig. 2.3 Deviations in presidential turnout rates, Indiana, 1860-1900

shows is a very high level of participation in presidential elections, combined with a small secular trend of increasing turnout. After 1876, only one election slipped below the mean level, and the elections of 1876 and 1896 reached turnout peaks near the 97 percent mark. Nearly the whole adult male population marched to the polls in these two elections.

Presidential turnout rates, of course, were high across the whole Midwest.[13] From Pennsylvania on the east to Kansas and Nebraska on the west, participation always reached above the 50 percent mark. Mean levels of turnout across these states, and their standard deviations, are shown in the two bottom rows of table 2.5, and the body of this table shows the turnout deviations from those mean levels. Consider first the mean levels themselves. Two states to the south that sent many settlers to Indiana—Kentucky and Tennessee—had average levels of citizen participation twenty to thirty percentage points lower than those among Hoosiers and with much wider fluctuations measured by their standard deviations. To the east, Pennsylvania and Ohio also

Table 2.4. Percentage Magnitude of Total Third-Party Voting in the Midwestern Region, 1872–1900

Election	Nation	Kan.	Neb.	Ind.	Ohio	Pa.	Ill.	Mich.	Wis.	Iowa	Minn.	Mo.	Ken.	Tenn.
1872	0.5	0.6	0.0	0.4	0.6	0.3	0.7	1.9	0.4	1.1	0.0	0.9	1.2	0.0
1876	1.1	6.4	7.6	2.2	0.7	1.1	3.4	3.1	0.6	3.1	1.9	1.0	1.0	0.0
1880	3.5	9.9	4.5	2.8	1.3	2.6	4.3	10.2	3.0	10.4	2.8	8.8	4.4	2.5
1884	3.6	12.5	6.7	2.3	3.3	2.5	3.9	5.4	6.5	3.0	6.2	4.4	1.7	2.0
1888	3.6	12.5	6.7	2.3	3.3	2.5	3.9	5.4	6.5	3.0	6.2	4.4	1.7	2.0
1892	11.0	51.6[a]	43.9[a]	6.4	4.8	3.5	5.5	8.8	6.2	6.1	16.3	8.4	8.8	10.6
1896	2.3	1.1	2.3	1.2	1.1	2.7	1.7	2.6	3.1	1.7	2.5	0.8	2.2	1.6
1900	2.8	1.5	2.3	2.8	2.0	3.1	2.7	3.0	4.0	2.6	4.1	2.6	1.3	2.1
Mean	3.5	11.9	8.7	2.6	2.0	2.4	3.2	6.2	3.5	3.6	4.8	3.4	2.8	2.4

SOURCE: Petersen, *Statistical History of the American Presidential Elections*, recomputed.
[a]Populist fusion with the Democrats.

Table 2.5. Deviations from Mean Turnout in the Midwestern Region, 1860–1900

Election	Tenn.	Ken.	Pa.	Ohio	Ind.	Ill.	Mich.	Wis.	Iowa	Minn.	Mo.	Neb.	Kan.
1860		−2.1	−4.4	−7.1	−2.6	−3.7	−3.6	−7.4	−3.1	−4.9	−5.3		
1864		−29.7	−0.8	−6.8	−8.5	−14.6	−15.0	−7.7	−21.2	−25.2	−35.9		
1868	−24.5	−6.6	2.8	−3.6	1.7	−6.5	−5.4	−6.5	−10.7	−9.1	−27.3	−22.5	−30.0
1872	−1.1	−8.1	−9.9	−4.6	−4.3	−8.7	−11.2	−4.9	−6.8	7.2	−3.0	−20.5	−3.4
1876	7.5	6.2	3.8	5.1	5.2	3.1	5.2	9.9	5.8	9.5	6.3	−12.2	−15.5
1880	7.6	0.6	6.9	4.8	4.8	5.2	1.5	3.2	2.5	7.3	7.8	3.0	−0.7
1884	6.4	−2.4	1.9	4.0	1.8	1.2	3.3	7.5	7.2	1.9	6.9	4.6	9.0
1888	12.4	8.8	3.6	2.8	3.6	0.9	9.0	6.2	5.2	10.3	11.9	13.8	16.4
1892	−2.8	2.0	−2.5	−2.9	−0.5	3.9	0.0	0.8	5.0	−2.5	7.4	3.5	7.0
1896	4.6	17.4	4.7	6.3	5.6	12.8	11.6	9.0	11.3	6.2	18.4	11.4	7.5
1900	−10.2	15.2	−2.7	2.2	2.7	5.8	5.3	0.0	4.9	−3.2	12.8	17.7	9.4
Mean	66.8	71.9	77.7	88.8	92.0	84.2	83.7	86.5	84.3	79.9	69.8	69.0	80.1
Variance	115.9	150.5	21.8	23.3	18.7	54.2	61.5	42.3	83.2	100.2	265.3	194.6	188.4
Standard deviation	10.8	12.3	4.6	4.8	4.3	7.4	7.8	6.5	9.1	10.0	16.3	14.0	13.7

SOURCE: ICPR election files

stood lower on this measure of civic duty. To the north and west, participation levels ranged from about 70 percent in Missouri and Nebraska to the mid-eighty percentiles in Michigan, Wisconsin, Illinois, and Iowa. But across all of these states Indiana's level of voter turnout remained unmatched.

The body of this table also shows some characteristics of turnout common to the midwestern states over presidential elections, marked by the negative and positive signs on the election-by-election turnout deviations. Not only in Indiana, but more generally across the states, turnout increased toward the end of the century. Between 1872 and 1876 there was comparable movement from below-average to above-average participation; this participation remained above average, except for 1892, and then reached a peak of turnout in 1896. In this fact is one key reason for the "critical" status of the 1896 election: it mobilized large numbers of new voters into the electorate over a wide array of states, just as had been the case twenty years earlier.[14]

Indiana's presidential elections can be compared not only to those in other states, but to Indiana's congressional elections as well. During the 1870s, congressmen were sent to Washington from Indiana at October elections. Congressional candidates ran in on-years with gubernatorial candidates and in off-years were paired with candidates for secretary of state. Though separated by a month from the national election, congressional turnout differences between the "high stimulus" presidential on-years and the "low stimulus" off-years are readily pictured by the saw-toothed line in the upper portion of figure 2.4.[15] Hoosiers sent their congressmen to the nation's capital backed by voter participation in the mid-90-percent range in presidential years and in the mid-80-percent range when presidential coattails were lacking. The lower line in this graph, which traces the Republican proportion of the congressional vote, shows the minor "wobble" induced by high turnout years, giving a slight advantage to Republican candidates.

If Indiana presidential elections were competitive affairs, congressional ones were even more so. Table 2.6 divides all congressional elections from 1860 to 1900 between the on-years and off-years, with the shift at each election measured from the

Chapter Two

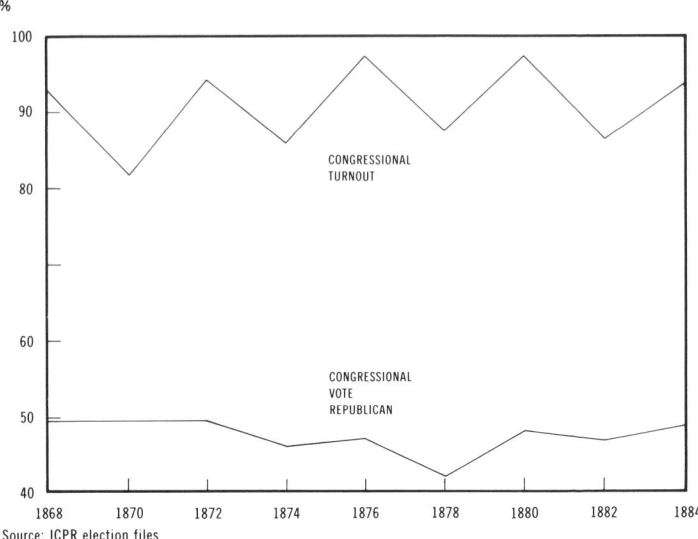

Fig. 2.4 Congressional turnout and Republican percentage of total vote, 1868-84

time-series mean. Viewed in this way, the state-wide vote for congressional candidates reveals even sharper party competition than the presidential series. Whether on-year or off, or over the full sequence, the mean two-party division hung within 1 percent of an equal split. In terms of the probability for opposition party victory, the on-year elections showed a one-in-three chance for victory by the Democrats and for off-year elections just less than a one-in-two chance for the Republicans. In all congressional elections, Hoosier candidates faced even keener competition at home than the presidential candidates who headed the national tickets. For Indiana, a betting politician would put the party's money into congressional contests where it could make the most difference.

The line of people at the polls on election days in Indiana was related to the legal conditions of suffrage. The state's legal system offered few barriers to voting participation among adult males until after the turn of the century. This meant that, aside from

Indiana's Electorate, 1860–1900

Table 2.6. Deviations from the Republican Mean, Indiana Congressional Elections, 1860–1900

Election Year	On-Year Deviations	Off-Year Deviations	All-Elections Deviations
1860	1.8		2.2
1862		−2.0	−2.5
1864	2.3		2.7
1866		2.0	1.5
1868	−0.9		−0.5
1870		1.1	0.6
1872	−0.8		−0.4
1874		−2.0	−2.5
1876	−1.4		−1.0
1878		−0.3	−0.8
1880	−0.3		0.1
1882		−1.5	−2.0
1884	−1.9		−1.5
1886		0.2	−0.3
1888	1.8		2.2
1890		−2.4	−2.9
1892	−1.3		−0.9
1894		4.5	4.0
1896	0.3		0.7
1898		0.8	0.3
1900	0.5		0.9
Series mean Republican	50.8	49.9	50.4
Variance	2.09	4.69	3.36
Standard deviation	1.5	2.16	1.83
Probability of a deviating election	.30	.48	.41

SOURCE: ICPR election files

new settlers entering the state and old residents leaving, largely the same persons were appearing at the polls on successive election days.

The system of suffrage had its basis in the state's first constitution, of 1816, which enfranchised all free, white, male inhabitants, twenty-one years of age and older, who had resided in the territory for one year and in the United States for two years, excepting only men enlisted in the United States Army.[16] It specified the county seat as the place of polling and replaced voice voting with the paper ballot. These legal conditions established few barriers to voting participation aside from sex, race, and age. While several attempts were made to alter them before midcentury, nothing was done beyond discussing the right of aliens to vote, the number of offices subject to direct election, residency requirements, and the proper place of voting. But the new constitution of 1851 contained two notable changes that eased even further these voting conditions. It modified residency requirements from one year to only six months within the state so that geographic mobility within the state's borders did not disenfranchise previous voters, and it modified the place of voting from the county seat to the township, thereby minimizing the distance of travel from home to the polling station. No literacy test, language clause, or other disenfranchising mechanism (other than those of age, sex, and race) was imposed, and for aliens the intent to become a naturalized citizen was defined as a sufficient condition to cast a ballot.[17]

After 1851, discussion moved in the opposite direction, that of possible restrictions on suffrage, in part because political leaders were concerned with election fraud. In 1858, for instance, the *Indianapolis Journal* reported that "election frauds have become as notorious as divorce cases. Immigration, transportation and double-voting were encouraged [in the last election] and the purity of the ballot box was a farce."[18] With the state's very liberal legal system allowing widespread participation, and with few checks on the identity of voters or the secrecy of the party-prepared ballot, the question of fraud plagued officials. Gubernatorial messages to the state General Assembly during the 1850s and 1860s repeatedly underscored potential misuse of the franchise for partisan gain, often linking the lack of local (rather than state) residency requirements, the lack of a voter registration system, party prepared ballots, and the presence of foreign-born voters with practices regarded as electoral fraud.[19]

A movement to enact local residency requirements and a voter registration law, as well as to grant suffrage to women, was begun in 1861. Under the urging of Republican governor Oliver P. Morton a voter registration law was passed by the General Assembly in 1867 but was declared unconstitutional by the state Supreme Court two years later.[20] To counter the court's ruling, Democratic governor Thomas A. Hendricks, in 1873, urged a constitutional amendment fixing local residency requirements and allowing the General Assembly the right to legislate a registration law. Pressed in 1875 and again in 1877, these and several other amendments were adopted by the General Assembly in 1879, to be sent to the voters for ratification. After a year's delay, they were finally passed in 1881.[21]

As amended in 1881, state law required for the first time six months' residency in the township and thirty days in the ward or precinct. It was also provided that the General Assembly might legislate a voter registration law. However, no registration law was enacted in Indiana until 1911, and the major electoral change, along with the admission of Negro citizens to the suffrage by federal decree in 1870, was the Australian ballot reform, stimulated by continuing intimations of fraud.[22] It was passed in 1889, and for the first time made voting a secret act. Thus, in spite of concerns to safeguard the ballot after mid-century, the legal conditions of suffrage remained exceedingly liberal in Indiana, encouraging widespread use of the franchise and involving few restrictive legal barriers, aside from the sex-based one, that would inhibit citizens from going to the polls.

Certainly, a combination of other factors contributed to high participation as well, including the relative maturity of the political system, strong southern influences from the early days of settlement, and highly competitive parties. Further, in rural areas election days were themselves special occasions, much like official holidays, that provided a chance for picnics, parades, and pleasurable visits to town. But the legal conditions that were pervasive to the state from the Civil War to the turn of the century were important because they provided so few barriers to the casting of ballots.

Indiana's parties were not simple state-wide ones but were organized within that state by counties. Counties were the smallest local political units that sent representatives to the state

Chapter Two

General Assembly. The Assembly itself elected Indiana's senators during the 1870s. All congressional districts, which elected members of Congress directly, were also each composed of several counties. County chairmen and other party leaders therefore regularly monitored the mood of their people and fed this information to district and state-wide leaders. For example, one Republican party leader in Cass County wrote in 1874 to Daniel P. Pratt, then senator from Indiana, apprising him of new developments. "We have a pretty correct understanding of the tendency and possible results of the Granger movement," he confided, and then continued, "At the meeting on the 8th [of January], we had reports and information from nearly all parts of the state, and, I think it may safely be assumed that there will be no Granger ticket for the state, nor in any but two Congressional districts (south). The Granger effort will be directed chiefly to county and local tickets."[23]

Appraisal of the state by county leaders was a regular part of party operations. As in this instance where Pratt's chance to return to Washington as senator was at stake, so in other instances party victory was dependent on how stable across counties were party competition and voter participation. As Pratt well knew, the electorate of every county had its own political complexion. Taken together, it was the counties that gave color and hue to the face of the state as a whole. The nine *People's Guide* counties, many of whose citizens recorded their party allegiance in the 1874 directories, were part of this pigmentation, themselves shaded by different degrees of party loyalty and civic duty.

How did the behavior of these nine counties measure up to the political behavior of all counties in Indiana? To ask this question is to ask how a "sample" of counties, admittedly selected by historical rather than probability methods, was related to all counties within the state. For just as Indiana had a larger Midwestern context in the late nineteenth century, so also did the nine *People's Guide* counties have a context within the Hoosier commonwealth, itself marked by physical, temporal, social, and political lines of development.

Three major regions within Indiana defined its physical land surface (see figure 2.5).[24] When Indiana gained statehood, the northernmost region was a marshy area, dotted with numerous small and shallow lakes, due to poor natural drainage. Several rivers and streams in this northern region entered the eastern St. Lawrence drainage system through Lake Michigan and Lake

Fig. 2.5 The nine *People's Guide* counties

Chapter Two

Erie while elsewhere nine-tenths of the state's natural water highways drained into the Mississippi River basin on the west. The area south of the Wabash River and north of the east fork of the White River was an expanse of level, rolling plains covered by rich, deep glacial till, oriented to the Mississippi by the Wabash and the east and west forks of the White River. Nowhere in this area did the height of land above sea level vary much, except for a slight "cant" to the surface stretching from the east-north-central downward toward the southwest. The state's level land surface from north to south was broken only in the south, by rugged, well-defined hills and small streams that entered the Ohio River on the Kentucky border. It was in this southern region that the early settlers met the greatest variety of land features.

The first American homes in Indiana were built in this southernmost region.[25] Early pioneers came up the Mississippi from the south or down the Wabash or Ohio from the north and east, making the southwestern corner of Indiana Territory the first area densely populated by whites. Then, after the buying of the "New Purchase" of land in the central part of the state from Indians, tiers of counties were organized in successive northward thrusts, generally following behind "the lines of Indian cessions and pioneer settlements."[26]

The movement of people on foot, by horse, in wagons, and on boats, however, was not northward only. The Erie Canal, completed across New York state in 1825, opened a way from the eastern seaboard to the interior Great Lakes region and brought people to Indiana who had access to eastern markets as opposed to those at New Orleans. The Erie Canal served in turn as a model for the Wabash-Maumee Canal (and the Whitewater), begun in 1832. These developments broke the gradual movement of population from the south, and at the 1831 revision of county boundaries by the General Assembly, the counties of Allen, St. Joseph, and Elkhart were all established in the north.[27]

While the canal projects stimulated this northern development, the railroads made it flourish. Rails reached Indiana in 1847 with the completion of track between Madison, on the Ohio River, and Indianapolis. By 1850, 228 miles of track connected Indianapolis with Terre Haute to the southwest and Lafayette to the northwest.

Another 2,163 miles were completed by 1860, thereafter virtually covering the entire state.[28] The canal projects (which were not completed) and the railroads shifted the direction and development of Indiana's population from the south to the east and north. In 1860, when several new counties were carved from earlier ones, the state comprised the ninety-two that endure to the present.

The nine *People's Guide* counties were all organized after the new purchase of 1818 and before the general revision of county boundaries in 1831.[29] By 1870 they had had a generation and a half of sustained population growth, drawing people from both north and south and from foreign areas as well. Rates of population growth for each of these nine counties are presented in table 2.7, where they can be compared to growth rates in the whole state, in the city of Indianapolis (Marion County), and in the United States. These comparisons indicate that Indiana's population more than doubled each decade from 1800 to 1840, and that until 1870 the number of Hoosiers increased at a rate faster than that for the United States as a whole. Between 1830 and 1840, in their first decade of recorded settlement, the nine *People's Guide* counties grew more rapidly than the state, but in the decades between 1850 and 1880 this growth fell behind the more general levels as newer areas of the state developed and as settlement in the United States moved increasingly westward. Before the end of the century, several of the these counties experienced slight declines in population, while the city of Indianapolis continued to surge.[30]

The growth of cities in Indiana was clearly paced by Indianapolis. With a population of 48,244 in 1870, Indianapolis ranked eighteenth in the nation, about the size of Pittsburgh or Detroit. All nine *People's Guide* counties were clustered around this great new metropolis. No other cities of such magnitude grew on Indiana soil even though the state held six cities with populations of more than 10,000 persons. Twenty-five others ranged in size from 2,500 to 10,000 inhabitants, and another 108 had 500 to 2,500 people. Several cities in these two smaller size-ranges were scattered within the nine *People's Guide* counties; the largest were Franklin City in Johnson County (2,707), Crawfordsville in

Table 2.7. Percentage Rates of Net Population Growth

	1800	1810	1820	1830	1840	1850	1860	1870	1880	1890	1900
United States		36.4	33.1	33.5	32.7	35.9	35.6	22.6	30.1	25.5	20.7
Indiana		334.7	500.2	133.1	99.9	44.1	36.6	24.5	17.7	10.8	14.8
Indianapolis (Marion County) (Dec. 31, 1822)					123.6	49.9	65.4	80.5	42.9	37.3	39.7
Bartholomew (Jan. 8, 1821)					83.4	23.8	43.8	18.3	7.8	4.8	3.1
Boone (Jan. 29, 1830)					1207.7	43.2	44.0	34.9	14.7	2.5	−1.0
Hamilton (Jan. 8, 1823)					460.9	28.7	36.5	20.6	18.8	5.3	14.5
Hendricks (Dec. 20, 1823)					183.4	25.0	20.4	19.6	13.3	−6.4	−1.0
Henry (Dec. 31, 1822)					132.9	16.4	14.3	14.3	4.5	−0.6	5.1
Johnson (Dec. 31, 1822)					132.7	29.4	22.8	23.6	6.4	0.1	3.4
Montgomery (Dec. 22, 1822)					97.3	25.3	15.5	13.8	14.9	2.6	7.3
Morgan (Dec. 31, 1821)					92.0	35.7	10.5	8.8	7.8	−1.4	9.7
Vermillion (Jan. 2, 1824)					45.4	4.7	8.8	15.1	10.9	9.4	15.9

SOURCE: Published federal census

Montgomery County (3,701) and Columbus in Bartholomew County (3,359), with several smaller towns in each of the other counties.[31]

In spite of the geographic clustering of the nine *People's Guide* counties around the state's only area of major urban growth, with all that meant for temporal and social development, the political behavior of these counties nonetheless captured quite well the political behavior of all counties in the state. The basic data summarizing county-level partisan voting within Indiana is presented in table 2.8, using all on-year congressional elections from 1860 to 1904. The entries in column (1) and column (2) of this table are the mean percentage Republican over all ninety-two counties at each election and its standard deviation, respectively. The figures in parentheses refer to the same calculations based only on the nine *People's Guide* counties. At the bottom of these columns, the time-series mean (of the election means) stands at 49.4 percent Republican, with an average standard deviation of 8.5 percent. The entire series of elections, across all counties, cluster closely about these summarizing values and underscore *within* the state the continuing competitiveness of Indiana's elections.

More important than this competitiveness, however, was how the *People's Guide* counties were related to all counties. First, compared to all counties within the state, the election-by-election means (parenthesized in column 1) for the nine *People's Guide* counties were consistently more Republican than the state as a whole; on average the difference in this part-to-whole relation was about 4 percent (shown in the final row). But the movement of these means from one election to the next precisely paralleled the movement in the state as a whole. Second, the standard deviations show a pattern of decrements in dispersion from the election of 1864 to 1900, and this change in dispersion was again paralleled by the dispersion measured from the nine sample counties, even though their magnitudes are slightly less (as parenthesized in column 2). These same patterns over time and between all counties and the *People's Guide* counties held for presidential and gubernatorial elections as well. Off-year congressional elections followed similar patterns but with slightly higher and more variable rates of dispersion.

Chapter Two

Table 2.8. Presidential-Year Measures of County-level Republican Congressional Election Distributions

Year	(1) Mean %	(2) Standard Deviation	(3) Pearson's r
1860	51.5 (54.7)[a]	9.1 (7.7)	—
1864	51.9 (59.9)	11.1 (10.4)	.85 (.90)
1868	48.8 (56.1)	9.4 (10.0)	.93 (.97)
1872	49.8 (55.0)	8.6 (8.6)	.97 (.99)
1876	47.4 (50.6)	8.7 (7.8)	.92 (.93)
1880	48.4 (51.8)	8.3 (7.3)	.93 (.88)
1884	48.3 (51.6)	7.9 (6.4)	.96 (.95)
1888	49.5 (53.3)	7.0 (4.9)	.97 (.94)
1892	45.9 (49.5)	6.9 (5.0)	.95 (.95)
1896	50.1 (52.6)	6.6 (5.6)	.95 (.96)
1900	49.7 (51.8)	6.8 (5.8)	.97 (.99)
1904	51.9 (53.8)	11.7 (5.8)	.92 (.94)
Time series mean	49.4 (53.4)	8.5 (7.1)	.938 (.946)
Nine-county difference from all counties	+4.0	−1.4	+.008

SOURCE: ICPR election files
[a]Values in parentheses are based on the nine-county *People's Guide* subset.

The Pearsonian correlation coefficients in column 3 measure the geographic stability of the partisan vote, entered in the table at the second congressional election in each pair. Thus, the stability of the vote between 1860 and 1864 was .85 of a maximum stability of 1.00. From 1864 through 1904 these coefficients were all above .90 and averaged nearly .94, indicating very strong geographic partisan stability indeed. And this stability was again matched in the sample counties, where the time-series average was .95 and where only one election pair, from 1872 to 1876, fell below .90. Again, both presidential and gubernatorial elections followed these patterns for all counties, with average correlations at the .95 level. Off-year congressional contests had much greater geographic movement, and the average correlation dropped to .84.

What these three independent measures all indicate is that the 1870s fell within a much longer era of stable, highly competitive partisan politics, in which the relative distribution of counties over the partisan terrain remained highly constant between each succeeding pair of elections.[32] The nine *People's Guide* counties captured both the immediate election-by-election aspects of this competition, displaced at the mean towards the Republicans, and the full temporal aspects of the geographic stability both in dispersion and interelection correlation.

In spite of the high election-to-election continuity shown by these measures, it is possible that they could mask a secular "decay" in the partisanship underlying the vote from the first to the third, from the first to the fourth, or from the first to the fifth election in the series—even though every successive pair remained quite stable. To test for this possibility again requires a mathematical model, one that specifies the "expected decay" in correlation coefficients as elections are further separated from each other in the time-series and that enables the "retarding of decay" to be attributed to sustained levels of partisanship.[33]

Table 2.9 is a matrix of all interelection correlation coefficients for the Republican percentage of the presidential vote in Indiana from 1860 to 1904. This matrix exhibits a standard "pitched-roof" form, with the high ridge of successive interelection coefficients formed along the main diagonal from the upper-left to the lower-right corners. The magnitudes of the coefficients then slope toward the lower left-hand corner, diagonal by diagonal. These successive diagonals yield relatively independent estimates of the correlation between elections removed in time from each other by one, two, three or more intervening elections, and so to the end of the time series. Row (1) at the bottom of the table is the mean correlation for these "elapsed time" estimates, averaged along the diagonals, and symbolized in row (2).

If each election in Indiana was only a simple function of the previous election, and if sustained levels of partisanship were not continuous across elections removed in time by intervening elections, then a simple null model of expected decay in partisan levels could be erected. Such a null model implies that elapsed-time coefficients for election pairs removed from each other by intervening elections will be a direct function of the number of such intervening elections.[34] Row (4) shows the expected correlations under this null model. By comparing row (1) with row (4), it

Table 2.9. Interelection Correlation Matrix: Republican Percentage of the County-level Presidential Vote.

	1860	1864	1868	1872	1876	1880	1884	1888	1892	1896	1900	1904
1860	.80											
1864	.83	.95										
1868	.81	.88	.95									
1872	.84	.91	.96	.95								
1876	.81	.91	.95	.92	.97							
1880	.76	.88	.93	.90	.96	.98						
1884	.73	.87	.92	.90	.95	.94	.97					
1888	.72	.86	.89	.86	.92	.92	.95	.96				
1892	.76	.86	.87	.84	.90	.91	.91	.92	.94			
1896	.77	.85	.89	.88	.93	.93	.93	.94	.95	.98		
1904	.81	.83	.88	.89	.90	.89	.88	.88	.87	.93	.96	
(1) Mean	.810	.800	.830	.840	.848	.863	.883	.903	.907	.924	.946	
(2) r_{1k}	$r_{1,12}$	$r_{1,11}$	$r_{1,10}$	$r_{1,9}$	$r_{1,8}$	$r_{1,7}$	$r_{1,6}$	$r_{1,5}$	$r_{1,4}$	$r_{1,3}$	$r_{1,2}$	
(3) No. of coefficients	1	2	3	4	5	6	7	8	9	10	11	
(4) Expected r_{1k}	.569	.599	.630	.663	.700	.735	.774	.815	.857	.900	.95	
(5) 9 counties	.900	.860	.877	.895	.908	.918	.919	.921	.922	.938	.963	
(6) Expected r_{1k}	.638	.665	.693	.722	.752	.783	.816	.850	.885	.922	.96	

Source: ICPR election files

is clear that the null model is false to this Indiana data: levels of partisanship among county electorates clearly intervened across elections in this time-span to "retard" the decay in elapsed-time correlations. Once again, this same retarding effect was present for the elapsed-time correlations based only on the *People's Guide* counties, which are shown in row (5). Partisan decay in these counties, which appeared to be slightly slower than in the state as a whole, was determined in part by the slightly higher mean correlation between initial election pairs (.96 in the nine-county sample; .95 in the full set of counties). The higher "expected" correlations are given in row (6). Essentially, however, both the full set and the sample subset behaved in much the same manner; both showed retarded rates of partisan decay. Indeed, these findings on the temporal behavior of the nine sample counties in relation to the behavior of all Indiana counties are fully consistent with a view that the same partisan processes were at work in this particular subset as in the state's counties as a whole. Both show the strong and sustained impact of continuing levels of partisan competition.

Where, then, were these nine counties located in the distribution of all county-level voting outcomes? Were they clustered in a Republican "wing" of counties, a Democratic one, in the center of the distribution of county partisan results, or were they spread over the terrain of outcomes at fairly regular intervals? Given the temporal stability of the county outcomes, these questions may be answered by viewing a more restricted time-series of elections in relation to a particular outcome at the onset of the 1870s. I have employed the six-year interval between 1862 and 1868, using the two off-year congressional elections of 1862 and 1866 and the two presidential elections of 1864 and 1868, as a basis for establishing Indiana's county mean-levels of partisanship leading into the 1870s. The choice of these elections was made to balance the effects of different offices and of "high" versus "low" turnout conditions.[35] Thus, over these four elections, the mean Republican vote and the mean turnout was calculated for each county and then compared to the actual Republican vote and the actual turnout in the off-year congressional election of 1870.

Figure 2.6 displays by a scattergram the distribution of the nine sample counties among all counties of Indiana, for the regression of the 1870 congressional percentage of the vote that was Republican on the 1862-68 mean percentage Republican. The scattergram makes visibly clear that the nine counties were distributed over a wide range of the partisan surface, in spite of their geographical clustering in the Tipton Till region. The grand state mean of the mean vote for all counties was near the fifty-fifty division point, and the grand state standard deviation showed average variability on the order of 10 percent. From these figures and the scattergram, we find that roughly four sample counties—Hendricks, Hamilton, Henry, and Vermillion—stand one standard deviation or more above the grand mean and that two sample counties—Bartholomew and Johnson—stand about one-half standard deviation below. Boone and Montgomery counties were quite near the state mean itself. Thus, while the nine sample counties are "weighted" by several highly Republican ones, they nonetheless distribute over the county-level partisan surface in such a way as to capture much of the variability exhibited by the full set of counties in the state.

A precisely parallel set of calculations was made for turnout variation. The key term in measuring turnout is the denominator that defines the eligible electorate, an estimate that must be based on the decennial census figures for each county. In 1860 and 1870 this figure represents the white, male inhabitants, twenty-one years of age and older, and therefore includes the foreign-born who by law were equally eligible. The estimated eligible electorate for intervening election years was made as a strict linear interpolation over the time-interval of the decade. It is difficult to conceive of any way in which the eligible electorate could be grossly underestimated by these calculations, except by underreporting in the census itself or by very high net population changes unevenly spread within the decade. I emphasize this question of measurement because Indiana's turnout rates were not only exceedingly high but in several instances exceeded 100 percent, again raising the issue of voting fraud.

The relative turnout location of the *People's Guide* counties is shown in the scattergram of figure 2.7, a regression of the 1870 congressional election turnout on the 1862-68 turnout mean. The

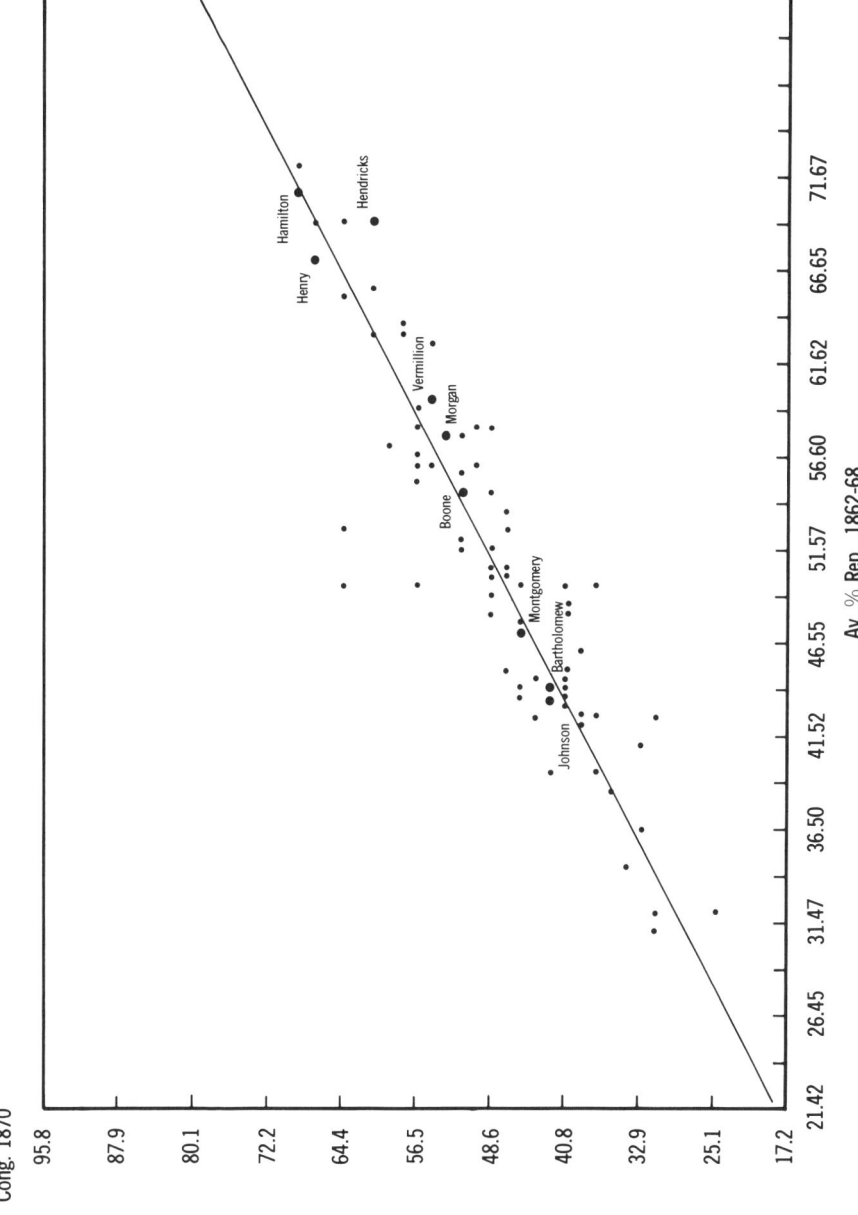

Fig. 2.6 County regression for the Republican vote

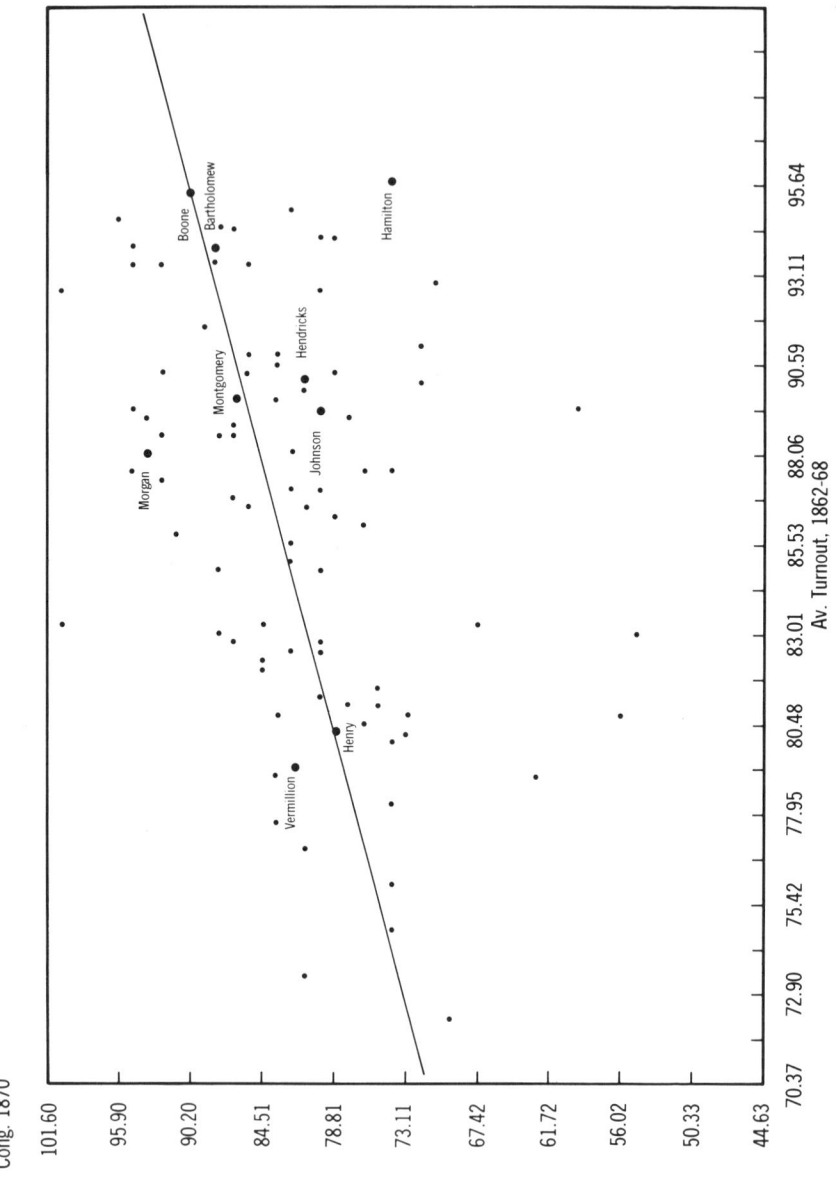

Fig. 2.7 County regression for turnout

generally high absolute levels of turnout are readily apparent, as well as the relatively wide scatter of counties about the regression line (though absolute scatter was small). The relative scatter is indicated by the moderate correlation coefficient, $r = .41$, while the underlying relationship, measured by Beta, is shown to be .67, due to lower off-year turnout. Again, however, we find that the nine-county sample distributes over much of the turnout surface in quite adequate fashion. At least two counties, Henry and Vermillion, stand about one-half of a standard deviation below the 1862-68 grand mean, and Montgomery, Hendricks, Bartholomew, Boone, and Hamilton stand one standard deviation or more above. These counties were neither unusually clustered about the regression line nor spread away from it, and in 1870 only Hamilton appeared as an unusual outlier with high average turnout and unusually low turnout in this congressional election. While the nine counties were again somewhat weighted by those with high turnout, they nonetheless extended widely over the turnout surface. Thus, both the partisan and turnout distributions for the nine counties, among all counties of Indiana, suggest that these nine counties can capture much of the variability within the state on both dimensions.

In sum, the *People's Guide* counties, whose structure we shall examine, were clustered geographically within Indiana. All lay within the central Tipton Till region of the state. These counties contained no large cities, although within them were located several smaller ones. They centered around Indianapolis, the state's single most rapidly growing urban area.

While these geographic differences remain obvious, others do not. The levels of partisan voting across these nine counties were widely distributed by 1870. Although not located at the extremes of partisan variation, they reflected much of its range, with a small Republican cast. In levels of turnout as well, the *People's Guide* counties were also distributed widely over the turnout terrain, at levels only a little higher than average.

We now come full circle. Indiana was only one state of the larger midwestern region. The comparative context of this state's voting behavior during the full length of the late nineteenth century has made clear how Hoosier voting differed from that of its nearer neighbors. What was true for Indiana voting dynamics during the 1870s may throw new light on these other states as well, but it cannot confirm that the same dynamics operated uniformly across them. Indeed, we know that each differed from Indiana in levels of party competition and in civic participation. A detailed study of Indiana, however, will show the kinds of questions about structure and process that may have been equally important elsewhere and to which further attention should be given. These questions can be raised because we have new data on the interior political and social structure of nine counties. It is the *People's Guide* counties and these new data for individual voters that now require attention.

3

The People's Guide Counties: A "Grass Roots" Sample of Individual Voters

Individual voters are the mass base of politics. They are the "grass roots" of power toward whose behavior other historians have pointed. Yet records of individual voting behavior rarely exist. I doubt that such records exist for Indiana in the 1870s even though fully secret voting was not instituted until several decades later.[1] Ballots were generally destroyed shortly after an election without the recording of individual decisions, and the vote was aggregated upward from precincts and townships to county and state totals. There was no party registration system, and there were no survey organizations to monitor systematically voter preferences or choices over large expanses of the electorate.

Occasionally, however, someone produced documents having to do with voting only indirectly, marking party preference or the vote for a candidate as a pertinent piece of information about a person. The *People's Guide*s are such documents, springing from the nature of rural life itself.[2] One farmer knew another down the road, and both knew the merchants and dealers in town with whom they dealt. But they knew only by name and place the people at a greater distance. County directories spanned the miles between these people by giving each one some background information about all the others, whether friends and neighbors close at hand, mere strangers several sections away, or persons living

Chapter Three

wholly unknown in the county's more remote villages—just as the county histories produced in this same period made the earlier pioneers "closer" in time.

The *People's Guide*s were printed and published at Indianapolis in 1874 by two men, Cline and McHaffie, who themselves lived in Hendricks county. No one told these men how to draw a probability sample of the state for later historical use. A simple random sample of all Hoosier voters would have served admirably, even though such a design becomes very inefficient for areas as large as a state.[3] A random sample of counties and then, within those counties, random samples of citizens would have been better and would have confined their canvass within a few counties, more widely dispersed than the nine counties they chose but still representing the whole state. If in addition, they had divided the voters in each sampled county by social classes, religious groups, and places of birth, and then sampled them, their work would have been even more efficient from a later point of view. But sampling was not their business in the first place, nor were they concerned with political or historical analysis. They sought instead to publish and make a profit, in a limited area of nine nearby counties and from as many different subscribers as possible, without knowledge of the survey techniques that were invented decades after they lived.

Every volume of the *People's Guide*s contained two parts. Initial pages were devoted to common material through all of the volumes, regardless of county: the United States Constitution, the platforms of parties in recent election campaigns, a few home remedies, recipes, and special state laws. The later pages gave information specific to each county: a brief county history, written sketches of each township, its major associations such as churches and lodges, and then alphabetical entries, by township, of (primarily) male residents. These entries listed each person by name, giving occupation, place of residence, state or country or birth, year of birth, date of settlement in the county, political party attachment, and religious affiliation, as follows:

ALLEE, O. S.; carpenter and builder; Lebanon. Born in Ind[iana] 1834; settled in B[oone] C[ounty] 1868. Rep[ublican]. Christian.

APGAR, F.; retired miller, Lebanon. Born in K[entucky] 1823; settled in B[oone] C[ounty] 1855. Rep[ublican]. Methodist.
ADAIR, JOHN; farmer; ½ m[ile] s[outh] e[ast] Lebanon. Born in N[ew] J[ersey] 1821; settled in B[oone] C[ounty] 1851. Dem[ocrat]. Christian.
ADAM, HENRY; leather store and tannery; Lebanon. Born in Europe 1835; settled in B[oone] C[ounty] 1866. Dem[ocrat]. Lutheran.[4]

How these guides were compiled, and why, apart from a profit motive, Cline and McHaffie published them, is only partially known. Bates Harrington, an all but unknown observer of the 1870s, reported that maps, atlases, county histories, and biographical sketchbooks fascinated readers across many parts of the country.[5] First in New England and then in the Midwest, these publications were printed by local entrepreneurs whose own profit depended on selling subscriptions. Since basic costs remained much the same for one hundred or a thousand copies, profit margins were a direct function of the number of subscribers. Harrington noted three strategies initiated by Captain T. H. Thompson and Major L. H. Everts, who sought to increase subscriptions to their map of Dubuque County, Iowa. Thompson and Everts first secured official endorsement from the Board of County Supervisors. Then, to broaden sales, the project was described in local newspapers as a public service to the community. Finally, "lightning canvassers," or agents, were sent out on a commission basis to bring in subscriptions. These tactics did not elsewhere follow one another easily, and occasionally even the pretense of putting off a project for lack of support was used to obtain a full, public endorsement from leading citizens and boards.[6]

Harrington's report, which was also an indictment, nowhere mentions Cline and McHaffie or the *People's Guide*s. Yet, his description of a project by Captain A. T. Andreas, who joined Thompson and Everts as a canvasser before setting out on his own, follows closely the form these directories took. Experimenting with county atlases and histories in Minnesota, Iowa, and Wisconsin, Andreas tried a new format in Knox County, Illinois. In tabular form, he published "the names of subscribers to the

Chapter Three

atlas, giving the section they resided on, or the town they lived in, their business or occupation, the State, county and Town they came from, and when they settled in Illinois."[7] Harrington estimated that the addition of individual names increased the sale of Andreas' atlases by 25 percent and that, beginning in 1870 with nothing, Andreas had, by 1875, published twenty-three county and two state atlases with total sales exceeding a million dollars. I believe, therefore, that Cline and McHaffie simply expanded on Andreas' tabular form for individuals by adding religious and political information.

After Cline and McHaffie advertised for agents, they sent them from house to house and town to town seeking information from individuals and subscriptions for the *People's Guide*. The task was a big one, covering large areas that were often lined with poor and difficult roads. Most people were helpful with information, of course, but some refused to give any at all.[8] With coverage of all people difficult at best, and with agents who were untrained in the work, the question arises: who was listed? How were those persons listed related to the total number of voting-age citizens in each county? Certainly the people listed in the *People's Guide*s were a sample. It was not, however, a sample of women, for few women were listed. Perhaps it was largely a sample of heads of households, except that boarders and sons living with their parents were also added. Quite clearly, the sample of individuals whom Cline and McHaffie listed in the *People's Guide*s was an ad hoc one; like their selection of counties, it was governed by their goals of publication and profit. What Cline and McHaffie might have done suggests what we must do in order to use their survey for our purposes. On the one hand, the composition and behavior of the nine counties they selected must be compared to all counties in the state, allowing us to see in what ways those counties were and were not representative of the state-wide county distributions. That task, begun in the last chapter, will continue in subsequent ones. On the other hand, a sample of citizens also must be constructed from the *People's Guide*s lists for each county so that it represents the voting-age citizens who lived in each of them. Then, when social groups are compared within this nine-county electorate, those groups will represent the nine-county electorates as fully as possible but will represent the rest of the state only in accord with how social groups in those nine counties themselves compared to the state-wide distributions of social groups for all counties.

Indiana had no voter registration law in the year when the *People's Guide*s were compiled and published. By federal statute, however, census-takers in 1870 were required to mark a special entry designating every eligible voting-age citizen.[9] By county, these census returns marking eligible voting-age citizens are the closest approximation to complete voter registration lists now available for the early 1870s and provide a basis for evaluating and using information contained in the *Guide*s.

In constructing a sample for the *People's Guide*s I pursued a deliberate two-phase strategy.[10] In the first phase, a large initial simple random sample of voting-age citizens was drawn from the 1870 manuscript census returns for each of the nine counties, in proportion to the size of the electorate of each county. This random selection covered all voters in these counties in 1870 and assured no initial bias.[11] The census provided information for every voter, by name: whether he was the head of a family, his age, race, occupation, assessed value of real estate, assessed value of personal estate, his state or country of birth, whether his parents were foreign-born, whether he was able to read and write, and whether he was disabled. Among these variables, each person's name, year of birth, occupation, and place of birth were also given in the *People's Guide*s. I then attempted to trace each voting-age citizen from the 1870 census sample to the 1874 directories, in order to match the same persons and link information about them from the two sources. The criteria by which entries were matched were several: the voter's last name, the first name or one or more initials, place of birth by state or country, and residence within the same township, because the directories were organized alphabetically within townships for each county. Success in matching led to a smaller subsample of voters who were traced between the two sources. The success rate for tracing was about 37 percent. Of 3,318 voters originally sampled, 1,216 were matched and linked to entries in the *People's Guide*s, a traced *Guide* sample about the size of many national surveys today.

Table 3.1 shows the initial proportionate stratified sampling

Chapter Three

design and the trace-rate within each county. The differences in these trace-rates, from a high of 42 percent in Vermillion County to a low of 30 percent in Johnson, are sufficiently large so that they cannot be due to sampling error. Outmigration and death, as well as incomplete listings in the *People's Guide*s, were very real factors that caused variation in the trace rates. If the *Guide* subsample was to represent the voting-age population within these counties, then the differences in tracing within each of them had to be taken into account.

By intent, the sampling design was treated as a two-phase process for just this reason.[12] Expecting the *People's Guide*s to be underrepresented among certain categories of voters when compared to the census, I used the census variables for all 3,318 voters sampled in 1870 to define subgroups by wealth, age, occupation, and several other factors. The difference between traced and nontraced voters could then be viewed as a function of combinations of these factors, in a second phase.[13] Assuming that the traced voters in each substratum formed by combinations of census variables were a random selection, I then reweighted the traced voters for the second phase, to accord with their relative incidence among all voters in 1870. This reweighting removed the most severe biases of tracing between the two sources but increased the measurement error on one known variable, age, in a striking and understandable way (see Appendix C).[14] The weighted, traced *Guide* sample of 1,216 voters included all variables from both the 1870 census and the 1874 *People's Guide*s, bending the original purposes of Cline and McHaffie to our later research needs.

The political content of the *People's Guide*s, of course, is what makes them special for our purposes. As political directories, these guides told county residents not the candidates that a person supported but the preference between the parties which he held. This party-preference information, not a particular vote, is probably as close as historians will ever come to knowing the grass roots of politics in the way Hoosiers a century ago themselves knew them. For by viewing individual party attachments in relation to other social characteristics for this sample of voters in these nine counties, we will obtain the first systematic survey of internal structure for any nineteenth-century electorate—a survey

The *People's Guide* Counties

Table 3.1. Nine-County Population of Indiana Voting-age Citizens

	Voting-age Citizens[a]	Census Sample Size[b]	County Weight[c]	*Guide* Subsample Size[d]	Trace Rate[e]
Bartholomew	4,852	400	.118	147	.367
Boone	5,013	415	.123	128	.308
Hamilton	4,694	390	.115	154	.395
Hendricks	4,623	385	.114	155	.403
Henry	5,397	445	.131	173	.390
Johnson	4,210	345	.102	102	.296
Montgomery	5,716	475	.140	146	.307
Morgan	3,874	320	.095	128	.400
Vermillion	2,507	210	.062	88	.419
Totals	40,886	3,385	1.000	1,221	
Final sample totals[f]		3,318		1,216	

[a]The number of voting-age citizens is found in the published census for 1870 as "male citizens 21 years and older."
[b]The sample size for each county was determined by the overall sampling fraction of .083, rounded to whole integers.
[c]The county weight is the ratio of the county size to the total size of the population represented by all of the counties.
[d]The *Guide* subsample represents those members of the original census sample who were subsequently traced to the *People's Guide*s.
[e]The trace rate is the proportion of the original sample for each county successfully traced.
[f]The final totals resulted after students, paupers, and blacks were eliminated from the population of interest.

that, admittedly, will be a biased one since it is based on nine counties that only partially represented the whole state.

The most critical variable whose meaning must be assessed for these Indiana voters is party attachment. The range and rate of political responses in the *Guide* sample is shown in table 3.2, by both unweighted and weighted proportions. Among unweighted responses, better than 80 percent of all voters indicated either Democratic or Republican responses. About 3 percent used the label "independent." Another 11 percent provided no partisan response at all. The remainder indicated one or another third-party response. Weighting the sample decreased slightly the Republican proportion and slightly increased the Democratic proportion.

Chapter Three

Table 3.2. Original Party Response Labels and Their Relative Frequency

Response Label	Unweighted N	Unweighted %
Republican	615	50.6
Democrat	390	32.1
No party label	141	11.6
"Independent"	37	3.0
Granger	18	1.5
Liberal	8	0.6
Granger Republican	3	0.2
Granger Democrat	2	0.2
Liberal Democrat	2	0.2
Total	1,216	100.0

Several considerations governed how I used these party labels. One immediate question was whether "no answer" provided a meaningful response. The absence of a response could simply indicate a complete refusal to give any information to a directory agent, or it could indicate no attachment to any party—a quite different response. In the first case, including "no answer" adds "noise" to the data; but in the second case, "no attachment" is important for making meaningful distinctions between voters holding party attachments and those standing outside the party system. Finding the boundary between undesirable "noise" and significant variation is a problem with no easy solution. Because other information was present for these voters, indicating that they did not simply refuse to talk with agents, my decision was to include the "no answer" category as indicating "no party attachment," in order to observe how this category behaved with regard to other variables.[15]

A second question was how the remaining labels should be conceived. Because better than 3 percent of the voters used "independent" as a label for themselves, and this could mean an independent party, the term was initially retained as a separate category. The remaining "liberal" and "Granger" answers, including those with a major party leaning, were combined into a single category that I labeled "third party" attachments. Thus recoded, the party attachment variable initially spanned the five categories presented in table 3.3.

The *People's Guide* Counties

Table 3.3. Recoded Party Response Categories and Their Weighted Relative Frequency

Party Response Category	Weighted N	Weighted %
Major parties		
(1) Republican	597	49.1
(2) Democrat	424	34.9
Minor parties		
(3) Third party	28	2.2
(4) "Independent"	38	3.2
No party label		
(5) No party attachment	129	10.6
Totals	1,216	100.0

These five categories of party response are a discrete, nominal classification. They may be combined and unfolded in a variety of ways. One combination of interest was the possible contrast between responses tuned to the major parties and all others. This dichotomy could be further unfolded by first distinguishing "no party attachment" from all party responses and then subsequently separating out the "independent" and "third party" responses. Unfolding the variable this way allowed a study of variation across all categories that contrasted with responses tuned to the major parties.

The primary construction of the party categories, however, relies on a psychological view of major party attachments and treats them as ordered categories. That individuals view themselves as members of different parties is nothing new.[16] Survey research in the twentieth century amply confirms this old insight by measuring in the electorate both partisan direction and the intensity of attachment to parties. Starting from clues offered by Charles E. Merriam, Angus Campbell and his colleagues developed a formal scale of party identification possessing characteristics that measured both direction and strength.[17] Their view of party allegiance in the mass, as a psychological identification, was presented in the following terms:

> Only in the exceptional case does the sense of individual attachment to party reflect a formal membership or an active connection with a party apparatus. Nor does it

simply denote a voting record, although the influence of party allegiance on electoral behavior is strong. Generally this tie is a psychological identification, which can persist without legal recognition or evidence of formal membership and even without a consistent record of party support. Most Americans have this sense of attachment with one party or the other [in the twentieth century]. And for the individual who does, the strength and direction of party identification are facts of central importance in accounting for [political] attitude and behavior.[18]

This view of party allegiance explicitly defines political parties as social-psychological groups in a broad, aggregate sense, involving as members those persons who share something of a common sense of belonging. Thus viewed, partisanship is a result of learned identification and has a group basis of its own in which the image of a group derived from small face-to-face membership situations is extended to include "any aggregation of individuals who share a sense of common characteristics or common goals."[19]

For the two-party system of post-Civil War Indiana, the psychological alternatives largely formed a single polar scale the endpoints of which were Republican and Democratic groups. Between these two polar groups I have arrayed all other voters, whom I have labeled "Independents" (with a capital "I"), and who stood independent of the two major parties.[20] Figure 3.1 shows how this ordering of a one-dimensional scale is conceived, by comparing the three ordered categories for our sample of Indiana voters with the wider scale that is now a standard tool in political research.[21] The psychological basis of this ordering is quite clear when the scale points proceed by strength as well as direction from "strong Republican" to "weak Republican," "Independent," "weak Democrat," and "strong Democrat." But such *degree* of identification is only a further refinement of the initial three-point scale, one to which the *People's Guide* responses were not fully sensitive but which makes clear their ordering nonetheless.[22]

We now have in hand a basic sample of individual voters drawn

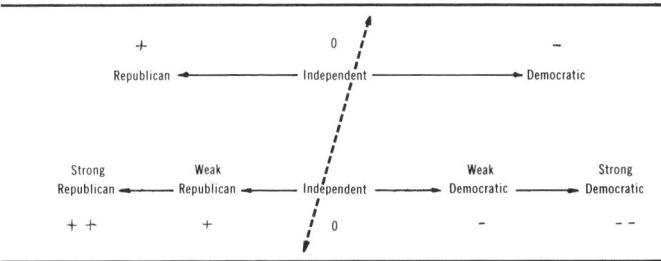

Fig. 3.1 Three-point and five-point scale of party identification

from nine counties in central Indiana, weighted for the relative incidence of these voters in 1870. We also have a view of the partisan labels which those data encode, and an understanding of how party attachments can be unfolded as a set of nominal categories indexing membership in Indiana's party system and of how they can be combined as an ordered scale of party allegiance. Therefore, it is now possible to ask about attachment to the party system and the dependence of party allegiance on other characteristics of these voters, and to measure the strength of association between party support and other aspects of the social structure. Because social class and occupational status are potentially among the most important of these relationships, we turn first to the effect on party attachments of class and status differences within this nine-county electorate.

4

Probing the Social and Economic Structure of Indiana's Rural Electorate

Indiana's party system was marked and shaped by differences in wealth, in status, and in places of living and working. Distorted by inflation following the Civil War, and by depression during the 1870s, these lines of difference nonetheless gave shape to party support and etched their imprint on the electorate. But whether they fully determined party support remains a question still debated and as yet unanswered. The answer, of course, depends on knowledge of the internal structure of the electorate. If inflation and depression touched most markedly the lower ranks of Hoosier society, then how party support varied by wealth, by status, and by places of work is fundamental to our understanding of election dynamics.

Inflation following the Civil War was closely tied to how that war was financed, the principal methods being the government's issuing of "greenback" paper currency and the taxing of foreign imports. By 1870, the currency question began to haunt Indiana's political leaders. Whether the federal government should repudiate its greenback debt, contracting and reducing it in favor of the gold standard, or expand the greenback currency were major issues that party leaders debated and that, together with conflicts over import tariffs, largely consumed their energy during the 1870s.[1] These issues were not easily resolved at elite levels. Until

The Rural Electorate: Social and Economic Structure

1872, leaders of both parties pitched their platforms on a fine line between contraction to the gold standard and the expansion of greenbacks, all the while fighting over which goods were to be taxed. But these issues struck the mass of Indiana's citizens only as the issues were further compounded by the onset of a long agricultural depression, one signaled nationally in September of 1873 with the dramatic financial collapse of Jay Cooke and Company, the nation's leading investment brokerage firm. The depression lasted in Indiana well into 1879.[2]

The response of Indiana's party leaders and its mass citizenry to this depression drama was described most graphically by William G. Carleton.[3] Though swept by depression winds, Indiana's political system did not crumble. Across its counties, major-party support held strong, smoothing the rough edges of voters' needs by small shifts in party positions. One the one hand, Carleton showed that "the position of the parties on the money question was a trustworthy barometer of economic conditions."[4] On the other hand, he marked the party vote of counties against their social and economic condition:

> The Democratic strength ... was in the poor south and in the poor counties of the north and of the central plain. Where the per capita wealth was small, the yield meager, the land value low, the size of the farms restricted, and the farms tilled by their impecunious owners the Democrats were usually in the majority....
> The Republican strength ... came from the wealthy counties, the counties of large farms, and from those where there was a tendency to a higher percentage of tenantry. Politically, this likeness in economic condition expressed itself in a sectional alliance of the central plain with the northwest.[5]

From his mapping of mass party strength, Carleton argued that "there was no need of a third party in Indiana" during the 1870s. The Democratic party, whose leaders espoused monetary expansion from 1874 onward, became in his view "the natural party of opposition" and "adjusted its policies and its creed to the interests and predilections of the people who composed it."[6]

The common ailment from which Carleton's analysis suffers is

Chapter Four

the inaccessibility of individual data for voters that can show historians the extent to which party support actually arose from differences in wealth and in status. Measures of wealth for counties are aggregate measures that average out most internal variation. They can indicate that high total wealth and high Republican support went together for counties and that poor counties showed high Democratic support. But these aggregate measures cannot show *why* this relationship obtained across counties unless the internal structure of wealth, status, and partisanship among voters is first observed.

The *People's Guide*s help make clear this internal structure among voters for Indiana's depression decade. What their examination shows is how the class structure of wealth and the steps marking occupational status in different places of work influenced party support in ways that otherwise remain quite invisible at the county level. It is worth reviewing at the outset, however, the county-level distributions of wealth from which Carleton's inferences were made, in order to see how stable they were and where the *People's Guide* counties stood in their level of wealth compared to all counties of the state.

The geographic distribution of average farm values across Indiana in 1870 is displayed in figure 4.1, where the darkly shaded counties are those whose average value was more than one-half standard deviation above the state mean. This mapping, of course, is only one way that wealth was distributed. How stable was this distribution in relation to other measures of county wealth during the 1870s? Part of the answer is given in table 4.1, which displays the county-level means, standard deviations, and correlation coefficients from 1870 to 1880 for several wealth-related measures of county composition.[7] A decade-long decline in mean levels is registered by several measures; the average value of farms, the average assessed value of property, and the average value of farm products all stood at lower levels in 1880 than in 1870, and with smaller dispersion across the counties. On the other hand, the percentage of farms larger than one hundred acres increased and showed a consolidation toward this new level by lower dispersion. The average value of capital invested in manufacturing and the average value of manufactured products

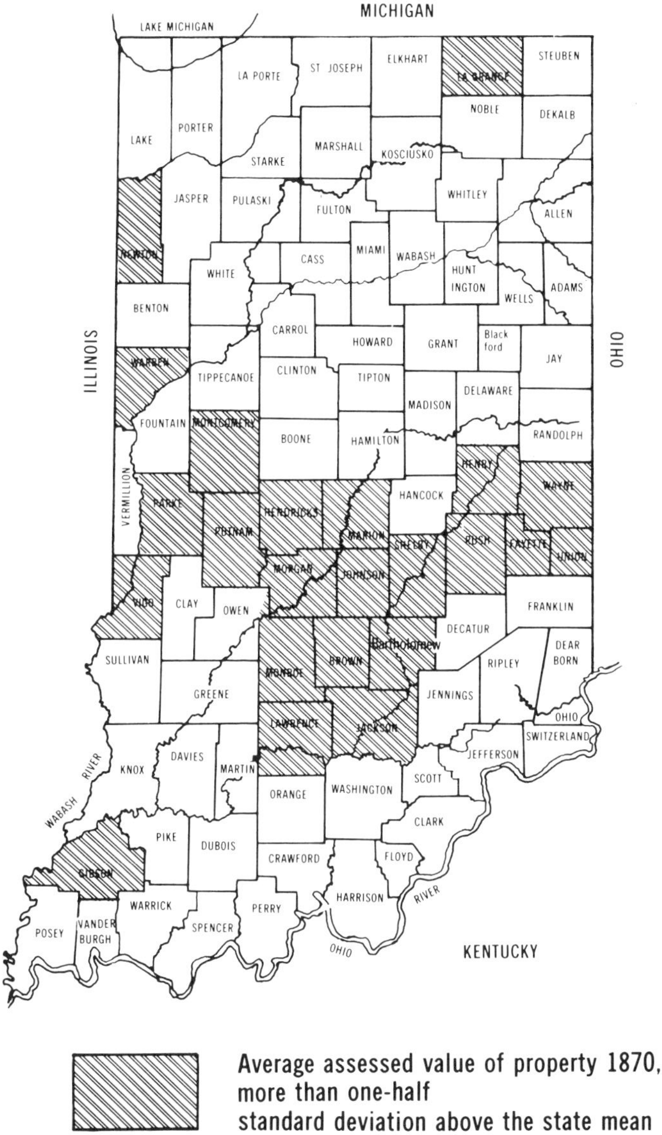

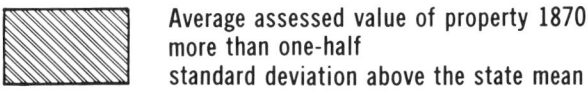

Fig. 4.1 Geographic distribution of average assessed value of property, 1870

Table 4.1. Measures of Wealth on All Counties, 1870 and 1880

Aggregate county measure	Pearson's r 1870–80	1870 Mean	s	1880 Mean	s
Average value of farms[b]	.86	$3,940	$1,623	$3,251	$1,252
Average assessed property[a]	.76	$1,657	$581	$1,358	$424
Average value of farm products[b]	.60	$785	$318	$590	$217
% of farms larger than 100 acres	.46	52.3%	11.9%	71.5%	6.1%
Average capital in manufacturing[c]	.78	$3,464	$2,607	$4,438	$3,899
Average value manufacturing products	.62	$7,420	$4,842	$9,715	$8,829

[a]Assessed value of property divided by the number of adult male citizens.
[b]Value of all farms divided by the number of farms.
[c]Capital employed in manufacturing divided by the number of manufacturing establishments.

The Rural Electorate: Social and Economic Structure

also increased but with greater variability. Over the decade, these changes could have meant that wealth among counties shifted dramatically from one end of the state to the other and differently for every measure of wealth. What, in fact, did the changes mean?

Part of their meaning is revealed by the correlation coefficients, all of which were below the .90 level, toward which the most highly stable geographic distributions usually tend, but were still a long way from zero (no stability) or a reversal to negative coefficients. The lowest one ($r = .46$) indicates that the geographic distribution of farms greater than one hundred acres shifted the most during this ten-year period, as small farms in 1870 were combined into larger farming units by 1880. This consolidation, and the ripples of depression, tended to affect the other coefficients as well, but not so severely. The average value of farm products ($r = .60$) and the average value of manufactured products ($r = .62$) showed greater stability in their geographic distribution during the decade than the size of farms. But even these were less stable than either the value of assessed property ($r = .76$) or the average capital invested in manufacturing ($r = .78$). Most stable of all, however, was the average value of farms ($r = .86$), which remained largely unaffected by shifts in farm size or the decline from the depression registered in the mean levels. There was, then, stability in wealth across Indiana, even if not at the very highest levels.

Do these measures index one or several dimensions of variation in wealth across Indiana's counties? This question can be explored by observing the intercorrelation matrix given in table 4.2. This matrix contains four main regions. The first is the upper triangular region that indicates how all six measures of wealth were interrelated in 1870 alone. The circled value in the lower right-hand corner of this region ($r = .92$) shows that average values of manufacturing capital and of manufacturing product varied together across Indiana. But the low entries for rows five and six also show that this variation was largely unrelated to agricultural wealth. Similarly, the four measures of agricultural wealth show a geographic overlay; where agricultural wealth was high on one measure it was also high on the others, with the average value of farms and the average assessed value of property most closely mapped to each other (r = .78). The triangular region of the matrix for 1880 contains very similar information, except that the percentage of large farms was no longer an index to the other agricultural distributions of wealth. To summarize, both in 1870 and in 1880, the two measures of manufacturing wealth followed similar geographic patterns across the counties and, at slightly lower levels of stability, so did those for agriculture. Agricultural wealth and wealth in manufacturing, however, were unrelated to each other. Thus, two prime dimensions of wealth were present.

The rectangular region of the matrix is one of intertemporal relationships that has for its main diagonal just those coefficients between 1870 and 1880 previously discussed. Among all coefficients in this region, the average value of farms (r = .86) was the most stable indicator of general agricultural wealth over the decade. The final region of this matrix adds several further measures of county composition to the previous ones. The percentage of the population living in urban areas in 1870 was high where manufacturing wealth was high but was not related to agricultural wealth. The percentage of farmers who owned their own farms in 1880 increased moderately as the average value of farms and farm products declined, and increased most dramatically in areas where the prior 1870 proportion of large farms was low (r = -.86). These relationships simply underscore again the two primary dimensions. Most interesting, perhaps, is that no wealth measures were related to population growth.

What these measures show, then, aside from mean level declines in agriculture due to the depression, is that at least two dimensions of wealth had significance across Indiana, one based on farming and its way of life and the other based on manufacturing and an urban way of life. It will not be grossly inaccurate, therefore, to assess where the nine *People's Guide* counties stood among all counties on the two relatively most stable distributions for these two major dimensions.

Figure 4.2 displays the regression of the average values of farms for 1880 on those for 1870 and locates the nine *People's Guide* counties in this joint distribution. With the exception of

Table 4.2. Intercorrelation of County Wealth Measures, 1870 and 1880

	1	2	3	4	5	6	7	8	9	10	11	12	13	14	15	16	17	18
1. % lg. frms. 70																		
2. Av. val. frms. 70	(63)																	
3. Av. assd. prp. 70	(66)	(69)																
4. Av. val. f. pr. 70	(59)	(78)	(60)															
5. Av. mfg. cap. 70	–.08	.20	.16	–.04														
6. Av. val. m. pr. 70	–.08	.15	.13	–.04	(.92)													
7. % lg. frms. 80	(.46)	.21	.17	.20	–.31	–.36												
8. Av. val. frms. 80	.43	(.86)	.50	.54	.25	.17	.21											
9. Av. assd. prp. 80	.54	.84	(.76)	.67	.26	.21	.06	(.77)										
10. Av. val. f. pr. 80	.49	.75	.58	(.60)	.15	.13	.20	.86	(.73)									
11. Av. mfg. cap. 80	–.08	.13	.04	–.06	(.78)	.70	–.22	.25	.19	.11								
12. Av. val. m. pr. 80	–.04	.17	.05	–.02	.62	(.62)	–.20	.29	.23	.16	(.83)							
13. % urban 70	–.04	.25	.19	.07	(.82)	(.81)	–.31	.30	.33	.24	(.71)	(.63)						
14. % frm. own. 80	–.36	–.44	–.43	–.60	.03	–.02	.10	–.33	–.46	(.56)	.12	.02	–.12					
15. Pop. growth	.05	.02	.06	.16	–.06	–.05	.11	.05	–.02	.18	–.07	–.01	–.05	–.44				
16. % lg. f. gro	(.86)	.62	.64	.55	.02	–.08	–.05	–.40	–.57	–.44	–.02	–.07	–.09	.43	.06			
17. Mfg. growth	.09	–.07	–.22	–.06	–.15	–.16	.12	.02	–.10	–.08	.38	.54	–.10	.12	.00	–.06		
18. Pop. dens. 70	–.09	.30	.14	.07	.75	.71	–.44	.35	.40	.20	.64	.57	(.81)	–.04	–.19	–.14	–.06	
19. Pop. dens. 80	–.09	.31	.14	.08	.74	.71	–.45	.37	.40	.23	.63	.58	(.80)	–.11	–.03	–.13	–.06	(.98)

1870 region

Region of intertemporal relationships

1880 region

Region of relationships to other measures

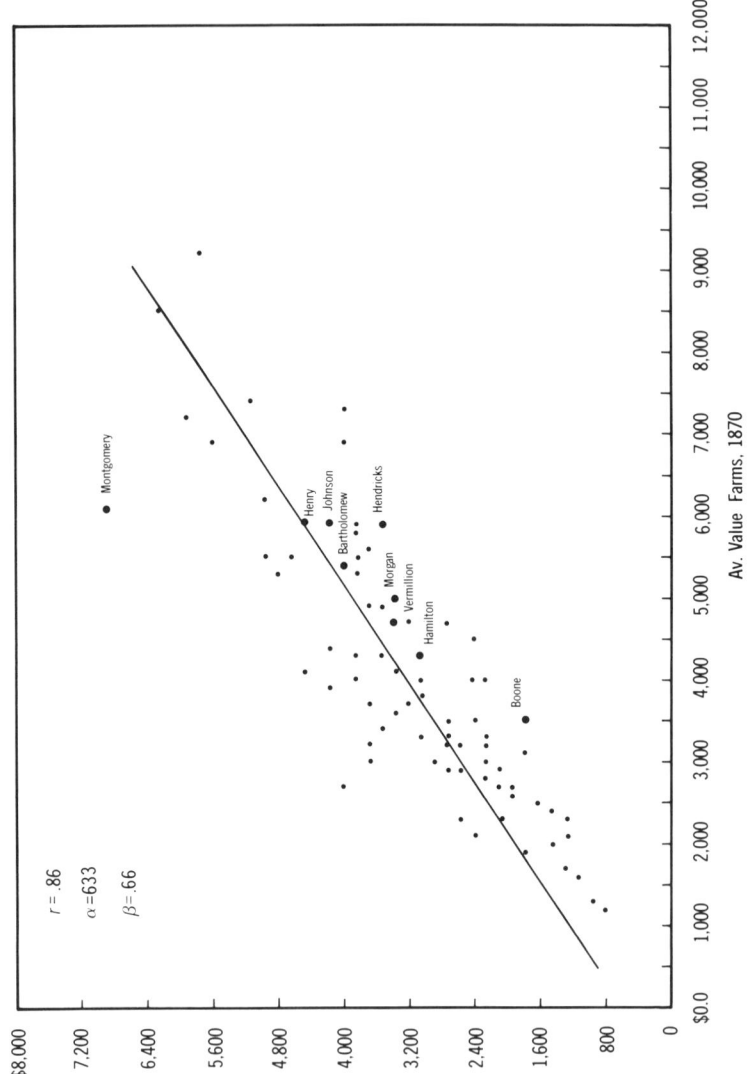

Fig. 4.2 Regression of average farm values in 1880 on average farm values in 1870

Montgomery County, which stood as a dramatically wealthier outlier in 1880 than in 1870, the nine counties covered the surface of agricultural wealth at levels of change only slightly lower than those defined by the regression line itself. This nine-county electorate, while more Republican than the state as a whole, was not, in general, wealthier. If anything, the counties which composed it shifted less rapidly in their farm values than other counties of the state.

Similarly, figure 4.3 displays the regression of the average value of capital invested in manufacturing for 1880 on the urban percentage for 1870. The nine *People's Guide* counties were distributed in the lower half of this joint distribution as a direct function of their rural character. Within the lower half, however, they again covered the main aspects of covariation. But the rural character of these sample counties, like their geographic location in the Tipton Till region, is a distinct bias. None of these counties contained a city with a population greater than 5,000 persons. This bias means that inferences from the *People's Guide*s about internal structure for the electorate apply most clearly to the rural-farming rather than the urban-manufacturing portion of Indiana, quite in accord with Carleton's earlier emphasis. In demographic terms, the rural-farm areas of Indiana contained about two-thirds of the state's population. It is to these voters in the rural areas that the *People's Guide*s apply, and to whom we now turn.

In their door-to-door canvass of central Indiana in June 1870, federal census-takers found many rural voters outwardly poor. Nearly half owned no real estate. Poverty, of course, cannot be measured directly by these figures but only by annual income from daily work and what it would buy for a family. Wealth reveals poverty indirectly, looking backwards, by the lack of accumulated savings, purchase of goods, and investment in land. But by these standards, one out of five rural Hoosier voters had no wealth at all.[8]

Table 4.3 shows the median and mean levels of wealth for the nine-county sample of individual voters. The large differences between median and mean levels, and the large standard deviation around the mean, point to inequality in the distribution of

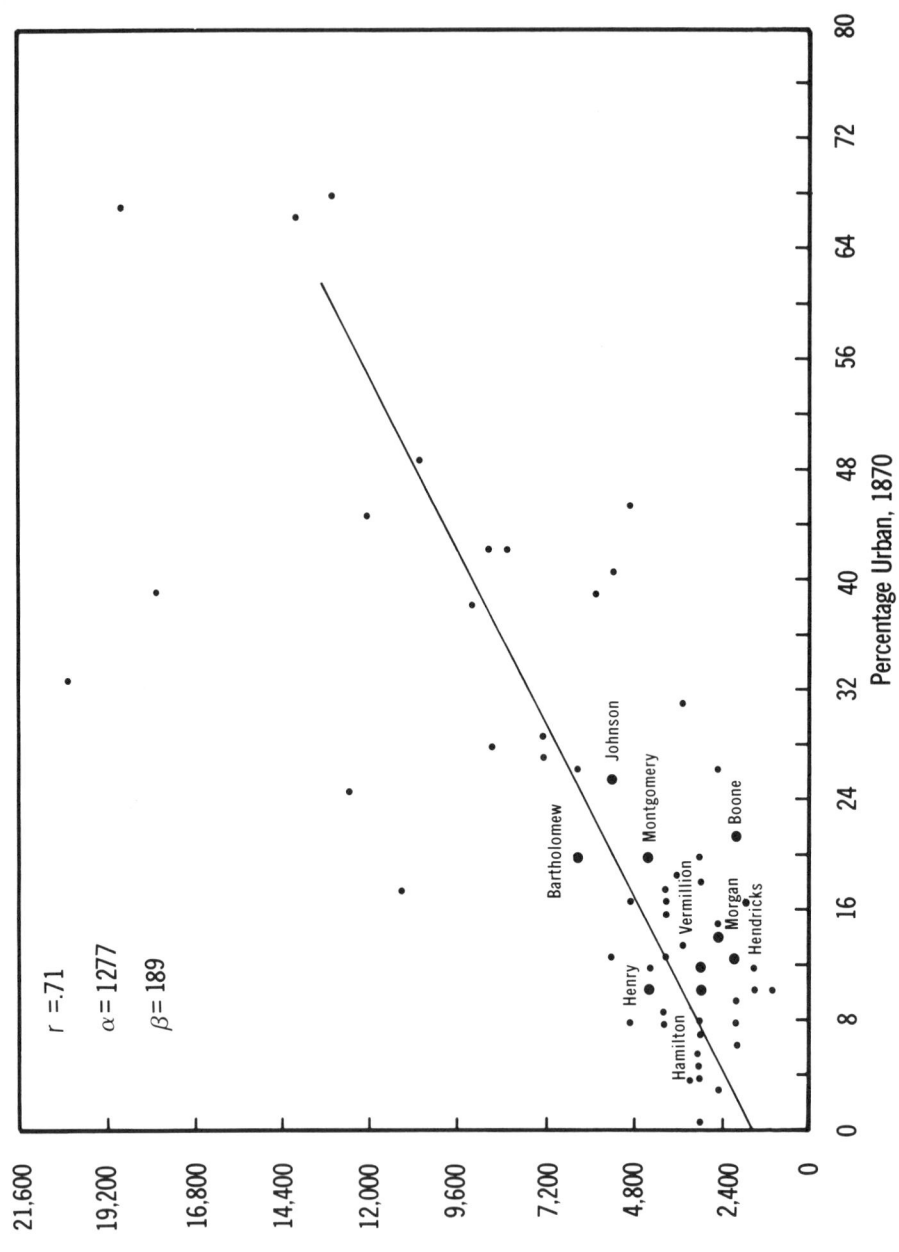

Fig. 4.3 Regression of average manufacturing capital in 1880 on percentage urban, 1870

The Rural Electorate: Social and Economic Structure

Table 4.3. Central Tendency and Dispersion for Three Types of Wealth

Distribution	Median	Mean	Standard deviation
Real estate owned	$800	$2,571	$5,933
Personal estate owned	$400	$779	$1,593
Total estate	$1,300	$3,350	$7,083
N = 3,318			

wealth. A picture of this inequality among voters is shown by the Lorenz curves graphed in figure 4.4 that jointly cumulate proportions of wealth and proportions of voters. A diagonal line has been added to indicate the "ideal line" of perfect equality along which each voter would enjoy an equal share of the total wealth.[9] Two measures serve to show how far from perfect equality the actual distribution was. The Gini index measures the area between the straight equality standard and the actual curves, and shows that wealth among these rural voters ranged from .73 to .80 toward complete inequality. A similar index, the equal-share coefficient, defined as the proportion of persons holding less than an equal share (that is, the mean), stood comparably high, at .72 for each distribution.[10]

Some of the reasons for this high degree of inequality are clear. Voters spanned all ages in the adult years, and wealth, accrued from current income, accumulated with the years and the kind of work a voter did. Both age and occupation helped form the outlines of inequality in wealth among Hoosiers. Of more immediate interest than explaining how these differences in wealth arose among voters, however, is showing whether they had any effects on party support. Were voters from different classes involved in the party system in different ways? Did voters in different wealth classes offer differing degrees of support to the major parties? Did extremes of wealth inequality lead to partisan polarization? In asking these questions, the term "class" itself poses a minor problem. I will not dwell long on its definition. The term is generally used, in the words of Milton Gordon, "to refer to the horizontal stratification of a population by means of factors related in some way to the economic life of society."[11]

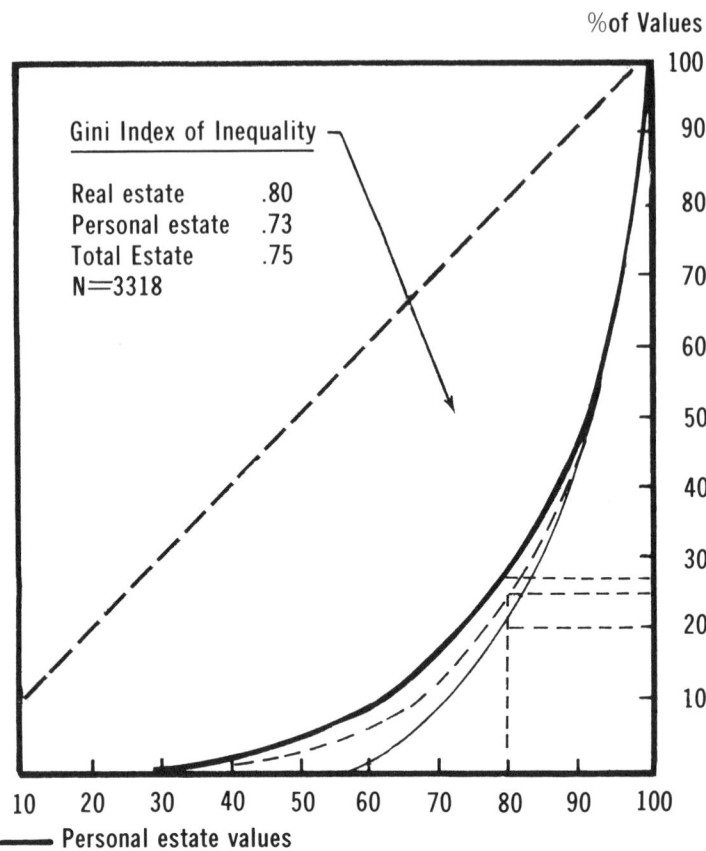

Fig. 4.4 Lorenz curves of wealth inequality

Richard Centers several years ago suggested distinguishing between subjective classes, as categories of people sharing a "consciousness of kind" or "a feeling of belonging" (in the same sense as party identification), and objective classes, as categories for people where boundaries must be imposed by the researcher quite apart from the individual's own perceptions of self.[12] In opera-

The Rural Electorate: Social and Economic Structure

Table 4.4. Party Involvement by Three Types of Wealth Classes (in percentages)

	Real Property	Real No Property	Personal Property	Personal No Property	Total Property	Total No Property	
Major parties	84	84	83	85	84	85	(84.0)
Minor parties	5	6	6	5	5	6	(5.4)
No answer	11	10	11	10	11	9	(10.6)
Total	100	100	100	100	100	100	
	(53.9)	(46.1)	(76.0)	(24.0)	(78.8)	(21.2)	
Significance level by chi-square =		(.88)		(.69)		(.75)	
N = 1,216							

tional terms, the available data allow only the objective categories that can be established from real, personal, and total wealth as reported in the census manuscripts.

Wealth categories formed from these objective measures may be developed in several ways, however. First, rural Indiana voters can be distinguished from the census reports into propertied and nonpropertied groups on each kind of wealth. I shall use the term "wealth classes" for this basic distinction. Second, additional wealth "strata" may also be distinguished among those who held property. If the mean is taken as the equal-share point in each distribution, then several groupings of wealth can be marked off by setting other boundaries at the half-share and double-share points of division, yielding a fivefold classification for each kind of wealth.[13] If political polarization based on the distribution of wealth was present in Indiana during the 1870s, it will appear for one or more of these wealth partitions as a moderate to high correlation coefficient.

As a first step, it is worth asking whether class differences in wealth led to any differences in the way individual voters were involved with the party system itself. As table 4.4 shows, major party commitments, minor party loyalties, and attachments to no

Chapter Four

party at all were kinds of involvement as likely for the nonpropertied as for the propertied, whether these classes were formed from real, personal, or total estate wealth. On no dimension of wealth was variation in these kinds of responses distinguishable from sampling error, nor was there any difference if those identifying themselves as "independents" were separated from other third-party adherents. Class lines of cleavage simply had no effect at all for these different kinds of involvement in the party system.

The scale of party allegiance alters these political responses to form an ordered scale with the two major parties at each end. How was party allegiance among voters affected by the different wealth classes? Consider the classes formed by the property distinction for real estate. Section (a) of table 4.5 shows that Republican allegiance increased from 49 percent among all voters to 53 percent among those owning land, and that Democratic allegiance increased from 35 percent to 40 percent among those without real property. These differences by real estate classes moved in opposing partisan directions, without affecting voters between the major party division—the Independents. They resulted in a Republican majority among holders of land and a balance of power within the landless class, as one source in wealth differences that helped shape party support at the polls. The similar division into two classes for distributions of personal estate and total estate revealed insufficient variation in party support from that among all rural Hoosiers to distinguish this variation from sampling error. Only one difference in party support by class, then, arose among Hoosiers; this was along a line of wealth dividing landholders and the landless.

How important for party allegiance was this line of cleavage? Was it like an unbridgeable river in a deep canyon—one that separated and polarized voters into distinctly partisan camps—or was it more like a shallow creek, easy to cross? These are questions about the extent of political polarization that depended on this wealth-class cleavage. They are answered by a correlation coefficient for the ordered categories of this table. Measured by gamma = .18, the degree of class-based political polarization in this electorate was low; the line of class cleavage was more like a small creek than a running stream or a foaming river. Certainly in

Table 4.5. Party Attachments by Three Types of Wealth Classes (in percentages)

	Real (a)		Personal (b)		Total (c)	
	Property	No Property	Property	No Property	Property	No Property
Republican	53	44	50	46	50	45	(49.1)
Independent	16	16	17	14	16	15	(16.0)
Democrat	31	40	33	40	34	40	(34.9)
Total	100	100	100	100	100	100	
	(53.9)	(46.1)	(76.0)	(24.0)	(78.8)	(21.2)	

Significance level by
  chi-square =   (.001)   (.13)   (.14)
Kendall's Tau$_b$ = .10
Gamma = .18
N = 1,216

Chapter Four

this respect, aggregate county-level measures of farm wealth are deceptive with respect to the internal sources of strong Republican support.

The extent of wealth inequality among Indiana's voters during the 1870s suggests that dividing them into two large classes may not have captured the real extremes of wealth difference, and therefore party support, that then existed. If one man owned five hundred dollars' worth of real estate and another held land valued at ten times that amount, then this difference is worth testing for any further consequences in the support offered to the parties. Table 4.6 shows, however, that the four additional wealth groupings among property-holding Hoosiers, when set alongside of the landless class, made little difference for variation in party support. The rate of independence from the two major parties increased from 16 to 18 percent, but neither Republican nor Democratic attachments followed directly along these further grades of wealth. Polarization, as measured by an order coefficient (gamma = .13), was even less than in the simpler two-class division. At best, the shallow creek between voters who owned land and those who did not was the only one worth noting. In terms of allegiance to party, rural Hoosier voters constituted no hierarchy based on wealth in land alone.

Census-takers asked not only how much wealth a person had but also what he did to earn his daily bread. Very few voters failed to report an occupation to the census-taker, for what a man did—whether in shops, stores, banks, classrooms, or on the farms—gave him an identity in rural society. Nearly everyone had some job he called his own, and the relations among men established by these jobs were powerful and persuasive, relating one person to another on a day-to-day or week-to-week basis. Coopers built the barrels used by farmers and merchants. Dealers arranged to purchase, store, and transport grains from the farms to market. Wagonmakers, harness and saddlemakers, blacksmiths, and teamsters provided the vehicles, implements, and labor for local transportation. Clergy gathered their flocks, baptized, married, and buried God's children. Merchants, grocers, and druggists stocked and sold locally needed goods. The variety of occupations among Hoosier voters was extensive but not

The Rural Electorate: Social and Economic Structure

Table 4.6. Party Attachments by Real Estate Strata (in percentages)

	Upper	Upper-Middle	Middle	Lower-Middle	Non-propertied	Row Totals
Republican	52	57	52	52	44	(49.1)
Independent	18	17	16	15	16	(16.0)
Democrat	30	26	32	33	40	(34.9)
Total	100	100	100	100.	100	
	(15.9)	(11.7)	(10.0)	(16.4)	(46.1)	

Significance level by chi-square = .05
Kendall's Tau$_b$ = .09
Gamma = .13
N = 1,216

endless and, compared to that of a more urban setting, was even perhaps quite restricted.[14] This variety was sufficient, however, to make for substantial differences in function and status, and it marked some of the steps of status within rural society itself.

The clearest line of demarcation among all occupations in rural central Indiana was a functional one between the agricultural and nonagricultural domains of work. Measured by sheer involvement in Indiana's party system, there was little difference among voters that depended on their placement in either of these domains. Rates of major party commitment, minor party loyalty, and no attachment to any party were comparable in both domains. On the scale of party allegiance, however, rates for Republican attachment increased from 49 percent among all voters to 61 percent among those who worked off-the-farms, while Democratic rates increased from 35 percent among all voters to 41 percent in the agricultural work-force (see table 4.7). These shifts in the rates were notably greater than for those based on the wealth classes. They heightened in the nonagricultural domain of work, one source of strong majority Republican support. The comparable order statistic, gamma = .35, also indicates that there were greater polarizing tendencies along this basic division of work than along lines of sheer wealth in land. Nonetheless, the balance of party strength between Republicans and Democrats within the farming community prevented any direct confrontation

Table 4.7. Party Attachments by Occupational Domain (in percentages)

	Nonagricultural	Agricultural	
Republican	61	43	(49.1)
Independent	16	16	(16.0)
Democrat	23	41	(34.9)
Total	100	100	
	(32.2)	(67.8)	
Significance level by chi-square = .001			
Kendall's Tau_b = .18			
Gamma = .35			
N = 1,216			

of the parties across this major work-force boundary, especially because the farming community contained two out of every three rural Hoosier voters.

What was the internal structure of this agricultural workforce? The first line of distinction was between farmers and farm laborers, who used these identity terms in reporting their occupation to the census-takers. Among farmers, the ownership or nonownership of land marked the class difference already observed in the electorate as a whole. But also important to a farmer was the amount of land that he controlled. Therefore, I classified Indiana's farming population into four categories that formed a status gradient: farm laborers at the lowest status level (a few of whom held land), then nonpropertied farmers (owning no land), small propertied farmers (owning less than the mean amount of land), and, at the highest level, large propertied farmers (owning more than the mean amount of land). The ranking of these categories in the form of a status gradient was itself confirmed by calculating for each group the proportion of voters who held more than the median amount of personal estate wealth. As shown in table 4.8, this proportion ran a rank-ordering from the low of 15 percent among farm laborers to the high of 93 percent among large propertied farmers.

Clearly, the distinction between farmers and farm laborers is a functional one of superordination and subordination. Such functional differences are more difficult to justify among all

The Rural Electorate: Social and Economic Structure

Table 4.8. Rank Order of Strata within the Agricultural Domain, Census Sample

	% with More than Median in Personal Estate	% of Population	Census N
Farmers—large property	93	22	735
Farmers—small property	72	12	396
Farmers—no property	51	18	587
Farm laborers	15	13	418

farmers as a group, although owning and not owning land (tenancy) may approach one. The grades of status by land among farmers are clear, however, and the status gradient extends readily to farm laborers as well, in terms of the amounts of personal estate that individual voters controlled. Thus, status grades within the agricultural work-force may be viewed as four steps on a ladder but of unequal size, for there were different numbers of persons engaged on each rung.

Of what political import were these steps? Figure 4.5 graphs the movement in party allegiance along the status grades from farm laborers to the large propertied farmers, where the two lines indicating Republican and Democratic levels of support open in a "scissors" shape, crisscrossing in the middle. The "handles" of this scissors-graph lie among farm laborers and show a spread from 32 percent Republican to 56 percent Democratic, then crisscross at the middle status levels, and show at the "blades," among large propertied farmers, a spread from 53 percent Republican to 30 percent Democratic. Quite clearly, Republican allegiance increased with farming status and Democratic allegiance increased as status declined. At the middle status levels—among nonpropertied farmers and those with small amounts of property—the balance of party support stood intact, characteristic of the farming community as a whole. Independents bulked largest among farmers who owned no land. Like the steps on the ladder within the agricultural work-force itself, status differences were a controlling factor for party support. They provided, in addition to the notable difference between the two

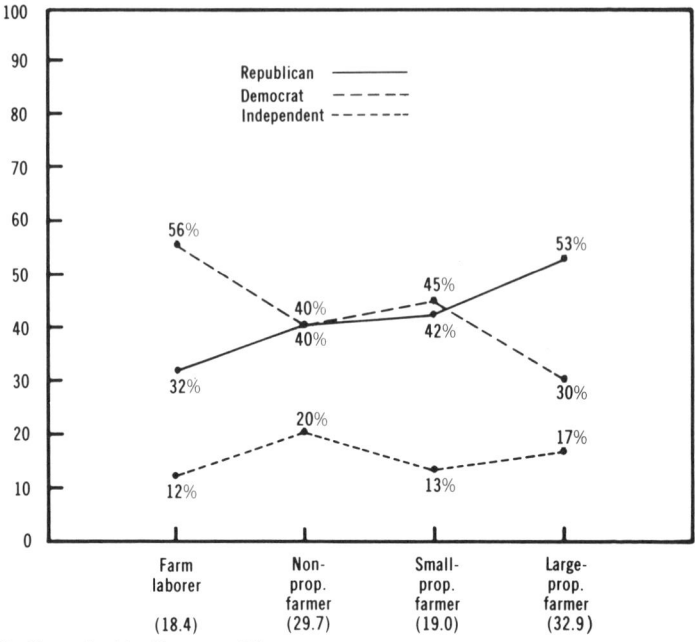

Fig. 4.5 Party attachments by ranked occupational strata within the agricultural domain

domains of work, a further important polar movement in party allegiance on-the-farms (gamma = .22) that was otherwise a basic balance of party power.

In large perspective, both the balance of power within the farm community as a whole and the interior movement toward polarization deserve stress. Hit by depression during a Republican administration, all farm groups could shift more Democratic, or into third parties, but none so readily as the nonpropertied farmers, among whom a large group of voters stood independent of the major party divisions. Any such movement, however, would also begin to cut the connection between high farm wealth and the high Republican support that Carleton mapped, without disrupting the Democratic connection at the lower end of the

The Rural Electorate: Social and Economic Structure

farm scale. Thus, the balance of power in the farm domain as a whole, and the small polar movement in support towards opposition parties, emerge as parts of a puzzle that asks to be solved: if not based on farmers of high wealth standing, then from among what groups of voters did strong Republican support come? Clearly, more pieces of the puzzle are needed and some of them can be put in place by looking at party support in work off-the-farms.

For work off-the-farms functional and rank-ordered groupings of occupations were developed separately.[15] Four functional groups were defined by global judgments of the kind of activity required by persons in each occupation, whether primarily merchandising, professional, or craft-specialty tasks, along with a residual category for those in other occupations that could not be readily classified in these ways. These are simple, nominal categories defined by the global functions that persons in each specific occupation were thought to perform. In contrast, rank-ordered groups were also established for the people working off-the-farms just as they were for the agricultural domain, again using as a criterion the proportion of members in each specific occupation who held more than the median amount of personal estate wealth.[16] From this ranking of occupations by personal estate, a gradient of three categories was formed—from low-status through middle-status to high-status occupations off-the-farm. Table 4.9 shows both the functional classification (with the number of persons in each occupation for the census sample) and the status-gradient classification (with the specific rank-score for each occupation).[17] This ladder of status, for occupations off-the-farm, involves only three steps, again of unequal size.

Levels of party allegiance quite parallel to those following the farm gradients characterized voters by status differences in work off-the-farms, extending upward in Republican support and downward in Democratic support. Seen alone, they took the shape of a "funnel," opening outward (see figure 4.6). At the narrow, low-status "neck" of the funnel, 55 percent Republican support was countered by 32 percent Democratic support. Then, the differences in support widened further to a "rim" of substantial spread between the parties, at 69 percent Republican to 15

Table 4.9. Rank Order and Functional Categories for the Nonagricultural Domain, Census Sample

Rank-Order Categories	Rank Score[a]	Functional Categories	Census N
Upper occupational stratum		*Mercantile occupations*	
Dry goods merchant	98	Agent	12
Merchant	92	Butcher	12
Grocer	91	Druggist	14
Lawyer	89	Dry goods merchant	48
Physician	87	Food merchant[b]	14
Druggist	86	General merchant[b]	29
		Grocer	21
Middle occupational stratum		Merchant	25
Trader	75	Miller	21
Agent	67	Store clerk	34
Clergyman	63	Trader	12
General merchant[b]	59		
Lawyer	59	*Professional occupations*	
Butcher	58	Clergyman	19
Miller	57	Lawyer	18
Saddlemaker	50	Personal services[b]	31
Personal services[b]	48	Physician	39
Blacksmith	42	Teacher	16
Teamster	42		
Wagonmaker	39	*Craft specialty occupations*	
Manufacturer[b]	38	Blacksmith	48
Carpenter	37	Cabinetmaker	13
Tailor	36	Carpenter	115
Food merchant[b]	36	Cooper	21
Cabinetmaker	31	Manufacturer[b]	61
Store clerk	27	Saddlemaker	16
		Tailor	11
		Shoemaker	13
		Lawyer	22
		Wagonmaker	26

percent Democratic among high-status voters in off-the-farm occupations. Independents, again, were most numerous at the middle occupational level. The increasing spread in support for the major parties was not, however, one of polarization within the nonagricultural work-force (gamma = .10). Across this whole

(Table 4.9 continued)

Low occupational stratum		Other occupations	
Railroad engineer	23	Brickmaker	10
Brickmason	23	Brickmason	13
Shoemaker	22	Day laborer	180
Teacher	19	Domestic service	10
Cooper	14	Factory worker	36
Painter	13	Painter	16
Factory worker	11	Plasterer	13
Brickmaker	10	Railroad engineer	13
Plasterer	8	Railroad hand	27
Day laborer	5	Teamster	24
Domestic service	0		
Railroad hand	0		

[a] The rank score is defined as the percentage in each occupational subgroup holding more than the median amount of personal estate wealth in the whole sample.
[b] Several occupational labels were combined for this category.

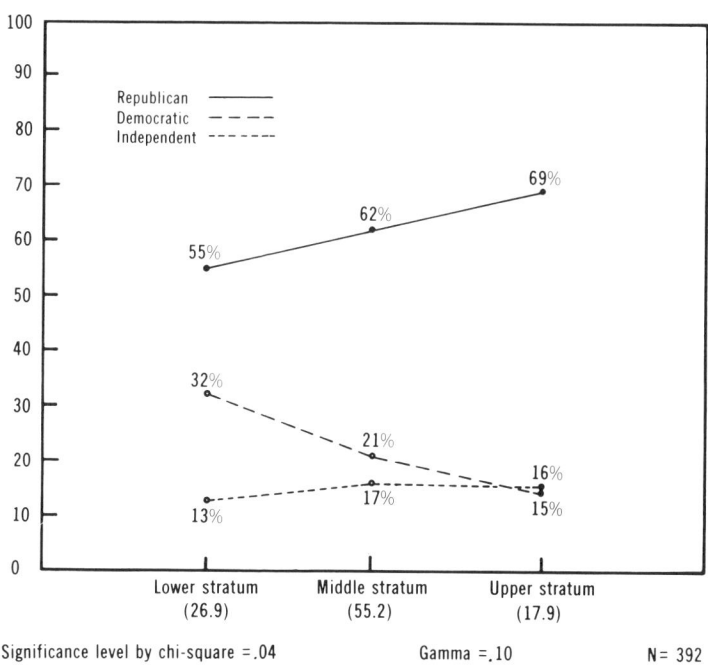

Fig. 4.6 Party attachments by ranked occupational strata within the nonagricultural domain

Chapter Four

off-the-farm gradient, Republican support was at a majority level, and this off-the-farm majority is a piece of the puzzle that no aggregate measures could readily tap. In fact, party support followed a nearly continuous gradient, across both agricultural and nonagricultural domains, quite hidden from any classification of counties by wealth alone or as urban or rural areas.

Perhaps the most graphic display of how occupational status levels affected support for the parties among rural Hoosiers can be shown by a composite picture of this electorate, putting the agricultural and nonagricultural domains of work side by side in one portrait. This composite picture is shown in figure 4.7, which combines into one the two previous graphs. What it shows are two main lines of party support that cut through and across Indiana's rural electorate, following, by level, the rungs of these two status ladders. The meaning of status among Indiana voters in the 1870s is clear: the higher in status was a voter's work within his domain, the more likely was his party allegiance to be a Republican one; the lower his status, the more likely was it to be Democratic. But the movement in party allegiance toward increased Republican support across all ranks of occupation was most pronounced off-the-farms, and at the very top of this work-scale we can quite properly speak of a Republican party norm.

One footnote to these findings must be appended. Functional groupings of nonfarm occupations added no additional insight and obscured variation in party support by gradients of status. In one respect, however, differences among functional groupings were worth noting. Both merchants and professionals were more likely than others outside of agriculture to hold no party attachments at all, a combination where both higher than average income and perhaps better than average education may have shaped independence from the two major parties.

As might be expected, the occupational domains of work were highly associated with residential location in these nine rural counties. Voters generally lived where they worked. The *People's Guide*s indicated the residential location of voters in terms of towns, cities, and distances from the nearest town or major crossroads. Since no large cities were included in these counties, the classification of residence was initially sought in a scale of five

The Rural Electorate: Social and Economic Structure

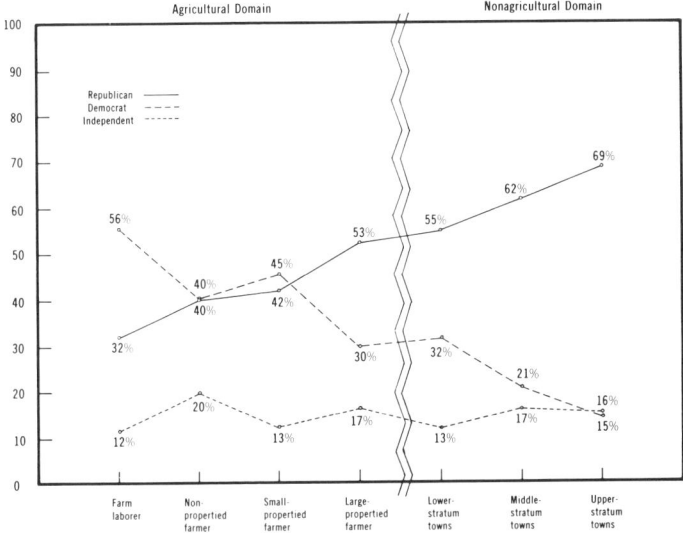

Fig. 4.7 Party attachments for combined occupational strata by domain

small increments: (1) the open countryside, denoting any place of residence marked by distance from a point of reference; (2) a hamlet, as any place with a population under 625 persons; (3) a village, as any place larger than a hamlet but having less than 1,250 persons; (4) a town, as a population center with betwen 1,250 and less than 2,500 persons; and (5) a small city, with a population between 2,500 and 5,000 persons. Since nearly two-thirds of all voters lived in the open countryside, the primary boundary clearly stood between the countryside and residence in the hamlets, villages, towns, and small cities of rural Indiana.

The relation between residence for this simple dichotomy and the two major occupational domains is presented in table 4.10. The major cells on the diagonal of this table show that 88 percent of those who worked on the farms lived in the open countryside, and a comparable proportion who had off-the-farm jobs lived in the towns. Because of this large overlap in occupation and residence, the rates of party allegiance between the two residence domains closely mirrored those for the occupational domains themselves, as shown in table 4.11. The Republicans held a clear

Table 4.10. Work Domains by Place of Residence (in percentages)

Work Domain	Small Towns	Open Countryside		
Nonagricultural	88	12	100	(32.1)
Agricultural	11	89	100	(67.9)
	(33.8)	(66.2)		
N = 1,216				

Table 4.11. Party Attachments by Place of Residence (in percentages)

	Small Towns	Open Countryside	
Republican	62	42	(49.1)
Independent	14	17	(16.0)
Democrat	24	41	(34.9)
Total	100	100	(100.0)
	(33.8)	(66.2)	
N = 1,216			

three-to-one majority over the Democrats in the small towns, comparable to their advantage in the nonagricultural domain of work. Similarly, in the farming countryside neither party was in the majority and those independent of the two major parties held the balance of power.

Table 4.12 considers residence and occupational domains jointly and makes clear that where voters lived as well as where they worked *both* influenced party allegiance. At the extremes of contrast, nonfarm work, combined with residence in town, produced a 64 percent Republican majority around which further variation was a product of the status differences already examined, but farm work and farm residence produced a near 40 percent Republican and 40 percent Democratic standoff, between which Independents who lived and worked on the farms were nearly a 20 percent minority.

We must now recast Carleton's earlier argument. Not only did party support in Indiana's mass electorate vary by average levels of farm wealth across counties, but it varied within them over several different cuttings of the electorate. Sheer wealth classes were not the most important groups distinguished by these

The Rural Electorate: Social and Economic Structure

Table 4.12. Polar Party Attachments by Residence and Work (in percentages)

	Town Nonagric.	Town Agric.	Country Nonagric.	Country Agric.	
Republican	64	56	54	41	(49.1)
Independent	15	11	17	17	(16.0)
Democrat	21	33	29	42	(34.9)
Total	100	100	100	100	(100.0)
	(25.8)	(8.0)	(6.3)	(59.9)	
N = 1,216					

cuttings, though ownership of land among voters was one basis for increased Republican support. Much more important were the status gradients established by what voters did for a living and where they lived. Differences in party allegiance between farm life and village life, between the open countryside and the small towns of rural Indiana, made this clear. Each contained further variation that followed quite directly on steps of status among Hoosier voters. But these same findings also offer a further problem in the puzzle: why was not political polarization greater, given both high wealth inequality and gradients of status that led in quite opposing partisan directions? The key to this puzzle lies among Indiana's farmers as political actors and with the balance of party power that largely characterized those who both lived on and worked the farms—an observation Carleton never could make working only from aggregate returns. We shall return to the problem this puzzle poses after first considering the ethnoreligious group-structure of Indiana's rural electorate.

5

Assessing the Ethnic and Religious Composition of Indiana's Rural Electorate

The "freezing" of Indiana's party system after the Civil War left several fissures and cracks in the body politic along regional, ethnic, and religious lines.[1] Allegiance to party during the 1870s was fitted to these fissures and cracks in no simple way. It ran through and across them in ways that were connected to, but not determined by, cultural group aspects of the social structure. Clearly, European and native backgrounds were important sources of differing involvement with the party system itself, and they also gave strong direction to party support. Regional identities among the native-born, however, made for little difference in support. While religious denominations structured group levels of Republican and Democratic support for members, many citizens were not denominational members. Denominations, therefore, were important for the whole electorate not for their particular theologies but as channels of communication that led to different levels of party involvement among both native and foreign-born citizens. Like the tip of an iceberg, only the surface "results" of these several internal lines of cleavage have been visible in aggregate election returns from the 1870s. Submerged and invisible, the interior mass structure of Indiana's electorate has remained largely hidden from view. The *People's Guide*s now allow us to probe this inner structure more fully than ever before,

The Rural Electorate: Ethnic and Religious Composition

to see the formations of party allegiance along cultural group lines and to measure the extent of party polarization and party support that followed from those lines.

This interior view of party support among Indiana's cultural groups challenges, in part, and then alters the most formidable reinterpretation of late nineteenth-century mass politics that has been offered in recent years. In the two decades since Lee Benson first examined voting patterns in New York State during the Jacksonian period, many historians have looked to ethnic and religious groups as a primary basis for political polarization.[2] The most persuasive such studies were those offered by Richard Jensen and Paul Kleppner. Each presented a major examination of late nineteenth-century midwestern politics that focused attention directly on ethnic and religious subgroups in the electorate and the levels of party allegiance that characterized them. "Partisan affiliations were not rooted in economic class distinctions," Kleppner argued, "they were [instead] political expressions of shared values derived from the voters' membership in, and commitment to, ethnic and religious groups."[3] Jensen argued along similar lines, suggesting that congregations and denominations organized men into cohesive groups "which exerted intense pressure toward uniformity of outlook."[4]

While neither Jensen nor Kleppner viewed congregations and denominations as totally partisan blocs, each took these organizations, along with the regional and ethnic backgrounds of voters, as a structural basis for determining a polarization in the underlying values characterizing the political party spectrum. "Those religious groups offering strong support to the Republican party were more pietistic, or evangelical, in their orientation than those offering similar support to the Democrats," was how Kleppner phrased this polarity.[5] In the strongest form of this argument, both authors claimed that the partisan subcultures of the Midwest from the 1870s through the 1880s were ranged on a "pietistic-ritualistic continuum" of opposing values (Kleppner) or a "pietistic-liturgical" one (Jensen), that had its most telling impact whenever the use of liquor, foreign languages, or sabbath practices became public issues.[6]

Most voting results marshalled in favor of party polarization

Chapter Five

based on ethnoreligious group loyalties have been drawn among ward, township, and county areas of high "culture-group" density. This special selection, of course, poses several questions, certainly one of which is how these special ethnoreligious enclaves were related to all other geographic areas of settlement. At the outset, this question is worth posing for Indiana and for the *People's Guide* counties in particular. Answering it shows how the state of Indiana was composed in ethnic and religious subgroup terms and whether or not the *People's Guide* counties were distributed, in their composition, along the state's main axes of cultural group polarization.

In sheer numbers, Indiana was a native-born stronghold.[7] Thirteen out of fourteen Hoosiers were born in the United States, and six out of ten within Indiana's own borders. Across counties of the state, these figures appear as mean percentages in 1870 that can be compared to those in 1880. Table 5.1 indicates that, on average across counties, a little better than 7 percent of all Hoosiers were born in Europe, and this mean, along with the means for the northern- and southern-born portions of the population, declined only slightly over the decade as new births increased the number of persons who called Indiana home. Because the Irish and Germans were especially important subgroups, their relative incidence across counties has been indicated by a ratio based on the size of the European-born population as a whole. Over this decade, the ratio for Irish declined two points, while it increased the same amount for Germans. In geographic terms these shifts in proportions between 1870 and 1880 were relatively unimportant, for the distribution of population by these regional and ethnic indicators was highly stable, as shown by correlation coefficients all above the .95 level.

European-born Hoosiers were clustered in the four corners of the state, as shown in figure 5.1, which maps the upper tail of the foreign-born distribution. Six counties in this "high-density" tail—Vandenburgh and Dubois in the southwest corner of the state, Porter, Lake, and La Porte in the northwest corner, and Allen in the northeast—had between one-in-five and one-in-three persons born in Europe. No county population was more than 30 percent foreign-born. The *People's Guide* counties were not

The Rural Electorate: Ethnic and Religious Composition

Table 5.1. Means, Standard Deviations, and Correlation Coefficients for Places of Birth, All Counties, 1870 and 1880

Aggregate County Measure	Pearson's r 1870–80	1870 Mean	S	1880 Mean	S
% Indiana-born	.97	63.4	9.8	69.8	9.3
% born in border-so.[a]	.97	6.3	3.9	4.7	3.2
% northern-born[b]	.99	16.7	11.0	13.3	8.9
% foreign-born	.97	7.3	6.3	6.4	5.4
Irish/foreign ratio	.96	26.5	17.2	23.9	16.3
German/foreign ratio	.98	45.8	18.9	47.5	19.8

[a]The states given in the census to form this measure were Kentucky, Virginia, and West Virginia.
[b]The states given in the census to form this measure were Ohio, Pennsylvania, and New York.

located in these areas of the most dense foreign immigration; in none of them was the proportion for foreign-born enclaves above the state mean.

The geographic distribution of native-born citizens in 1870 followed the state's earlier settlement pattern.[8] The map in figure 5.2 shows that persons who knew Indiana as their first home, together with those who came from the states bordering Indiana on the south, were most strongly settled in the southern and central regions of the state, leaving northern-born influence strongest in the northern region. The nine *People's Guide* counties were located along these native-born lines of settlement rather than in the foreign-born enclaves.

Table 5.2 offers the intercorrelation matrix of these measures of population composition, along with three measures of religious composition. Because the main diagonal in the second region of this matrix reports the high geographic stability of composition from 1870 to 1880, essentially the same information about how these measures were related to each other is contained in the first and third regions. Therefore, only the region of the matrix for 1870 needs to be examined in detail.

Two strong polarities in foreign-born and native-born settlement patterns are shown by several high negative correlation coefficients. First, the strong negative relation between the Irish

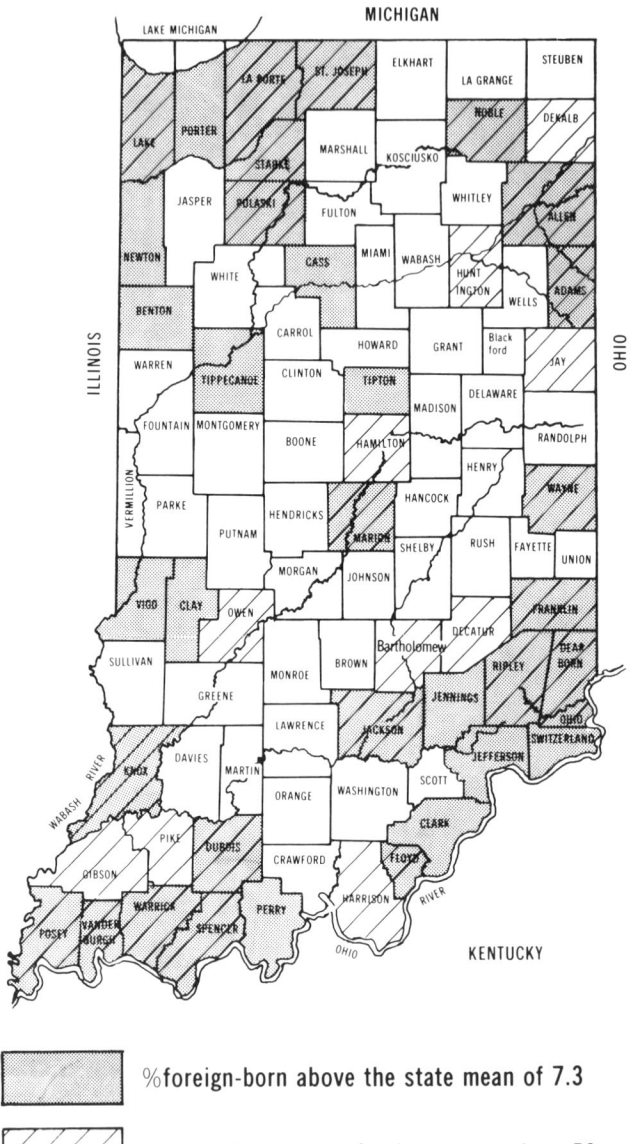

Fig. 5.1 Geographic distribution of foreign-born Indianans, 1870

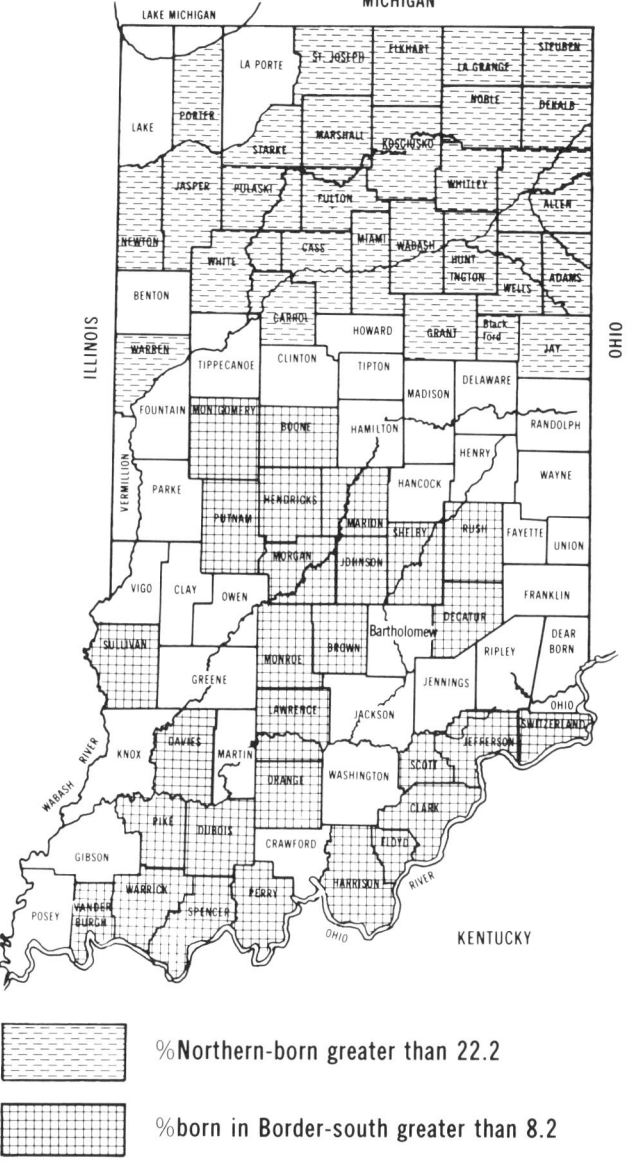

Fig. 5.2 Geographic distribution of native-born Indianans, 1870

Table 5.2. Intercorrelation of County Birthplace Measures, 1870 and 1880

	1	2	3	4	5	6	7	8	9	10	11	12	13	14	15
1. % Indiana 70															
2. % border-so. 70	.59														
3. % north 70	-.78	-.74													
4. % foreign 70	-.49	-.24	-.05												
5. Ir./foreign 70	.29	.39	-.20	-.45											
6. Ger./foreign 70	-.10	-.19	-.06	.51	-.79										
7. % Indiana 80	.97	.60	-.72	-.52	.28	-.08									
8. % border-so. 80	.53	.97	-.73	-.12	.31	-.11	.51								
9. % north 80	-.77	-.74	.99	.04	-.20	-.04	-.72	-.73							
10. % foreign 80	-.55	-.31	-.03	.97	-.44	.44	-.61	-.21	.03						
11. Ir./foreign 80	.33	.39	-.21	-.47	.96	-.74	.33	.33	-.20	-.47					
12. Ger./foreign 80	-.10	-.17	-.07	.51	-.76	.98	-.08	-.08	-.05	.45	-.73				
13. % pietistic 70	.22	.21	-.15	-.33	.25	-.25	.21	.15	-.15	-.32	.26	-.27			
14. % liturg. 70	-.32	-.32	.16	.54	-.47	.49	-.31	-.26	.17	.52	-.45	.51	-.62		
15. % Ch. seat 70	.33	.08	-.21	-.23	.22	-.10	.34	.16	-.18	-.27	.24	-.10	-.14	-.10	
16. % urban 70	-.30	.17	-.09	.54	-.02	.10	-.33	.21	-.07	.50	-.04	.11	-.15	.06	-.15

1870 region — Region of intertemporal relationships — 1880 region — Region of relationships to other measures

and German ratios (r = -.79) indicates that these two immigrant groups largely resided in distinct geographic areas. In counties where the Irish were the foreignborn mainstay, few Germans lived; and where many Germans settled, there were fewer Irish. Further, where Germans lived, others of European birth were also settled (r = .51), but in these same enclaves of the foreign-born, Irish density was low (r = -.45). Rather than clustering among others of foreign birth, the Irish settled instead across areas populated by the southern and Indiana-born, where Germans were less prominent.

Second, the polarization of settlement among the native population was quite as strong as that between Germans and Irish. As the earlier map showed, northern-born settlers were established in areas different than those settled by persons of southern background (r = -.74) or of Indiana birth (r = -.78). Given the priority in time of southern migration to Indiana, it is not surprising to find a positive relation between those born in the southern border area and the Indiana-born (r = .59), suggesting that the descendants of earlier southern immigrants dominated the Indiana-born population.

The three county-level measures of religious composition were also related to these cultural group polarities and appear in the lower region of the matrix. As attempts to measure the religious composition of the counties, they require special comment. The county religious statistics that were published by the census bureau were *not* gathered by detailed surveys done by the bureau itself but were furnished to the bureau as reports by the various denominations. Denominations differed in the criteria they used for membership, for property valuation, and the like, and there was no effort from the census bureau to standardize these reports.[9] Therefore, detailed denominational comparisons across counties remain difficult to draw. I simply defined the percentage, according to the census, of Quaker, Methodist, and Baptist organizations out of all religious organizations as an index of the relative incidence of the more pietistic religious groups across counties, and the percentage of Lutheran and Roman Catholic organizations as an index of the strength of liturgical ones.[10] The relatively high inverse relation (r = -.62) between these two indices shows

Chapter Five

that the different types of religious organization tended to dominate relatively distinct areas of the state, generally aligned with native and foreign-born settlement patterns, and that these types were therefore related, indirectly, to the German and Irish polarity.

For the third measure I used the total number of seats available in churches of all denominations, relative to the county population, as an index of religious involvement within each county. The strongest relation it sustained in 1870, at quite moderate levels, was to the percentage born in Indiana ($r = .33$), perhaps as a function of the relative timing and duration of native-born settlement. It was related indirectly, then, to the northern and southern-born polarity.

The two main cultural group polarities that were in evidence across all counties of Indiana afford one basis for assessing the *People's Guide* counties in relation to all counties of the state. Figure 5.3 displays the regression of Germans among the foreign-born on the Irish ratio for 1870. The *People's Guide* counties were well distributed over the length of this inverse relationship, with high and low concentrations relative to the foreign-born represented for each group on each side of the regression line. The nine-county electorate covered, therefore, the main aspects of state-wide variation between the two groups, even though it was below average in the proportion of the foreign-born population as a whole.

Figure 5.4 shows the regression of the percentage born in the north on the percentage born in the south, for 1870. This inverse relationship between opposing regional concentrations of people was a curvilinear one (estimated by the curved line) because the size of each group was also a function of births increasing the proportion who were born in Indiana itself. The nine *People's Guide* counties, located at a geographic crossroads of these demographic changes, tended to stand below the mean for the Indiana-born (not shown) and were slightly more southern- than northern-born in their composition. No county among them stood above the northern-born mean.

From this summary of aggregate population relationships it is clear that the nine *People's Guide* counties composed an

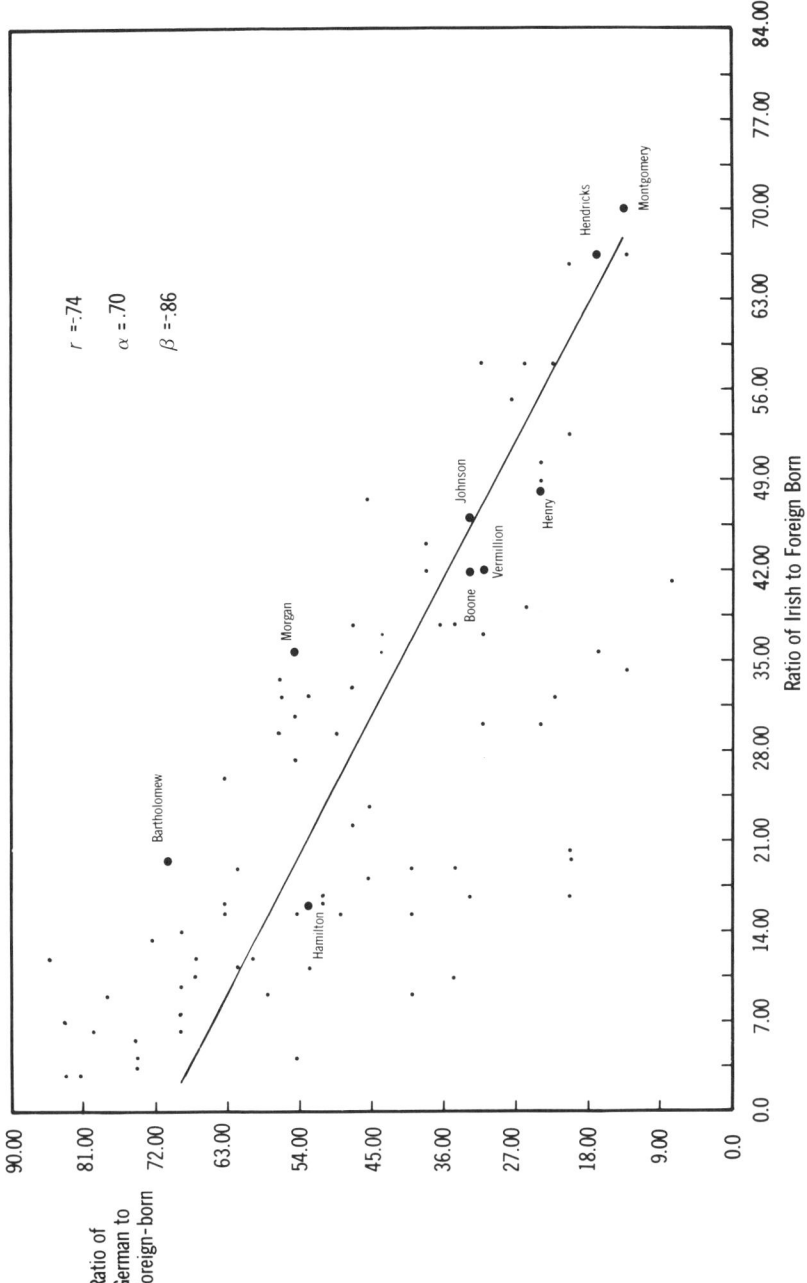

Fig. 5.3 Regression of German percentage of foreign-born on Irish percentage of the foreign-born, 1870

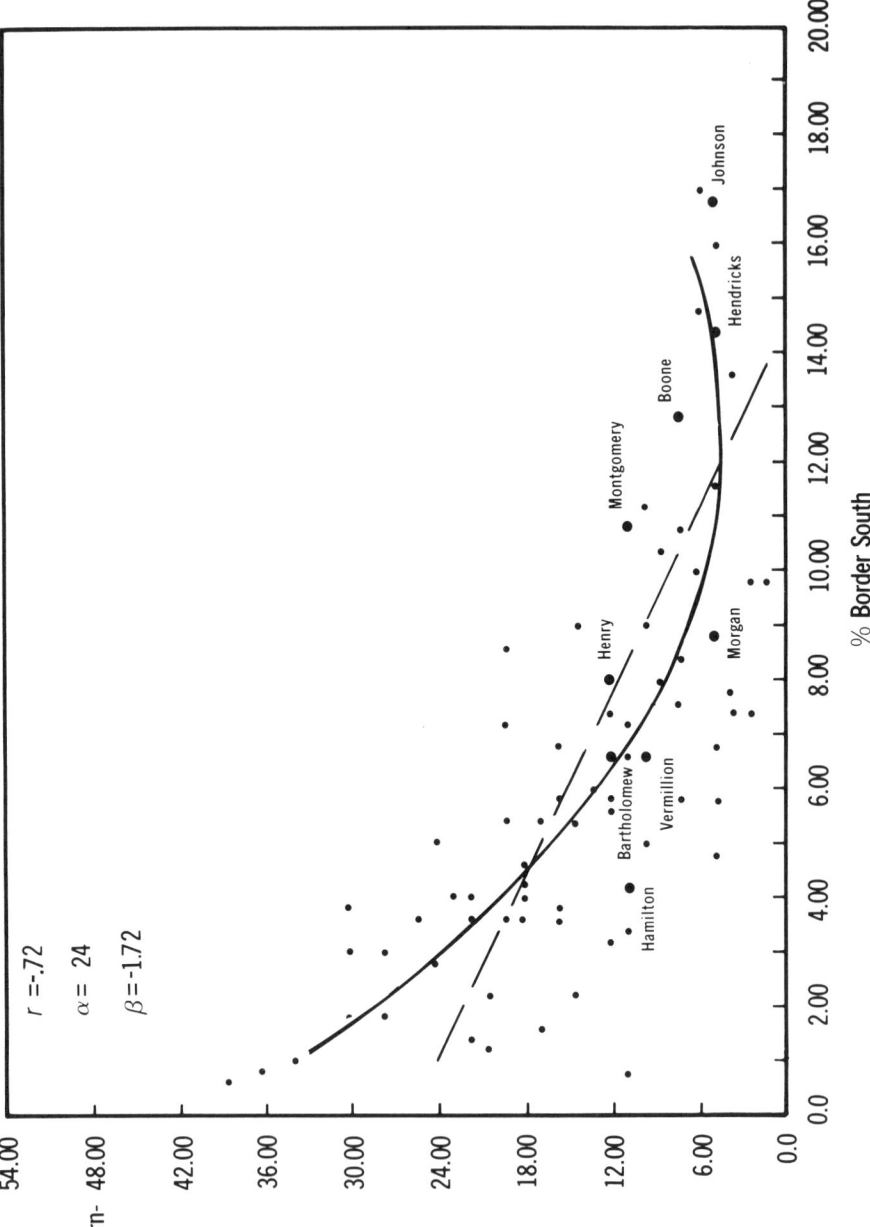

Fig. 5.4 Regression of percentage northern-born on the percentage born in the border-south, 1870

The Rural Electorate: Ethnic and Religious Composition

electorate less foreign-born, less northern-born, less Indiana-born, and more strongly influenced by persons from the south than the average across all counties of the state. This electorate was also more pietistic in the cast of its religious organizations. Like its central location in the Tipton Till region, and its rural character, these are additional biases of social composition, distinguishing the *People's Guide* sample of counties from all counties of the state.

Given the strong cultural group polarities across all counties of Indiana, it should come as no surprise that censustakers, when knocking on doors in central Indiana during June of 1870, found families living near one another who were from the same state or country of origin—a cluster from Ohio, Kentucky, Ireland, Germany or elsewhere. Residential propinquity was common within the counties as well as across them. These places of birth were also recorded by compilers of the *People's Guide*s (and were used as one criterion for matching voters in the two sources). Table 5.3 shows the relative incidence of places of origin by state and country, as detailed in the census sample. About four out of ten central Indiana voters were themselves Hoosiers by birth. Otherwise, most voters whose birth was outside of Indiana had their origins in the contiguous states of Ohio and Kentucky and then, at another step in distance, in the nearby states of North Carolina, Virginia, and Pennsylvania.[11] Altogether, one in three of these voters were born in the south or border states and one in five called some northern state their home. Only one in fourteen came from European countries, both English and non-English-speaking, and a small handful had returned eastward from Illinois or states further west (these are classified with the northern-born).

These regional and ethnic background identities, along with the religious attachments of voters, provided lines of cultural group cleavage that were important for involvement in Indiana's party system and for levels of major-party support. Table 5.4 probes native-born and foreign-born voters for their involvement in the party system itself and shows that foreign birth was something of a barrier to learning major-party attachments. In a comparison of foreign-born voters with all voters, major-party attachments declined from 84 to 71 percent among those who remembered

Chapter Five

Table 5.3. Voting-age Citizens by Place of Birth, 1870

Place of Birth	Sample Cases	% of Sample
Indiana	1,365	41.7
North		21.7
Connecticut	5	
Maine	2	
Massachusetts	9	
New Hampshire	4	
Rhode Island	1	
Vermont	1	
Delaware	9	
New Jersey	32	
New York	47	
Pennsylvania	135	
Ohio	451	
Wisconsin	2	
Illinois	19	
Iowa	2	
Missouri	2	
South		30.0
Alabama	2	
Georgia	6	
Louisiana	1	
North Carolina	281	
South Carolina	16	
Virginia	168	
West Virginia	7	
Kentucky	409	
Maryland	32	
Tennessee	78	
District of Columbia	1	
English-speaking foreign		3.6
Ireland	91	
England-Wales	13	
Scotland	12	
Canada	4	

The Rural Electorate: Ethnic and Religious Composition

(Table 5.3 continued)

Non-English-speaking		3.3
Bavaria	10	
Germany	45	
Prussia	38	
France	4	
Other	14	
Total	3,318	100.0

Table 5.4. Party Involvement by Nativity (in percentages)

	Native-born	Foreign-born	
Major-party involvement	85	71	(84.0)
Minor-party involvement	5	11	(5.4)
No answer	10	18	(10.6)
Total	100	100	(100.0)
	(94.6)	(5.4)	
Significance level by chi-square = .01			
N = 1,216			

Europe as their homeland, minor-party responses increased from 5 to 11 percent (all but one of these responses were "independent"), and responses indicating no party attachment increased from 11 to 18 percent. This decline in major-party attachments was not consistent across all foreign-born groups, however, but varied in a way that suggests language itself as a factor in the extent of decline. In table 5.5, the foreign-born alone are compared in two ways, first by origin from English or non-English-speaking countries, and second by the two most prominent subgroups encompassing this language distinction. Part (a) of this table shows that, in a comparison with all foreign-born voters, major party attachments increased from 71 to 77 percent among the English-speaking but declined to 66 percent among the non-English-speaking. Distinguishing in part (b) between the Irish and German subgroups shows that the Irish approached the levels of major-party involvement common to all voters but that the Germans and the residual group of others (French, Swiss, English, Scandinavians) continued

Chapter Five

Table 5.5. Party Involvement by Language Groups among the Foreign-born (in percentages)

	(a)		(b)			
	English-speaking	Non-English-speaking	Irish	German	Other	
Major-party involvement	77	66	84	66	61	(71.0)
Minor-party involvement	8	14	11	14	0	(17.8)
No answer	15	20	5	20	39	(11.3)
Total	100	100	100	100	100	
	(40.9)	(59.1)	(31.1)	(55.6)	(13.2)	
Significance level by chi-square =				(.19)		
N = 66						

to follow the German decline (though these differences were insufficient, for this small sample, to reject the null hypothesis).

It is worth recalling now that at least three sources of lowered involvement with the major-party system have been identified. The first source was among farmers in the open countryside, most notably among those without property; the second source was among merchants and professionals in Indiana's small towns, persons likely to be of higher than average income and education; and the third source was among the foreignborn, most especially among the non-English-speaking foreignborn, who in Indiana were largely of German background. What did this lowered involvement with the party system mean? Recall that, on the scale of party allegiance, both minor-party responses (including "independent") and the category of voters giving no attachment to a party, were combined as the single category of "Independents." What is now clear is that these "Independent" responses had sources of higher incidence in several different parts of the electorate and that these parts need to be considered for their larger import. In an older "classical" tradition, voters independent of the major parties were often viewed as well-educated and highly informed voters; they were, if you will, the unbridled

The Rural Electorate: Ethnic and Religious Composition

"mugwumps" of the electorate, who chose to vote for "the man" rather than "the party."[12] This view of "high standing" as the social sources for party independents is congruent with the higher Independent rates among merchants and professionals in Indiana's small towns. On the other hand, mid-twentieth-century survey research, while noting a small handful of highly informed Independent voters, has also shown that most Independents have tended to be less educated, less interested in politics, less informed, and less involved than their more partisan counterparts. These kinds of independents are the less involved "floating voters" of the electorate.[13] A language barrier among German-born Hoosiers and the status-level of nonpropertied farmers both suggest the social sources for a higher incidence of these "floating voter" Independents who moved with election tides.

Not only was involvement with the party system itself different between native-born and foreign-born Hoosiers, but these two groups also were aligned in opposing partisan directions, as shown in table 5.6. Compared to all voters, those of native-birth were just 2 percent more Republican—enough of a difference to reach a Republican majority—while those of foreign birth had Republican rates that declined from 49 to 23 percent and Democratic rates that increased from 35 to 48 percent. Nearly one in three of the foreign-born stood independent of the two major parties; most of these Independents were of non-Irish background. These differences represented, not a small fissure but something of a crack in the body politic, comparable in their polarizing tendency (gamma $= .38$) to the line between those who worked on the farms and off the farms. There was this difference, however: in Indiana the line between domains of work and residence split the electorate into two rather large chunks, while this line between native and foreign-born citizens cut off a small, albeit important, chip of the larger iceberg. In Indiana, nativeborn citizens comprised more than nine out of ten voters.

What, then, of this remaining mass? Were there further differences in levels of support between the parties that depended on native voters' regions of birth? Two issues should be kept in mind when observing party allegiance among these native-born voters. First, because Indiana was the most southern of the

Chapter Five

Table 5.6. Party Attachment for the Native and Foreign-born (in percentages)

	Native-born	Foreign-born	
Republican	51	23	(49.1)
Independent	15	29	(16.0)
Democrat	34	48	(34.9)
Total	100	100	
	(94.6)	(5.4)	(100.0)

Significance level by chi-square = .001
Lambda = .03
Kendall's Tau_b = .11
Gamma = .38
N = 1,216

northern states, several writers have pointed to the continuing impact of the Democratic party in voting returns for southern counties of the state, settled earliest by migrants streaming from the south. The natural inference has been that these southern migrants carried with them Democratic attachments and that the composition of Indiana's southern counties remained distinctly southern in terms of the regional backgrounds of later voters, who were therefore Democratic, politically.[14] This inference from county-level voting patterns to the party attachments of individuals within the counties is, of course, the classic ecological fallacy, where a relationship across aggregate units is assumed to hold for the individuals within those units as well.[15] It is therefore worth examining the extent of Democratic support among southern-born voters in this sample electorate.

Second, the long and peculiar history of voting experience among white southerners has suggested in recent times a greater strength of attachment to the major parties for this group as compared to other regional groups, even though participation levels have been lower.[16] The minor-party and no-attachment rates between northern-born, Indiana-born, and southern-born voters in Indiana showed that southern-born voters were the lowest in both categories, a fact summarized in their level of Independent allegiance. This result appears in table 5.7, which separates voters by their regions of birth and displays the levels of Republican and Democratic support pertinent to the ecological inference as well.

The Rural Electorate: Ethnic and Religious Composition

Table 5.7. Party Attachments by Region of Birth (in percentages)

	North	Indiana	South	
Republican	55	49	50	(51.0)
Independent	15	18	12	(15.0)
Democrat	30	33	39	(34.0)
Total	100	100	100	100.0)
N = 1,150				

This table shows that Republican support increased from 51 to 55 percent among those born in northern states; that Independent support increased from 15 to 18 percent among the Indiana-born and declined to 12 percent among the southern-born, and that Democratic support increased from 34 to 39 percent among the southern-born and declined to 30 percent for those born in the northern region. Contrary to earlier discussions using county-level correlations alone, which showed high Democratic support among counties high in their proportions of population born in the south, these individual-level data indicate that birth in the South did not, by itself, produce even a Democratic majority level of support in these nine counties. In fact, regions of birth had only a small impact in providing partisan lines of cleavage within this electorate; among voters from different regions, levels of party support varied only slightly and provided little basis for polarization.

By law, federal census-takers did not ask citizens about their religious attachments in 1870, but a few years later the compilers of the *People's Guides* did. We must therefore rely on the *People's Guides* of 1874 for information about religious attachments. Table 5.8 shows quite clearly the general Protestant cast of this rural electorate. One out of four Hoosiers, in fact, reported the term "Protestant" as their own religious self-designation. One out of two of central Indiana's voters indicated a specific denominational attachment, spanning a wide range of groups, the two largest of which were the Methodist and the Christian (Disciples of Christ) churches. No other denomination was specified by as many as 10 percent of these voters, indicating something of the fragmentation within this large denominational camp. Baptists, for instance, responded in four different groups, Methodists in

Chapter Five

Table 5.8. Religious Groups by *Guide* Frequency

Religious Label	Weighted N	Weighted Subsample %
"Protestant"	321	26.4
No religious affiliation	260	21.3
Methodist	181	19.9
Christians (Disciples of Christ)	168	13.8
Friends (Quakers)	68	5.6
Presbyterian	38	3.1
Mission Baptist	32	2.6
Lutheran	25	2.1
Baptist	20	1.7
United Brethren	17	1.4
Regular Baptist	16	1.3
Wesleyan Methodist	15	1.3
Roman Catholic	13	1.1
Universalist	11	.9
German Baptist	10	.8
Moravian	4	
Dunkard	4	
Spiritualist	6	
Evangelical	1	
Mennonite	1	
Adventist	4	
Jewish	1	(1.9)
Total	1,216	100.0

two. A number of smaller groups in the area—Moravians, Dunkards, and Spiritualists—were represented by only a few members, classified here among "other" Protestant varieties. Roman Catholics constituted only a little better than 1 percent of the voters in this area, and only one voter reported a Jewish identification. Finally, about one out of five voters reported no religious attachment at all.

In recent studies of midwestern politics, denominational groups have been fundamental to descriptions of party polarization. In particular, Richard Jensen and Paul Kleppner each developed a polar continuum of ethnic and denominational groups. As described in both accounts, this continuum shows the Roman Catholics of various ethnic origins and the German Lutherans at the

"Democratic-ritualistic" end of the polarity; the several Protestant denominations made up of native-born members (particularly those influenced by American revivals and the antislavery movement) and a few foreign-born evangelical groups are at the "Republican-pietistic" end.[17]

How this continuum was first constructed, however, is not fully clear in either account. Both authors illustrate the continuum by showing ethnocultural groups ordered by estimates of major party support. Neither one validates this ordering by criteria that might measure each group's pietistic or liturgical proclivities, independent of party support itself (setting Jensen's doctrinal arguments aside).[18] Ordering groups by levels of party support alone surely maximizes party polarization, and in the arguments of Kleppner and Jensen the inference is clear that polarization was high (although they do not measure it). If I have understood the implications of their procedure correctly, it is equivalent to ordering occupational groups by party support, thereby maximizing party polarization based on them, and then positing an underlying unmeasured continuum, like prestige, as the basis for polarization.[19]

Table 5.9 replicates this maximizing strategy among Hoosier voters, using denominational subgroups for which at least ten cases were available, and orders the denominations by levels of Republican support. If this ordering—from Quakers, Presbyterians, and the United Brethren on the one end to Lutherans, Regular Baptists, and Roman Catholics on the other—was also a pietistic-liturgical continuum, then the degree of polarization between parties offered by this structure of the electorate was moderately strong (gamma = .48). But denominations could also be ordered by Democratic levels of support (a different ordering) or by levels of independence from the parties (another different ordering), neither of which would validate a pietistic-liturgical continuum any more than does a Republican ordering. The problem is this: without further criteria beyond party support itself, denominations are inherently nominal, not ordered, categories. To show that party support from denominational groups was important, especially at the most local levels, does not require that they be arranged on a continuum. In fact, as unordered denominational groups, they still had a small but quite measurable polarizing impact on party support, as shown by a nominal summary statistic (lambda$_b$ = .12).

Even more important than the problem of order among denominational subgroups is the fact that not all citizens were members of such groups. The pietistic-liturgical continuum implies that every voter can be classified into one or another denominational group—an assumption that, like the basis for the continuum itself, is not clearly visible when the data are precinct, township, and county aggregates. Among Hoosier voters, the line between those who identified themselves with a specific denominational subgroup and those who did not very nearly split the electorate in two. Almost half did not consider themselves members of any denomination. And among voters who did not report a specific denominational attachment, about half described themselves with the general term "Protestant" while the remainder indicated no religious attachment at all. Thus, the religious structure of this rural electorate was even more complex than the pietistic-liturgical continuum suggests, and needs to be considered initially in the simplest terms.

The three primary kinds of religious response among Indiana voters offer a simple and clearly ordered scale of categories measuring directly the involvement of citizens with religious institutions, ranging from a low level of involvement among Hoosiers lacking religious attachments, to a middle level of involvement among voters who viewed themselves more generally as Protestant, to a high level of involvement with religious institutions among citizens who viewed themselves directly as members of denominational subgroups. The lines between these categories are quite global in two senses. On the one hand, they do not distinguish between an active and an inactive Presbyterian; the involvement measured on this scale is not "religion specific" in terms of the content of belief and practice but rather is "institutional" in terms of the degree of identification and contact that voters had with others through whom religious information flowed.[20] On the other hand, the categories are also global with respect to the middle category, for the term "Protestant" was often used by Hoosiers as a contrast to "Catholic"; there was no

The Rural Electorate: Ethnic and Religious Composition

Table 5.9. Party Attachment by Denominational Group, Ordered by Percentage Republican

	Republican	Independent	Democrat	Total	% All Groups
Quaker	98	2	0	100	(10.7)
Presbyterian	80	8	12	100	(5.9)
United Brethren	74	3	23	100	(2.6)
Wesleyan Methodist	73	11	16	100	(2.4)
Methodist	62	11	27	100	(28.7)
Disciples of Christ	56	11	33	100	(26.4)
German Baptist	53	21	26	100	(1.5)
Universalist	50	9	41	100	(1.7)
Mission Baptist	49	5	46	100	(5.0)
Baptist	35	25	40	100	(3.2)
"Other"	33	30	37	100	(3.3)
Lutheran	22	16	62	100	(4.0)
Regular Baptist	10	7	83	100	(2.5)
Roman Catholic	7	20	73	100	(2.0)
Total	(59.0)	(10.9)	(30.1)		(100.0)

Significance level
 by chi-square = .001
Kendall's Tau$_b$ = .33
Gamma = .48
Lambda = .12
N = 634

covering term like "Protestant" that distinguished "nominal" Catholics from those more institutionally involved. All who reported themselves as Catholics, therefore, are classified as institutionally involved at the same level as those of other denominations.

Table 5.10 shows that levels of religious involvement were important for how Indiana voters were related to the party system itself. Involvement with the major parties increased from 84 percent among all voters, to 86 percent among those considering themselves Protestants, to 89 percent among those involved with specific denominational subgroups, but declined to 69 percent among voters who did not consider themselves at all attached to religious institutions. Variation in minor-party involvement was minimal; but the level of no-party attachment increased from 11

Table 5.10. Party Involvement by Levels of Institutional Religious Involvement (in percentages)

	Denominational Attachment	Protestant	No Religious Attachment	
Major party	89	86	69	(84.0)
Minor party	5	7	5	(10.6)
No party	6	7	26	(5.4)
Total	100	100	100	
	(52.2)	(26.4)	(21.4)	(100.0)

Significance level by chi-square = .001
Kendall's Tau_b = .16
Gamma = .36
N = 1,216

percent among all voters to 26 percent among those lacking attachment to religious institutions, resulting in a polarization of involvement with the party system itself (gamma =.36) that was of import comparable to other cleavages along the scale of party allegiance alone.

The categories of minor-party attachment and no-party attachment sum, in the scale of party allegiance, to the category of voters whom we have labeled as Independents. Table 5.11 shows that, in this summary form, levels of religious involvement were a fourth source of variation in levels of Independent support. The level of Independent support increased from 16 to 30 percent among those who did not view themselves as attached to religious institutions, declined to 14 percent among general Protestants, and then declined to 11 percent among those most closely involved with denominational subgroups. Like merchants and professionals in the small towns, farmers without property, and the foreign-born generally, voters who lacked involvement with the churches tended also to be *less inclined* toward one or another of the two major parties. Table 5.11 also shows that Republican support followed this same gradient of religious involvement, reaching a majority level at 59 percent among citizens indicating a denominational attachment. Democratic support varied less than Republican support, leaving a balance of party power among

The Rural Electorate: Ethnic and Religious Composition

Table 5.11. Party Attachment by Levels of Institutional Religious Involvement (in percentages)

	Denominational Attachment	Protestant	No Religious Attachment	
Republican	59	45	30	(49.1)
Independent	11	14	30	(16.0)
Democrat	30	41	40	(34.9)
Total	100	100	100	
	(52.2)	(26.4)	(21.4)	(100.0)

Significance level
 by chi-square = .001
Kendall's Tau_b = .17
Gamma = .27
Lambda = .04
N = 1,216

both Protestants and those lacking religious attachments. These levels of major party support, however, deserve closer scrutiny.

In Indiana's party system, the fissure or crack between native and foreign-born voters was an important one, if only as setting off something of a chip within this Indiana electorate. On the one hand, it sent major party support in different directions; on the other, it made for differences in involvement with the party system itself, with those of foreign birth being more likely to stand independent of the major parties. Among the foreign-born alone, involvement with the party system also varied between English and non-English-speaking immigrant groups such that not only foreign birth but language as well might be viewed as something of a barrier to learning major-party attachments. Now, among all voters, the lack of a religious institutional attachment also has appeared as something of a barrier to one set of channels through which partisan cues were communicated. If major institutions, among which religious ones stood prominent in rural Indiana, provided channels through which information flowed, including partisan information, then among the foreign-born who lacked denominational attachments a double barrier was in effect. Table 5.12 shows the entire electorate of these nine counties cast in general terms between the native and foreign-

Chapter Five

Table 5.12. Party Attachments by Levels of Institutional Religious for Native and Foreign-born (in percentages)

	Native-born			Foreign-born			
	Denom. Attach-ment	Prot.	No Relig. Attach-ment	No Relig. Attach-ment	Prot.	Denom. Attach-ment	
Republican	62	46	30	19	29	22	(49.1)
Independent	10	13	29	54	38	18	(16.0)
Democrat	28	41	41	27	33	60	(34.9)
Total	100	100	100	100	100	100	
	(48.8)	(25.5)	(20.4)	(1.1)	(1.0)	(3.4)	(100.0)
Significance level							
by chi-square = .001				.09			
Kendall's Tau$_b$ = .19				−.19			
Gamma = .30				−.30			
N = 1,150				N = 66			

born, by levels of involvement with religious institutions. I have rearranged the involvement categories for the two halves of this table in accord with the differing partisan direction between the native and foreign-born, thereby also "centering" the categories indicating no religious attachment within the table as a whole.

Three comparisons within this table are important. First, among the native-born the level of Republican support increased from 49 percent among all voters to a strong majority level of 62 percent among denominationally attached voters, and then declined in a gradient to 46 percent for general Protestants and further declined to 30 percent among voters lacking religious attachments. Second, and in polar contrast, among the foreign-born the level of Democratic support increased from 35 percent among all voters to a strong majority level of 60 percent among denominationally attached voters, and then declined in a gradient to 33 percent for general Protestants and further declined to 27 percent among voters holding no religious attachment at all. These two polar movements are quite consistent with the notion that religious institutions channeled party support in opposing directions between the two nativity domains. But the third aspect

The Rural Electorate: Ethnic and Religious Composition

Table 5.13. Ethnic and Ethnoreligious Comparisons (in percentages)

	(a) Irish	(a) German	(b) German Lutheran	(b) German and Irish Roman Catholics
Republican	36	13	8	0
Independent	16	34	21	21
Democrat	48	53	71	79
Total	100	100	100	100
Actual N	(21)	(38)	(13)	(11)

of this table is equally striking, which shows the variation in rates for voters who stood independent of the two major parties. Among both the native-born and the European-born, Independent levels increased with decreasing institutional involvement, where the effect of lowered involvement with religious institutions among the foreign-born ranged nearly twice that for the native-born. Clearly, for the flow of partisan cues, involvement with religious institutions was a gradient of crucial import. It produced a balance of power between the major parties at each institutional level below explicit attachment to a denominational subgroup, and did so in both nativity domains.

For the larger Midwest it is now clear how, as a construct, the pietistic-liturgical continuum was born. Religious institutions were one important set of channels in the nineteenth century through which partisan information flowed. But they were important, politically, not for their doctrinal content so much as for their exposure, in terms of communication, of one member to another. Perhaps this can be made clear by two examples that lend themselves as well to showing how the pietistic-liturgical construct arose. First, the two largest ethnic groups in Indiana, the Irish and the Germans, both offered more support to the Democrats than to the Republicans, as shown in table 5.13. But when members of these two groups were also tied to a tighter network of people by their attachment to religious institutions, as among German Lutherans and Irish and German Roman Catholics, then that support moved strongly to a majority level, as also shown in this table, and appeared as a Democratic party

Table 5.14. General Religious and Specific Denominational Comparisons (in percentages)

	(a)		(b)	
	All Denominations	"Protestants"	Quakers	Presbyterians
Republican	62	46	98	80
Independent	10	13	2	8
Democrat	28	41	0	12
Total	100	100	100	100
Actual N	(612)	(296)	(87)	(41)

norm. Second, and on the native-born side, all general Protestants offered more support to the Republicans than to the Democrats. Then, when this support was tied to specific denominational subgroups, as among Quakers and Presbyterians in central rural Indiana, there was a further strong movement toward Republican norm levels (see table 5.14). These are the kinds of polar cases toward which the pietistic-liturgical continuum has pointed. What it has failed to capture, however, is the wide variation between these endpoints, where denominations were *not* ordered in and of themselves and where nearly half of all voters were not even denominational subgroup members.

The ethnic and religious structure of Indiana was less complex than elsewhere in the Midwest. The foreign-born and those identified with the Roman Catholic, the Lutheran, or other nonnative churches were but a small portion of the state's electorate. Had they been more numerous, the Democrats would have been more numerous too, if the same patterns of support held true elsewhere as within this nine-county sample. The "error" in the pietistic-liturgical continuum lies not in the size of these groups in the state's electorate or in the divisions among its foreign-born groups but in the assumptions of ordering among denominations and the assumptions about the classification of all voters as members of them. Differing levels of cultural group support were clearly present but were no more a basis for strong polarization in and of themselves than other cuttings of the electorate. More interesting is the fact that foreign birth appeared as at least a

The Rural Electorate: Ethnic and Religious Composition

partial barrier to learning major-party identifications in Indiana, as did the lack of attachment to religious institutions among both the native and foreign-born. To phrase these matters positively, party support moved in opposing directions between Indiana's native-born citizens and Hoosiers of foreign birth, where party cues were most strong among denominational members on both sides of this cleavage, pointing clearly to religious institutions as mechanisms for political information and political involvement. For party support in Indiana it was less important what a Hoosier voter believed, religiously, than whether or not his religious beliefs led him to join a church at all.

6

Party Allegiance among Indiana's Farmers and Townsmen

Differences between farmers and townsmen within rural Indiana were important and pervasive. They were more important than differences between wealth classes, occupational strata, regional and ethnic backgrounds, or religious groups, because each of these other cleavages were heightened within and between farm and village more than across them. But neither farm life nor town life created partisan polarization. Rather, this structural cleavage in rural life served to distinguish farmers as political actors from their village counterparts and defined that line which gave rise to the farmer's independent movement and the Greenback party, the movements that kept Indiana's rural turnout rates unusually high during the 1870s.

Social organization among Indiana's farmers was in its infancy during the 1870s.[1] Farmers were not a small special-interest group but the dominant numbers of society. Of every four Hoosiers in the 1870s, three lived in the countryside beyond village, town, and city. Most worked on family farms, either as family members or as boarders or laborers. Collectively a work force, they were bound together in a seasonal round—planting, cultivating, harvesting. These were necessary tasks that scheduled their daily duties according to the seasons of the year. It was often a hard, monotonous life. Only winter months brought a brief respite and time for leisure. As one participant put it: "Few who have not been residents of the country can rightly understand the monotony of the farmer's life. Day after day the farmer and his family pursue the same appointed round of toil. There is no change save for the regular recurrence of the Sabbath, and attendance upon religious services where such privileges are accessible."[2]

Three aspects of farm life appear characteristic of rural Indiana in the 1870s. One was the sheer physical distance between farms. Farming in Indiana was not conducted according to the tradition of nuclear villages, as among earlier Puritans or contemporary Mormons, or from line villages, but according to the much more isolated farming homestead pattern where each farmer's home was separated from its neighbors by intervening fields and networks of unpaved roads.[3] The extent of physical separation varied, of course, depending on the average size of farms and the amount of land that was cleared, plowed, and planted. The larger, more expansive and speculative farms were opened in the northwest plains section of the state, while the smaller, more intensive farms were located in the southern hills region.[4]

Physical separation bred social isolation because the calendar of work and the distance discouraged social contact in groups larger or more diverse than the homestead itself. While not unknown, large gatherings among farmers were occasions of special note—church services, a weekly trip to town, local picnics, elections, or state-sponsored fairs. Indeed, efforts to organize farmers in the 1870s, 1880s and 1890s were almost as much attempts to enrich social life as to prepare the farmers for new commercial, marketing, and political developments.[5]

Physical separation and social isolation reinforced the psychological individualism for which farmers were noted. A farmer was often viewed as a man unto himself, concerned with his own particular needs, regardless of how others in his occupational category were faring, and little given to easy conversation about wider developments.[6] Farm journals, such as the *Indiana Farmer,* which began in 1866, increasingly challenged this individualism by pointing to a wider context of knowledge, solutions to common problems, and the promise of scientific farming.[7] The

Chapter Six

state Board of Agriculture moved in similar directions, sponsoring annual state fairs at Indianapolis and supporting county agricultural societies.[8] Still, change was slow in the short-run, if not in longer spans of time, and farmers largely continued their characteristic way of life. They were less a cohesive community than an aggregate of persons, a category of voters.

The most notable event among farmers in Indiana during the 1870s was the rise of the National Grange of the Patrons of Husbandry.[9] On a national basis this organization was the creation of Oliver H. Kelley, a Minnesota farmer ensconced in the federal government's Department of Agriculture. Kelley knew firsthand the isolation and remoteness of farm life, its economic problems, and the failure of previous attempts at farm organization. Directing his attention to the social needs of farmers, he sought to build an organization that would survive its first fateful years and hold its members. From his own background in Masonry, he drew up the new order's ritual, hoping its mystery and secrecy would bind both men and women into permanent local Grange chapters.[10]

The beginnings were not auspicious. In Indiana the first Grange was organized at Honey Creek, Vigo County, in December of 1869. It was another three years before local chapters were sufficient to charter the state Grange, when, by December of 1872, there were fifty-four branches dotting several northwestern counties.[11] Suddenly the organization took hold. With the increasing severity of the agricultural depression after 1873, affecting all crops and markets, there was a dramatic increase in the growth of Granges. On July 1, 1874, the national office reported 1,968 subordinate Granges for Indiana, a number second only to that for Iowa.[12] Perhaps at the zenith of its growth in 1875, the Grange in Indiana would claim 3,000 chapters, collecting dues from about 60,000 members.[13] Thereafter, its numbers declined though its effects continued, for by all accounts this explosion in local farm organization was matched in degree by the movement of farmers into independent political action, support for the Greenback party, and shifts in their voting between the two major parties.[14]

The *People's Guide* directories were published before the onset

Party Allegiance: Farmers and Townsmen

of major Grange activity and its subsequent political unrest. Several responses that we have categorized as third-party ones did indicate "Republican Granger" or "Democratic Granger," but these were so few that separate categories for them could not be established.[15] We have no count, then, of the number of farmers who joined the Grange as a social organization, or of those who subsequently entered any third-party political movement. We know only the proportion who, in 1874 (standardized to 1870 population composition), thought of themselves as Republicans and Democrats, or whose response was "no answer," "independent," or for some third party, all of which we have categorized as independent of the major party division.

The nine *People's Guide* counties were not at the root of Indiana's subsequent Greenback party, though all of them, with the exception of Bartholomew County only, provided a Greenback congressional vote in 1878 higher than the state mean. It is difficult to assess what this might mean for any bias with regard to this nine-county electorate, for over the three election-years of its existence, the vote for the Greenback party was generally small and widely variable over counties of the state. In congressional elections, if there was no district Greenback candidate there was no Greenback vote, and in others either a Republican or a Democratic fusion candidate ran.

Figure 6.1 shows the Greenback party's prevalence and geographic impact in the state for the congressional election of 1878, by counties that produced more than a 10 percent Greenback vote (out of 73 counties where its candidates were slated). This was the height of its strength. The party had developed from roots put down by several independent candidacies in 1874 and had placed its own candidates on the ballot in 1876.[16] The center of strength had been in the west-central region of the state, around Vigo County, and then spread north and eastward, having the least impact in the stronger German foreign-born areas.

During the brief history of the Greenback party, few factors of county social composition were consistent correlates of its strength. The coefficients presented in table 6.1 show only that the movement gained its congressional support of 1876 in areas of pietistic strength ($r = .20$), areas of settlement by persons born in

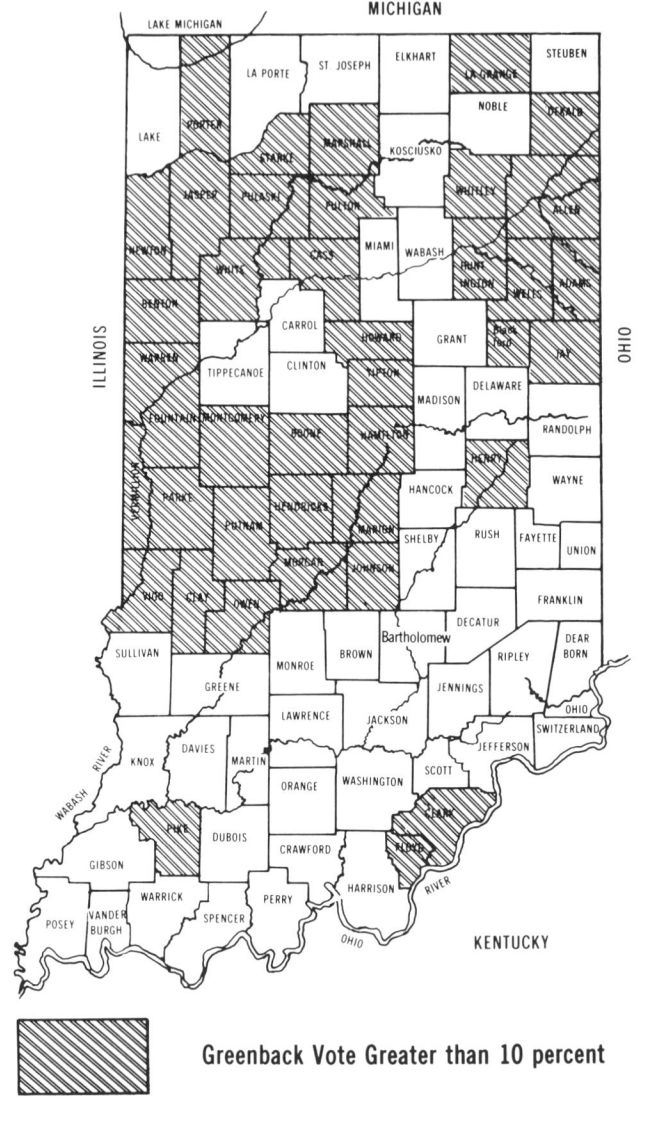

Fig. 6.1 Areas of Greenback strength in the congressional election of 1878

Party Allegiance: Farmers and Townsmen

Table 6.1. Correlation Coefficients between the Greenback Vote and Measures of Social Composition, All Counties with a Greenback Vote, 1876–80

Compositional Measure	Congress 1876	President 1876	Congress 1878	Congress 1880	President 1880
Av. val. farms	.08	.03	−.02	−.05	−.13
% lg. farms	.03	−.05	−.09	−.26	−.25
Av. ass'd prop.	.24	.20	.09	−.13	−.05
Av. val. fm. prds.	.32	.17	.01	.00	−.03
Av. mfg. cap.	.10	.00	−.02	−.08	−.10
% Ind.-born	.09	.08	−.24	−.05	−.12
% north.-born	−.11	−.10	.21	.31	.15
% bdr.-south	.29	.29	−.11	.12	−.01
% tor.-born	−.16	−.26	.04	−.22	−.16
Ir./for. ratio	.23	.23	−.07	.03	−.01
Ger./for. ratio	−.27	−.27	−.20	−.20	−.15
% church seats	−.01	−.04	−.31	−.20	−.14
% pietistic orgs.	.12	.20	.03	−.03	−.10
% liturgical orgs.	−.26	−.26	−.03	−.01	−.06
% rural	−.18	−.10	−.04	.06	.08
Pop. growth	.20	.17	.39	.31	.20
Lg. fm. increase	.20	.04	.30	.40	.41
% farm owners	−.28	−.27	−.27	−.11	−.13

the border-south (r = .29), areas where the assessed value of property was high (r = .24), and areas of high population growth during the decade (r = .20). Its intrusions were least where the percentage of farm owners was high (r = −.28) and where the German foreign-born were strong (r = −.27). But these coefficients were highly unstable from one election to the next, even reversing signs. Only the relationship to population growth, to the percentage of farm owners and to the ratio of Germans to the foreign-born remained at all consistent from 1876 to 1880. There was no effective correlation to the rural percentage, or over time to other measures of farm size, value, or product. To the extent that the Greenback party was a farmer's party, it therefore drew support among farmers from the most rural to the most urban counties as well as across other farm-related differences in county social composition. Since origin and support cannot easily be attributed to these differences in county composition, it is difficult to know what biases, if any, the *People's Guide* electorate had with respect to these subsequent developments.

Perhaps one effect of the Greenback movement was a small increase in already high levels of turnout, for in the time-series of turnout for president over the whole late nineteenth century, there was an increasing trend that could be located with 1876 as the point of change. The *People's Guide* counties, however, distributed rather well over the turnout surface and do not appear noticeably biased on that account. They were, however, more rural than most counties of the state, and, within the state, turnout was higher wherever rural populations dominated counties. Figure 6.2 shows the geographic variation in levels of turnout during the 1870s, taken as an average over both on-year and off-year elections.[17] This mean turnout across all counties was an exceedingly high 89.5 percent of the eligible electorate, with a small average variation measured by a standard deviation of 4.8 percent. The darkly shaded counties were those whose average turnout was greater than one-half standard deviation above the state mean. Except in the southeast and southwest, both areas of early southern settlement, the areas of highest average turnout during the decade were counties of the western interior of the state, running north and south, overlapping but not coterminous with areas of Greenback strength.

The correlates of the decade average turnout over the counties are given in table 6.2 for the several contextual factors measured at each end of the decade. Using measures from 1870 as a base, the table shows that voter participation in elections during the decade was higher where the proportion born in Indiana was high ($r=.48$), where the percentage born in the border-south was high ($r=.26$), and where the number of seats in churches was high ($r=.34$). These variables, I have suggested, may be seen as measures of the temporal development and the maturity of social organization in county populations; longer established and more fully organized counties tended to have increased levels of voter participation as measured by turnout. Unlike measures of the size, wealth, and product of farming, which were largely unassociated with turnout, where the rural percentage was high, turnout tended to be high as well ($r=.41$), suggesting one possible effect

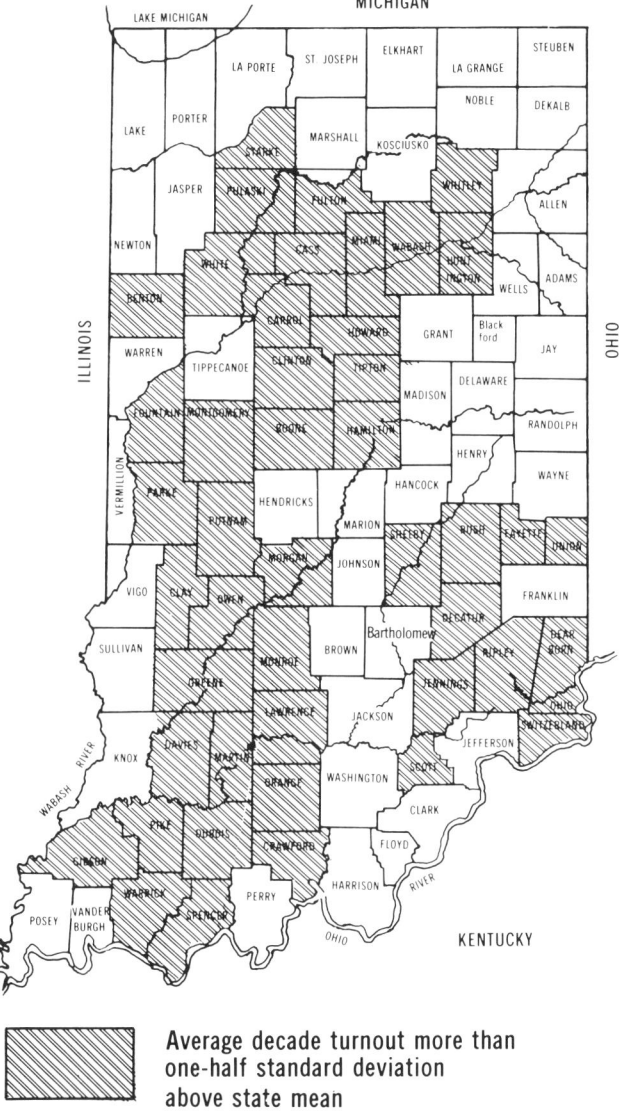

Fig. 6.2 Turnout strength, 1870–80

Chapter Six

Table 6.2. Correlation Coefficients between Average Decade Turnout and Indicators of Social Composition, All Counties

Social Indicator	1870	1880
% large farms	.10	.13
Av. value of farms	−.07	−.21
Av. value of farm products	.12	−.14
Av. assessed value of property	−.02	−.10
Av. manufacturing capital	−.41	−.42
Av. value of mfg'd products	−.41	−.50
Population density	−.32	−.32
% Indiana-born	.48	.51
% born in border-south	.26	.19
% northern-born	−.24	−.26
% foreign-born	−.41	−.40
Ratio of Irish to foreign	.24	.24
Ratio of German to foreign	−.08	−.08
% Pietistic organizations	−.05	
% Liturgical organizations	−.08	
% rural	.41	
Population growth	−.01	
% church seats	.34	
% farm owners		−.07
% growth, large farms		−.05
% mfg. growth		−.21
Mean average decade turnout = 89.5		
Standard deviation = 4.8		

of the Greenback movement as a stimulus to voter mobilization in rural areas. On the other hand, average decade turnout was lower where average manufacturing capital and product were high ($r = -.41$), where the percentage born in the north was high ($r = -.24$), and where the foreign-born were strong ($r = -.41$). This combination of factors, all relatively urban, tended to mark areas attracting new immigrants and areas with residents whose backgrounds were with European rather than American political institutions and norms.

What kind of voters were farmers? Were they highly politicized and conscious of themselves as a class? What were the likely sources of their third-party action and support for the Greenback party? National studies of agrarian political behavior in the mid-

Party Allegiance: Farmers and Townsmen

twentieth century have suggested that farmers, as political actors, have differed quite markedly from their urban counterparts.[18] On the one hand, the partisan choices farmers have made appear more fluid from one election to the next than have those of urban voters, and on the other hand, their voting turnout also appears more irregular. Characteristically, these two aspects of voting behavior have involved a status gradient among urban voters, with *partisan variability* more likely among upper-status urban voters (like merchants and professionals in Indiana's small towns) and *turnout variability* more likely among urban voters of lower status. But among farmers, both kinds of variability have come together, mutually reinforcing each other. In addition, the responsiveness of farmers to economic events has also appeared unusual, depending largely on the individual farmer's own condition without much reference to how others in the same occupational category were faring. This has made the farm vote variegated and disparate, in no sense a "bloc" vote except under one condition. When economic pressures have been highly pervasive across markets, crops, and individuals, then a protest farm vote has been most visible; the farm community has responded to pervasive economic events en masse, with an explosive quality that has been unique among categories of voters—a response with great force but with little duration.[19] Thus, in being *least restrained* by strong partisan loyalties and in their responsiveness to massive economic events, mid-twentieth century farmers have appeared relatively distinctive as political actors.

Among voters in rural central Indiana one hundred years ago the measure of party allegiance available in the *People's Guide*s does not tap strength as well as direction of attachment; this means a direct test of partisan strength as a motivational characteristic among farmers cannot easily be made. Nor can we make direct comparisons to a fully urban electorate. Our data, however, suggest two tactics. First, as a surrogate measure of strength we can let the balance of power in which neither major party reaches a majority stand as a very imperfect indicator of "weak" rather than "strong" attachments, with increasing strength indicated as partisan majorities or norms characterize subgroups. Second, we can compare farmers in the open countryside to their

Chapter Six

village and town counterparts who, while not "urban" by present-day standards, nonetheless offered a way of life different than that of the farms. Village life was more diverse and was integrated across institutions. In a relative sense, the hundreds of villages, towns, and small cities of Indiana, ranging upward in size from less than a hundred people to four or five thousand, were the "urban" centers of the rural population. They provided the farming countryside with needed banks, warehouses, hardware, shoes, wagons, and tombstones, and contained Masonic lodges, Odd Fellows halls, and a multitude of churches.[20] Shops, stores, a county or township courthouse, all provided public places of meeting. The small towns offered mail delivery and connections by rail to Indianapolis, Chicago, Toledo, or Cincinnati, and on to the world markets. Thus, much like the larger cities, but less subject to their dislocations, Indiana's small towns were centers of social diversity, organizational networks, and a fairly steady flow of information.[21] Townsmen, like farmers, were a category of voter.

Comparison between these two categories of voters requires the control of background conditions and the removal of other special subgroups from it. In particular, the foreign-born were one distinctive subgroup and constituted a small though highly salient component of Indiana's total electorate. Between the European and the native-born, levels of party support differed quite noticeably, and no more so than in their relation to institutional religious involvement. Among the foreign-born, voters who lacked denominational attachments were characterized by the balance of power and high rates of response in our category of Independents. This combination, we suggest, indicates both relatively weak major-party attachments and normally low turnout (or high mobilization potential), relationships which are quite in keeping with aggregate indicators of turnout for the foreign-born across all counties. The denominationally involved foreign-born were quite different, however, and gave strong Democratic majority support. That this pattern was based most fully on subgroup norms among German Lutherans and Irish and German Roman Catholics has been shown elsewhere.[22] Thus, the foreign-born, heterogeneous within the group by levels of religious involvement,

Party Allegiance: Farmers and Townsmen

Table 6.3. Polar Party Attachments by Occupational Domains, Native-born (in percentages)

	Agricultural Domain	Nonagricultural Domain	
Republican	44	65	(52.1)
Independent	16	13	(14.8)
Democrat	40	22	(33.1)
Total	100	100	
	(61.3)	(38.7)	
Significance level by chi-square = .001			
N = 1,150			

were a subgroup of special interest. The comparison between farmers and villagers, however, can be focused best by excluding these distinctive foreign-born subgroups.

Table 6.3 shows the global differences that remained between American-born voters engaged in farming occupations and those in nonfarm occupations. Differences in levels of party support between these two domains of work were as significant without the foreign-born as when they were included. Native-born voters in nonfarm occupations produced a substantial 65 percent Republican majority, in contrast to the balance of power and higher Independent rates for the farm domain. As among the foreign-born without denominational attachments, this balance of power in the farm domain suggests weaker attachments to the major parties and susceptibility to lower turnout (or higher potential for mobilization) even at this global level. Table 6.4 makes the basic comparison even more specific, by showing residence controlled for occupational domain. For native-born Hoosiers who lived where they worked, the combination of town residence and a village occupation led to a high 68 percent Republican majority, while residence in the open countryside and a farm occupation led to an even more well-defined balance of power.

Finally, the difference between farmers in the open countryside and their small-town counterparts can be explored by separating out farm laborers. Table 6.5 makes clear that farm laborers were a small Democratic subgroup, although without the

Table 6.4. Polar Party Attachments by Residence, Native-born, Controlled for Occupational Domains (in percentages)

	Agricultural Domain			Nonagricultural Domain		
	Open countryside	Small towns		Open countryside	Small towns	
Republican	42	61	(44.2)	52	68	(64.8)
Independent	17	11	(16.4)	15	12	(12.9)
Democrat	41	28	(39.5)	33	20	(22.3)
Total	100	100		100	100	
	(89.0)	(11.0)		(20.6)	(79.4)	
Significance level by chi-square = .01				Significance level by chi-square = .03		
N = 705				N = 445		

Table 6.5. Polar Party Attachments between Farmers and Farm Laborers, Open Countryside of the Agricultural Domain, Native-born Only (in percentages)

	Farmers	Farm Laborers	
Republican	45	31	(42.1)
Independent	18	13	(17.1)
Democrat	37	56	(40.8)
Total	100	100	
	(80.8)	(19.2)	
Significance level by chi-square = .001			
N = 705			

evidence of norms provided by the foreign-born German Lutherans and Irish and German Roman Catholics. Southern birth, lack of real property, lack of denominational attachment, and increasing age each magnified slightly this Democratic majority among farm laborers.

The several special subgroups that otherwise cloud a comparison between farmers in the open countryside and their village counterparts have now been removed. We are left with the basic contrasts. In terms of sheer size, these were the two largest categories of voters in rural Indiana, dominated by two farmers to every townsman. How did the internal structure of these two

Party Allegiance: Farmers and Townsmen

Table 6.6. Polar Party Attachments by Region and Birth, Controlled for Residence and Occupational Domain, Native-born, Farm Laborers Excluded (in percentages)

	Open Countryside				Small Towns			
	No.	Ind.	So.		No.	Ind.	So.	
Republican	42	42	49	(44.8)	70	70	63	(68.1)
Independent	15	22	15	(18.0)	15	13	8	(12.3)
Democrat	43	36	36	(37.2)	15	17	29	(19.7)
Total	100	100	100		100	100	100	
	(19.6)	(44.5)	(35.8)		(33.9)	(40.4)	(25.7)	
Significance level by chi-square = .20					Significance level by chi-square = .16			
N = 569					N = 284			

large aggregates affect their party attachments? Table 6.6 shows the internal composition of farmers and villagers by regions of birth. For neither category was variation in region of birth a significant factor in levels of party allegiance; every regional subgroup among villagers attained a Republican majority but sustained a balance of power among farmers in the open countryside, so that internal rates showed little variation around the levels characteristic of each group as a whole.

Similarly, broad age-groupings had no effect on the majority rates among townsmen. While the balance of power remained intact among farmers, significant differences by age-groups did result because younger farmers held higher Independent rates than older ones. But because younger farmers were also less likely to own property, these age differences were largely captured by variation due to status and property, where polar party attachments were related to property classes among farmers but not among their village counterparts.

Both the age and property relationships were fully captured by the two scales of occupational socioeconomic status, as shown in table 6.7. In both groups variation led to decreasing Republican rates with decreasing status. The comparisons of importance are those between farmers and villagers at similar status levels. High-status villagers attained a high 77 percent Republican norm, while high-status propertied farmers, with a 53 percent Republi-

Chapter Six

Table 6.7. Polar Party Attachments by Occupational Status, Controlled for Residence and Occupational Domain, Native-born, Farm Laborers Excluded (in percentages)

	Open Countryside				Small Towns			
	High farm	Medium farm	Low farm		High non-farm	Medium non-farm	Low non-farm	
Republican	53	42	38	(44.8)	77	71	55	(68.1)
Independent	16	15	22	(18.0)	14	13	10	(12.3)
Democrat	31	43	40	(37.2)	9	16	35	(19.7)
Total	100	100	100		100	100	100	
	(39.9)	(23.5)	(36.6)		(19.3)	(56.3)	(24.4)	
Significance level by chi-square = .02					Significance level by chi-square = .005			
$Tau_b = .10$					$Tau_b = .18$			
Gamma = .16					Gamma = .33			
N = 569					N = 284			

can majority, were a full 24 percent lower. Otherwise, farmers attained no partisan majority when compared to their village counterparts at similar status levels. Indeed, the Republican majority for the lowest occupational status level among townsmen was higher than that for high propertied farmers. Farmers, of course, were more consistently Democratic than their town counterparts, but they did not attain Democratic majorities, nor did these Democratic rates follow consistently the status gradients, as they did among villagers. Farmers' rates invariably clung close to a balance of power.

Further, levels of support for the Independent category were related to these status gradients in opposing directions. Independence from the two major parties reached its highest magnitude among low-status farmers but increased in magnitude by increasing status among villagers (and toward the lowest rates for farmers). The balance of power, therefore, was characteristic of farmers and, coupled with their levels of Independent support, suggests the presence of weak rather than strong attachments to the major parties quite in keeping with twentieth-century relationships.

Like occupational status differences, variation by levels of

Party Allegiance: Farmers and Townsmen

Table 6.8. Polar Party Attachments by Religious Involvement, Controlled for Residence and Occupational Domain, Native-born, Farm Laborers Excluded (in percentages)

	Open Countryside				Small Towns			
	Denom. attachment	"Prot."	No attachment		Denom. attachment	"Prot."	No attachment	
Republican	57	36	23	(44.8)	77	69	45	(68.1)
Independent	11	19	36	(18.0)	7	7	32	(12.3)
Democrat	32	45	41	(37.2)	16	24	23	(19.7)
Total	100	100	100		100	100	100	
	(54.1)	(24.2)	(21.7)		(50.5)	(28.0)	(21.5)	
Significance level by chi-square = .001					Significance level by chi-square = .001			
Tau_b = .20					Tau_b = .20			
Gamma = .30					Gamma = .33			
N = 569					N = 284			

institutional religious involvement among both farmers and their village counterparts was also significant. Table 6.8 shows these involvement gradients and their effect on partisan levels between these two categories of voters. For both villagers and farmers, Republican rates increased with increasing levels of involvement, and for denominationally involved farmers reached a maximum 57 percent Republican majority. At this same involvement level, however, farmers were still fully 22 percent lower than the 77 percent majority attained among denominationally involved townsmen. Again, farmers were more Democratic than villagers at comparable involvement levels, but these Democratic rates did not reach a majority.

The most interesting comparison by far, however, is for levels of independence from the two major parties. Among both farmers and villagers these rates increased with decreasing institutional religious involvement and approached or exceeded one-in-three of all voters in both camps who indicated no religious attachment at all. Among villagers, this suggests that voters lacking a sense of religious ties to existing institutions were, like the plurality of farmers, weak in their major-party allegiance and

in this respect makes the two kinds of political actors comparable without altering the major contrast. In terms of sheer demographics, nearly one-in-two farmers, but only one-in-five villagers were caught in the balance of power. Farmers were not highly politicized, but quite the contrary. They were weakly attached to the existing parties and in their standing relation to the parties not at all a group of cohesive character.

We could, of course, press these data further on a step-by-step basis, each time observing the comparison between farmers and townsmen in terms of a third variable. A slightly different strategy, however, will allow us to make a more global assessment of the total partisan structure in rural Indiana and the place of farmers in it. The vehicle for this assessment is similar to multiple correlation but operates on the nominal classifications appropriate to this data and allows us to assess all background characteristics among all voters.

The procedure (called Automatic Interaction Detection, or AID) is an iterative one that partitions the electorate into homogeneous subgroups through a series of steps; these subgroups can be diagrammed as a "tree chart" and the steps followed from beginning to end.[23] The tree chart may have one, two, or several main trunks from which reach much smaller "branches." These branches provide the terminal subgroups whose partisan homogeneity is such that further branches cannot be formed. Thus, the collection of terminal subgroups provides that set of fine-grained partitions which most fully account for the partisan variation. The variation in partisan rates between terminal subgroups compared to the total variation in the electorate provides a measure of the variation explained. In this sense, the routine affords a measure of multiple correlation.

The purpose of diagramming the tree charts is not necessarily to produce a high multiple correlation, which, given the nearly continuous presence of the balance of power pattern within the large subgroup of farmers, is not likely anyway. Certainly this coefficient is of interest as a total summary of polarization, but the purpose is also to show the range of variables that intersected with each other to form a structure with regard to partisan allegiance. AID tree charts will be displayed using two forms of the party-attachment variable, with other variables serving as the

Party Allegiance: Farmers and Townsmen

predictors. The first form sets members who identified themselves as Democrats over against those indicating Republican attachment, excluding for the moment the partisan Independents. The second form then brings the partisan Independents into the analysis with reference to the same social factors but with the additional variation in partisanship those Independents provided. The social characteristics used as predictors are listed in table 6.9.[24]

The initial AID tree chart in figure 6.3 displays the structure of partisanship in rural central Indiana in 1870, distinguishing only Democrats and Republicans. The origin-cell, or "root" of the tree, indicates that of all major partisans about 58 percent were Republicans. The first branch removes all of the Quakers, who were 100 percent Republican. The next split defines the two main trunks of the tree from which all subsequent branches emerged and follows the distinction based on place of residence. The set of members living in the small towns (trunk A) held a continuous Republican advantage, with one exception, where, among the foreign-born in the small towns the Republican segment sank to a low of 36 percent. Otherwise, subcells simply branched off as smaller Republican majorities, such as the southern-born in the small towns (61 percent), remaining small-town voters of low occupational status (59 percent), and then the Protestants (75 percent). Thus, the last remaining subcell defining the main trunk of voters in the small towns included the northern and Indiana-born, of middle and high occupational status, who were denominationally affiliated. They held a 92 percent Republican rate over against their Democratic opposition.

The other main trunk of the tree (trunk B) was defined by voters living in the open countryside. Though this trunk becomes increasingly Democratic, the rates tend to remain rather close to the fifty-fifty division characteristic of the balance of power pattern. Thus, with the Quakers split off and the Independents excluded, the Republicans lost the majority they held in the towns and showed a rate of 47 percent. The main trunk in the open countryside had only one branch of increasing Republicanism, among the Methodists (67 percent Republican). Otherwise, the remaining branches each represented a more Democratic subcell.

Chapter Six

Table 6.9. Background Variables Employed as Dichotomies for AID Analysis of Party Allegiance

1. High real estate wealth	18. Presbyterian
2. No real estate wealth	19. Small denominations
3. High personal estate wealth	20. Lutheran and Roman Catholic
4. No personal estate wealth	21. Disciples of Christ
5. High total estate wealth	22. No religious attachment
6. No total estate wealth	23. "Protestant"
7. High occupational status	24. Town/countryside residence
8. Low occupational status	25. Agricultural/nonagricultural domain
9. Propertied farmer	26. Northern-born
10. Nonpropertied farmer	27. Indiana-born
11. Farm laborer	28. Southern-born
12. Crafts and other occupations	29. Foreign-born
13. Professional or merchant	30. U.S.-born parent/foreign-born parent
14. Nonagricultural laborer	31. 21–30 years old
15. Methodist or Wesleyan Methodist	32. 31–40 years old
16. Quaker (Friends)	33. 41–50 years old
17. Baptist	34. 51 years and older

First the farm laborers split off (31 percent Republican), later the remaining Roman Catholics and Lutherans (15 percent). Then, of those remaining, voters lacking religious attachments formed a branch subcell (38 percent), then the Protestants (45 percent), and the Baptists (41 percent). Consequently, the last cell of the main trunk in the open countryside included the remaining denominationally affiliated voters who were not farm laborers, a group in which there was a 64 percent Republican majority.

This initial tree chart defines rather clearly the primary subcultural distinctions that distinguished voters by their partisanship in rural central Indiana in 1870. As was anticipated, these distinctions did not result in a dramatic multiple correlation, due in part to the balance of partisan power among farmers in the open countryside. Of the total variance, the distinctions represented by this tree chart produced a reduction in variance of about 21 percent, or a multiple correlation on the order of .46. Thus, given this structure of partisanship, nearly 80 percent of the variation in major-party attachment remained unexplained after these primary social factors were taken into account.

This basic structure to partisanship was not altered in its major

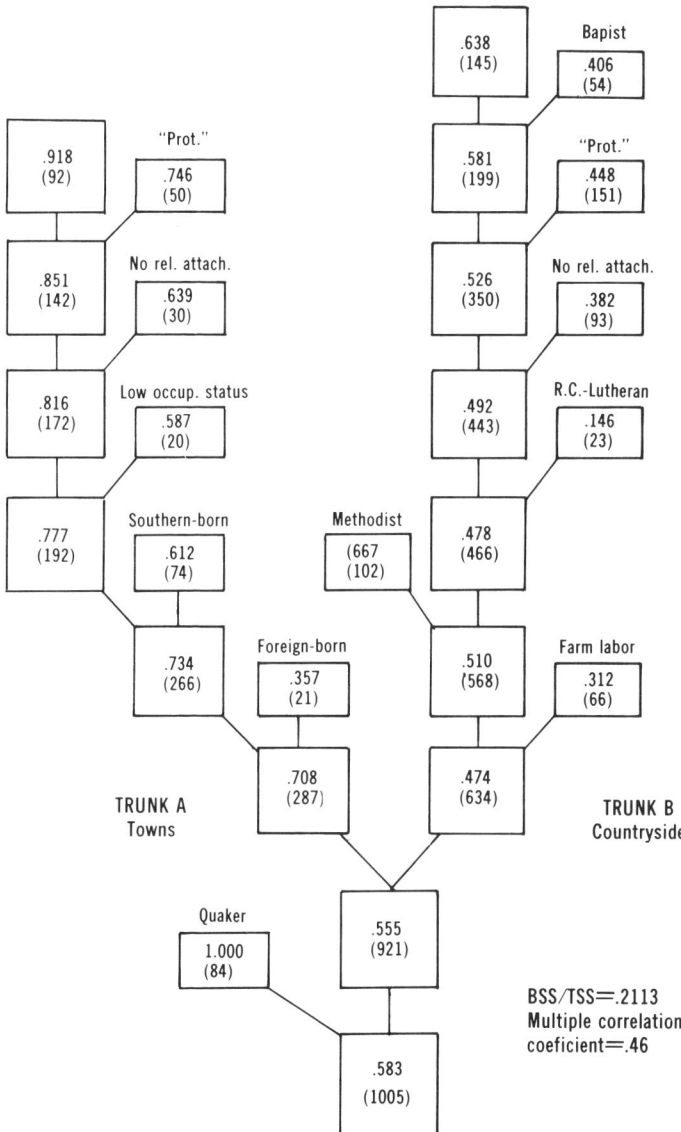

Fig. 6.3 AID tree chart, Republicans and Democrats (Independents excluded)

Chapter Six

outlines even when the Independent partisans were brought into the analysis. Adding these members involves making a further assumption beyond the ordering of parties on a threefold scale. This further assumption is that, psychologically, voters with Republican attachments were equally as distant from Independents as were those with Democratic attachments. Essentially, this is an assumption of ratio-level scaling and allows Republicans to be defined by a positive unit of value (+1) and Democrats to be defined by a negative unit of value (-1), with the Independents at the zero (0) midpoint.[25] If the scale is defined as ratio-level measurement, the Independents may be brought into the analysis directly, thereby increasing the total variation. The cells in the tree chart, in this case, will give the proportionate advantage of one major party over the other, on a base that includes the Independents, where positive proportions indicate a Republican advantage and negative ones a Democratic advantage. Thus, relative proximity to the zero-point on this three-valued scale tends to indicate how closely the balance of power pattern was approximated.

In the tree chart of figure 6.4, the Quakers again split off as a strong Republican branch. Then the two main trunks appeared, which distinguished between voters in the small towns (trunk A) and those in the open countryside (trunk B). Among townsmen the foreign-born were a Democratic branch (-18 percent Democratic advantage). For the remainder, voters in the small towns comprised a series of Republican branches, where that party's advantage was at a minimum in two of the branches—among those without religious attachments (17 percent), and among those born in the South (19 percent). The Republican advantage reached its maximum in the small towns among the native-born from Indiana and the northern states who were either Protestants or held specific denominational attachments, and who possessed some real estate (73 percent advantage).

In contrast to the increasingly Republican main trunk among town voters, the main trunk defined by voters in the open countryside (trunk B) centered closely on the balance of power pattern. The cell entries following one another along this main trunk oscillated only slightly to the Democratic side of an absolute zero stand-off point. This main trunk defined the largest single por-

Party Allegiance: Farmers and Townsmen

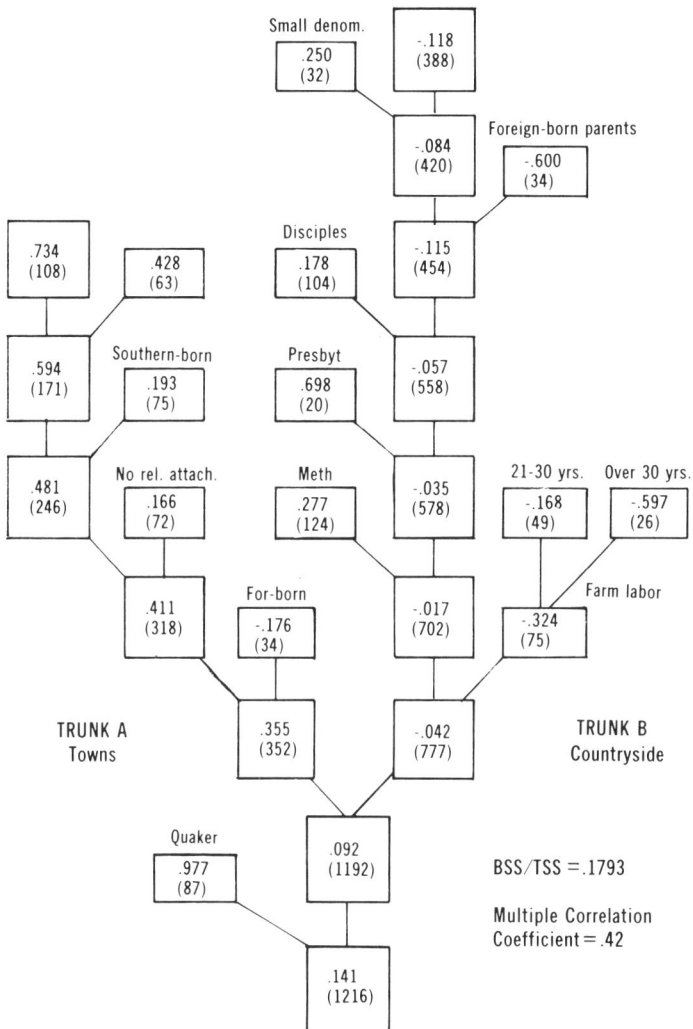

Fig. 6.4 AID tree chart. Republicans = +1, Independents = 0, Democrats = -1

tion of the whole electorate, nearly one-third of all rural central Indiana voters. It defined the primary stratum of the least partisan political actors.

Chapter Six

Three small branches of stronger partisans split off from this main trunk. The first were the farm laborers who held a Democratic advantage (-32 percent), among whom further "twigging" indicates that the older farm laborers gave the Democratic party an even greater advantage (-.60 percent). Second, of three denominational subgroups, a Republican advantage was most clearly defined among Presbyterians (at 70 percent). Third, among the remaining subcells, a second one with a Democratic advantage was defined by farmers with foreign-born parents (-60 percent). All the other subcells remained relatively close to the main trunk, whose final cell comprised voters who were farmers, both propertied and nonpropertied, who reported themselves as Protestants or lacking religious attachments. These farmers, as political actors, were defined most clearly by the balance of power pattern characteristic of the open countryside. Their lack of institutional subgroup ties thus becomes extremely clear.

The inclusion of those voters independent of the major parties in the analysis, which increased the total variation, also meant that the variation in party allegiance accounted for by the same background social characteristics was less than in the initial assessment, on the order of 18 percent. This results in a multiple correlation coefficient of about .43, indicating the full extent to which party allegiance in rural central Indiana had a life of its own, unaccounted for by social background factors.

Thus, to the extent that a subgroup balance of party allegiance indexed the relative incidence of weak as opposed to strong major-party attachments, these data confirm that farmers of the open countryside were distinctive political actors. In any case, it was not farmers who gave a Republican cast to rural Indiana, nor was it farmers who offered strong Democratic support. Rather, these rural farmers, as a category of voters, were without any strong partisan direction at all. They lacked the continuing, diverse, and multiple bases of group life that elsewhere sustained and nurtured strong political interest and partisan directionality. The farm itself as the very basis of social organization in the open countryside, rather than altering the farmer's physical, social, and psychological remoteness, served instead to reinforce it. A largely self-contained social unit, the farmstead had few mem-

Party Allegiance: Farmers and Townsmen

bers, each of whom, in work or family maintenance, was little dependent on others from outside the farm. Thus, in part due to their occupational role and the total way of life it required, farmers came to be characterized by their independence even from peers as well as from the large variety of associations and linking institutions which channeled political communication in other settings. They required pervasive, simultaneous, and individually felt "outside" forces during the 1870s, in the form of a deep agricultural depression, to drive them to action—through Grange organization, third-party formations, and partisan voting against the national party in power and its local representatives. It is to this understanding of Indiana's partisan voting that we now turn.

7

Indiana's Election Dynamics and the Power of Party Allegiance, 1868-1880

Elections in Indiana during the 1870s were decided largely by voters whose allegiance was to the two major parties. Yet so competitive were the two major parties within the state, and so close were successive elections from 1868 to 1880, that even the most minor shift of voters between the parties meant victory for one and defeat for the other. It was within this balance of competition between Republicans and Democrats among Hoosiers that the farmer's independent movement and the Greenback party had its most telling impact, causing county election returns to depart from their usual course over the series of presidential and off-year congressional elections.

Counties were the primary political aggregates for which local party leaders were everywhere in the state responsible, and in this sense the counties were themselves the most important political (and geographic) "masses" of voters. Party leaders anticipated and monitored the vote of these masses as they sought to insure local, district, and state-wide party victory. And county chairmen of both parties, like Justus C. Adams of the Marion County Republicans, took steps to insure voting loyalty among party regulars and to encourage irregular voters toward a "correct" party marking of the ballot. "Go to the polls early and remain until the last ballot is in the box," was how Adams instructed his county committeemen and poll-watchers. "See to it that every Republican vote is polled, and assist in persuading the doubtful and indifferent voter to vote with us, keeping in view ... that the effective [party] work is done at the polls on the day of the election."[1]

Allegiance to the major parties among voters within each county had an immense influence on the actual vote across all counties of Indiana. Taken alone, allegiance within each county summarized the different levels of party support that arose from other divisions and subgroups in these same masses and mapped their standing strength across the state. Allegiance to the major parties, therefore, was one factor that anchored and constrained each county's partisan vote division during the 1870s. On the other hand, the different candidates in each campaign and the issues and events of the decade determined the level of turnout and the extent of defection that led to departures in the vote toward one or another of the parties. These departures from the vote that was expected on the basis of party allegiance among voters within counties showed the effects of farmers as political actors who were weak in their party attachments and the effects of lowered party involvement among those large segments of Indiana's population, both on the farms and off them, that lacked attachment to religious institutions.

It is not my intention to describe each election during the decade of the 1870s as a totally separate affair. The continuity and competitiveness of the results were much too patent to warrant such idiosyncratic treatment.[2] Rather, I will instead show how the election results of this decade may be understood by means of an interpretative quantitative model, one that highlights those campaigns in which Indiana's third-party movements had their greatest impact, disrupting the usual bonds of party allegiance.[3] Why that disruption occurred, and its particular pattern, may then be seen as a product of rural and farm unrest during the depression decade.

This effort to understand the voting results across all of Indiana's counties (with our knowledge of how party allegiance was distributed within the social structure of nine of them), rests on important conceptual foundations that require initial discussion.

Chapter Seven

In a penetrating analysis several years ago, Philip Converse directed attention to what he called the "normal vote"—an aggregate estimator of the expected partisan division of the vote based directly on party attachments among individual voters within the national electorate.[4] In his period of research among American voters—the 1950s and 1960s—Converse observed that the national division of the two-party vote, measured biennially (the presidential vote and, alternately, the cumulated votes for Congress in the off-year elections), showed an oscillation as strong as any in the previous century. Raising the question of how such dramatic swings between elections might be understood and evaluated, he posited the need for a baseline which would establish the "expected state" of the partisan division and from which change in actual election outcomes might be viewed.

Converse had available to him survey data from across the whole series of elections of his interest, in which direct questions had been used to probe the partisan attachments of each sampled citizen. In complete contrast to the wide oscillations in aggregate outcomes, the distributions of these partisan attachments among citizens were strikingly stable and, as among Indiana voters a century ago, were almost as fixed as demographic attributes. This stability of attachment was itself confirmed for the voters within these distributions by panel studies reinterviewing the same persons over time. As Converse observed:

> This picture of dramatic short-term variation [in the aggregate vote from election to election] becomes more interesting as we discover, in sequences of sample surveys across precisely the same period, a serene stability in the distribution of party loyalties expressed by the same public.... Furthermore, this is not the sort of net stability which conceals gross turnover of individual partisanship over time. "Panel" studies, which involve the reinterview of a national cross-section sample after intervals of two and four years, confirm to a remarkable degree individual stability in party identification, even in this period of extravagant [aggregate] vote change.[5]

In view of these findings, Converse suggested a reconsideration of any aggregate vote outcome as the effect of two major components: (1) the long-term, normal, or "baseline" division of the vote, to be expected by aggregating the underlying distribution of party attachments for any electorate or subgroup (other things, such as turnout, being equal), and (2) the short-term, current departures from the normal vote, taken as the effect of the immediate campaign circumstances of the specific election. In his words, "The election outcome in the population or subpopulation, then, may be construed as the result of short-term forces acting upon a certain distribution of party loyalties which have characterized the population."[6]

This view of voting behavior as a result of two components led, in turn, to a new understanding of several dynamic features of party allegiance, when both strength of allegiance as well as direction were measured. One of these dynamic features was the probability of "defection" from the "home party" to vote for the opposition. In every contemporary election of survey record some voters departed from their nominal party attachment to vote for candidates of the opposition, all the while retaining their original allegiance and returning to the candidates of their home party after the issues compelling their departure receded. Such "defection" should not be confused with partisan "conversion." Measured on the same individuals over time, a report of change in underlying party allegiance gauges conversion, while opposition voting under the original allegiance gauges defection. Though never absent at any time, conversion was seen as a decidedly rare phenomenon when compared to election-by-election defection, despite the strong movement of the whole electorate first in one direction and then the other.

The first dynamic property of voting behavior measured by the full party-identification scale is that the *probability of defection* occurs in a gradient.[7] Under the impact of immediate election tides favoring one party and then another, rates of defection vary inversely with the strength of party affiliation. In his work on the normal vote, Converse illustrated these gradients schematically, as follows (see figure 7.1).

Conditions (a) and (b) depict unidirectional election swings favoring one or the other major party. Under these conditions, voting departures toward the advantaged party, by levels of

Chapter Seven

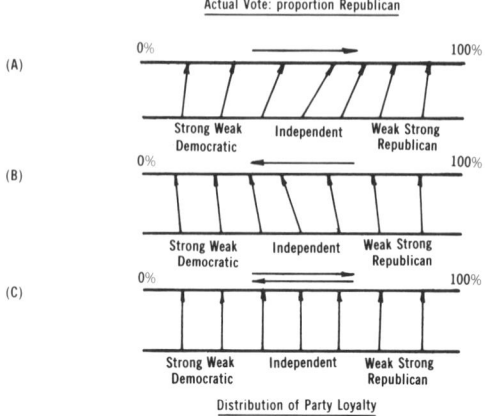

Source: Converse, "Normal Vote," p. 17.

Fig. 7.1 Varying strains induced on party loyalties by short-term net partisan forces. (*a*) Strong pro-Republican forces. (*b*) Mild pro-Democratic forces. (*c*) No forces; balance of forces

strength of party attachment, were largest among Independents and weakly identified voters in the central portion of the scale and least (though not absent) among the strongly identified categories on either end. Thus, *variability in the partisan division of the vote* from one election to the next has had its most highly visible source in the more volatile central portion of the electorate, when voters are spread over a scale by strength of party identification.

The second dynamic feature of voting behavior measured by the strength of underlying party attachments is that the *probability of turning out to vote* in the first place also exhibits characteristic gradients.[8] When general turnout rates were high, nearly all strength categories of party attachment showed voter response at the polls in about the same proportions. On the other hand, when general turnout rates declined, the decline in category-specific rates was most rapid in the central portions of the party identification scale. Figure 7.2 illustrates this shift in the turnout probabilities—from the nearly equal turnout within each category of party identifier for elections of high overall turnout, to the category-specific decline in turnout as general turnout levels have dropped. Thus, *variability in turnout* among voters by categories

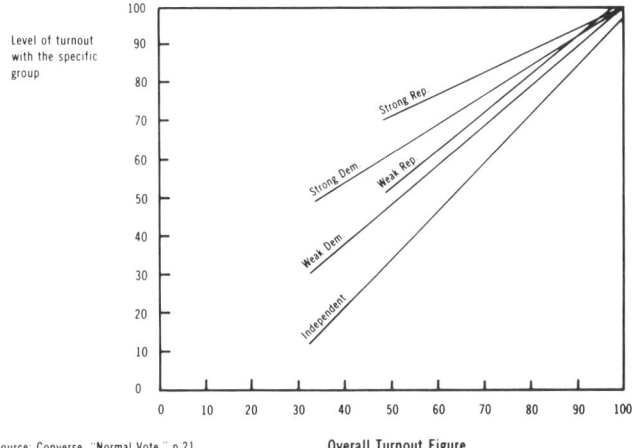

Fig. 7.2 Turnout within classes of party identifiers as a function of overall turnout in five national elections. (Source: Converse, "Normal Vote," p. 21.)

of party identification also has had its most highly visible source in the more volatile central portion of the electorate. From these observations it is a simple conclusion that citizens independent of the major parties are generally the most responsive "floating voters" in the electorate. It is equally important, however, that defection and shifts from one party to another occur all along the scale of identification, not only or simply among the Independents.

The normal vote model of stable long-term party attachments and of short-term voting behavior that varies from election to election was built on defection and turnout as two basic dynamic features of voting that were revealed by the full scale of party identification. What Converse called the "normal vote" at any time was the interpolation of a partisan division between the major parties based strictly on party attachments under conditions of a net balance of partisan tides for a hypothetical election on the low side of high turnout. Under these conditions, the normal vote was offered as a baseline party division, one expected by simply aggregating voters' attachments within gross party-attachment categories.[9]

Chapter Seven

Several deductions about the partisan division of the vote between presidential and off-year congressional elections follow from this basic model and the underlying dynamics on which it rests. Consider first this model's implications for presidential and off-year congressional elections according to the patterns of high and low turnout characterizing them. The model suggests that as turnout declines from high-stimulus presidential turnout levels to the lower turnout levels for off-year congressional elections, the Independents will tend to leave the electorate at a faster rate than either weak or strong partisans. Under this turnout decline, and with a balance of partisan forces, the off-year electorate in effect "shrinks" toward its basic core of voters. The dropout of active voters, most severe among Independents, therefore tends to strengthen any preexisting majority in underlying attachments, resulting in an off-year partisan vote slightly more favorable to the majority party than the normal vote itself.

Now consider the effect of *strong* short-term tides favoring one of the major parties, but with precisely the same turnout decline from presidential to off-year congressional elections. With strong short-term partisan forces moving the electorate during each campaign, the off-year election will then depart less far from the normal vote than in the preceding presidential election, because cause in the on-year election increased turnout moves the Independents most rapidly toward the advantaged party's position, increasing its margin. Thus, over a series of presidential and off-year congressional elections, where short-term tides favor one party or the other, this model implies that the presidential series of election outcomes will be more variable (departing further from the normal vote) than an off-year series (all other things equal).

Anchored by the allegiance of strong partisans on the one hand, and with independents as the most frequent "floating voters" on the other, some election series of strong tides nonetheless reverse this pattern of greater departures from the normal vote in presidential election than in off-year congressional ones. Converse has himself argued that one additional dimension in the structure of the electorate and several special conditions in the electoral situation must be recognized in order to account for these apparent "reversals" from the usual normal vote dynamics.[10] In his account, voters are not only characterized, politically, by the strength of their party allegiance but by their level of political involvement and political information as well, gradients (often measured by amounts of formal education) which also tend to define the intake of new political information among twentieth-century voters. Susceptibility to change from party allegiance to the actual vote cast in an election is higher at higher information and involvement levels while it is least at low levels (that is, among the less educated or least politically involved citizens). Voters of low information or involvement are a class of voters·least likely to monitor and act on new political events or issues. This view offers a direct refinement of the simple floating-voter hypothesis by conceiving that voting dynamics are "anchored" in two ways—first by strength of party allegiance and second by levels of information and involvement with politics. Strong party-attachment on the one hand and low political information on the other both provide "inertial" components of voting behavior, where low information or involvement levels, if measured on an educational scale, ranked much larger a century ago than today and with a much larger impact in constraining election outcomes.[11]

If citizens of low information and involvement are relatively stable from their party allegiance to the vote itself and, like strong partisans, provide inertia against change within the electorate, then the normal vote model must be refined to include this second anchoring term as well. This refinement shows how a "reversal" of the general pattern of election departures from the normal vote baseline occurs, causing off-year congressional elections to depart further from it than their presidential counterparts. All that is required is a moderate positive correlation between the strength of party allegiance and levels of political involvement or information, and the onset of new political issues and events giving rise to partisan tides. In particular, if new political information penetrates the mass electorate from the top of the involvement-information gradient on downward, then both anchoring classes of voters will shift least from their prior party attachments to the vote itself.[12] Thus, while those citizens stand-

Chapter Seven

ing independent of the major parties in the initial formulation appear as the voters most likely to shift their vote toward the party advantaged at the moment, those Independents receiving little new information are *the most unlikely* of all voters *to shift* at all, and, if they turn out to vote, will split their vote in proportions between the parties common to their class. The result is that low-information voters will stabilize the partisan division of the vote more by their presence in higher-turnout presidential elections than in the lower-turnout off-year congressional ones, and the latter elections, under strong partisan tides, will depart more from the normal vote baseline than the presidential series.

The refinement of the floating-voter hypothesis under the normal vote model provides our initial entry to Indiana's elections from 1868 to 1880. For the rise of independent candidates and the Greenback party in Indiana during the 1870s were responses to depression issues and events that had not been adequately captured in the platforms of the two major parties. From the dynamics of voting just described, it follows quite directly that the composition of these third-party movements was unlikely to be drawn from among voters who were strong partisans on the one hand or from those of low political information and involvement on the other, and that the shifts in major party fortunes at the polls depended on the communication of political information among Democrats and Republicans as party leaders altered their positions over this depression decade in response to the third-party threat. Therefore, under the normal vote model, our expectation is that as the least informed and involved voters dropped out of the active electorate in off-year elections, the weak partisans and Independents who remained in the active electorate would accelerate the amplitude of change from the normal-vote baseline, in a direct reversal of the usual normal-vote dynamics, with departures from the normal-vote baseline greater in the off-year congressional elections than in the presidential ones. In fact, Indiana's independent and Greenback movements made their greatest inroads in the off-year congressional elections of 1874 and 1878, quite in keeping with this apparent reversal. Whether or not the normal-vote model applies to Indiana during the 1870s at all, however, is itself a major question quite worth

Election Dynamics and Party Allegiance, 1868-1880

Table 7.1. Party Attachment by County, Nine *People's Guide* Counties, 1870

County	% Republican	% Independent	% Democrat	Total	Weighted Sample N
Bartholomew	34.5	11.2	54.3	100	144
Boone	53.1	15.9	31.0	100	148
Hamilton	63.1	22.0	14.8	100	140
Hendricks	59.2	9.5	31.2	100	139
Henry	61.7	26.9	11.4	100	160
Johnson	40.2	5.2	54.6	100	124
Montgomery	38.2	18.5	43.4	100	168
Morgan	39.4	14.3	46.3	100	117
Vermillion	51.4	18.0	30.6	100	76
Total	49.1	16.0	34.9	100	1,216

Significance level by chi-square = .001
Lambda$_a$ = .10

asking and trying to answer. From this conceptual background we must now turn to that question.

Indiana's counties were the one set of subgroups within the state for which all actual voting totals were consistently reported. These counties, of course, were geographic aggregates of voters that were quite heterogeneous but whose interior structure for nine of them we now know. Since the normal-vote model was not qualified in its application to specific subgroups, it can be applied to these county aggregates equally as well as to social classes, religious groups, or ideological camps. And it is just for these county aggregates that we have not only the levels of party support in nine counties for 1870 but also the record of their vote over sequences of elections before and after this date for our benchmark sample.

Table 7.1 presents the rates of party allegiance among voters for each of the nine counties from which the 1870 sample was drawn. Clearly, levels of party support varied across counties. While county of residence alone did not determine these levels any more than other divisions of the electorate, the strength of association between party support and county of residence was about as strong as for any other nominal classification of voters (lambda$_a$ = .10). The county, as a unit of aggregation, was there-

Chapter Seven

Table 7.2. Correlation Coefficients between Percent Independent (*Guide* sample) and Voting Turnout, *People's Guide* Counties

Election and Office	Pearson's r
1862 congressional	−.75
1864 presidential	.40
1864 gubernatorial	.19
1864 congressional	−.09
1866 congressional	−.29
1868 presidential	.01
1868 gubernatorial	.03
1868 congressional	−.04
1870 congressional	−.52
1872 presidential	.08
1872 gubernatorial	−.01
1872 congressional	.00
1874 congressional	−.53
1876 presidential	−.09
1876 gubernatorial	−.15
1876 congressional	−.21
1878 congressional	−.25
1880 presidential	.42
1880 gubernatorial	.23
1880 congressional	.18

fore itself a meaningful one for differences in party allegiance. And some county electorates, like those for Hamilton and Henry counties, even showed norming patterns in their support that elsewhere we have taken to suggest cohesive grouplike formations, while others, like Montgomery and Morgan, showed the balance of power pattern. How, then, were the direct measures of underlying party allegiance among voters in these nine *People's Guide* counties related to actual election outcomes over time?

If we follow the normal-vote model and simply aggregate party attachments as a set of proportions characterizing each county as a subgroup, then the relation between underlying party attachments and election results can be viewed by a series of correlation coefficients. Table 7.2 displays the correlation between the percentage of voters who turned out to vote in each election from 1862 to 1880 and the percentage of voters classified as Independent in our 1870 sample for each of the nine counties. These coefficients exhibit generally low values, as they should, reflecting in part Indiana's high average turnout and its geographic variability over the series of elections. The prevailing pattern, however, depends on the difference between on-year and off-year elections. the highest *negative* coefficients all occur for the low-turnout off-year congressional elections. In these off-year elections there was a tendency for turnout to remain high in those counties where the *People's Guide* proportion of Independents was low, quite in keeping with the idea that turnout in the off-years was inversely related to the size of this middle category. When turnout declined across these counties, it declined in relation to the proportion of voters independent of the two major parties.

Now observe the correlations between the *People's Guide* proportions of underlying major-party attachments and the major-party voting results for these same offices and period of time, as shown in table 7.3. All of these coefficients are gratifyingly high, regardless of party, office, or election. They are consistent with the notion that the tides of short-term partisan swing flowed everywhere in these nine counties pretty much the same for each election at these office levels. The coefficients are especially high in the elections immediately surrounding 1870, the point in time to which the sample itself pertains. Only two small patterns of decay in these coefficients appear, one related to the Democratic correlations antedating the election of 1868, the other to the Republican correlations following the election of 1872. This small decay seems sufficiently distant in time from the direct *People's Guide* measure of party attachments in 1870 to suggest that population change may be partly responsible; and both patterns of decay are counterbalanced by higher correlations for the opposite party. Thus, I believe there can be little doubt that these high correlations all indicate the sustained, long-term net impact of underlying major-party attachments in these nine counties as predictors of the partisan vote.

Within these nine counties, the level of support given to Re-

Chapter Seven

Table 7.3. Correlation Coefficients between Percent Major Parties (*Guide* Sample) and Percent Division of the Vote, *People's Guide* Counties

Election and Office	Pearson's r	
	Republican	Democrat
1862 congressional	.88	.78
1864 presidential	.94	.88
1864 gubernatorial	.92	.88
1864 congressional	.93	.87
1866 congressional	.92	.85
1868 presidential	.91	.92
1868 gubernatorial	.92	.92
1868 congressional	.93	.92
1870 congressional	.92	.95
1872 presidential	.90	.91
1872 gubernatorial	.92	.94
1872 congressional	.93	.93
1874 congressional	.84	.86
1876 presidential	.87	.95
1876 gubernatorial	.81	.96
1876 congressional	.86	.67
1878 congressional	.82	.88
1880 presidential	.77	.96
1880 gubernatorial	.78	.96
1880 congressional	.76	.94

publicans, Independents, and Democrats, as measured by party allegiance, has already been described. For each county the different levels of subgroup support have now been summarized in their impact on voting results by the measure of party allegiance aggregated to the county level itself. Our next task, rather than to decompose these results for the nine counties once again, is to extend the normal vote expected on the basis of long-term party attachments to all Indiana counties, not only for 1870 but for the successive national elections of the decade. The accomplishment of this task requires that the normal vote, based on underlying party attachments, be estimated prior to each election, first as a surrogate for the nine-county sample and then for all counties of the state. To estimate the normal vote, Converse himself suggested forming a special kind of time-series mean together with its variance, one that would include a balance of partisan tides for a (hypothetical) election on the low side of high turnout. For his purposes he used a series of presidential and off-year congressional elections to make this estimate. Several comparable strategies, all of them involving time-series averages, have been pursued by Kabaker, Zingale, and others in making normal-vote estimates for county aggregates.[13] I shall pursue a similar strategy.

In constructing a county-level measure of the expected normal vote as a surrogate for underlying party attachments I have included a four-election sequence, spanning six years, prior to each specific election year of interest in the 1870s and have included two off-year elections and two presidential-year elections in order that the normal vote estimator might balance the partisan forces of specific elections and stand on the low side of high turnout. I have also tried to remove the major effects of national offices from this estimator by employing the gubernatorial vote in presidential years and, for the 1870s, by using the off-year vote for secretary of state.[14] Thus, the normal-vote estimator was designed to cycle forward in time with each succeeding election year (like a series of aggregated samples) but was based solely on the four immediately preceding contests that tended to balance the partisan tides as well as the highs and lows of turnout.

How did this surrogate estimator of the normal vote compare to our direct measures of underlying party attachments for the *People's Guide* sample of counties? Table 7.4 shows the Republican normal-vote estimate for each of the nine counties for each election year, taken as a mean over four preceding elections. The decade average of these estimates is given as the final column. For most of these counties there is a secular decline in the estimated Republican normal vote from 1870 to 1880, due in part to the presence of third-party activity and Democratic tides in the latter half of the decade. How good these surrogate estimators are, however, is shown by table 7.5. This table displays slope coefficients and correlation coefficients for the regression of the Republican normal-vote estimate on the percentage of Repub-

Table 7.4. Estimated Normal Vote Republican for Nine *People's Guide* Counties, by Election Year, 1870–80

County	Estimated % Normal Vote Republican						Decade Average	*Guide* % Republican
	1870	1872	1874	1876	1878	1880		
Bartholomew	44.7	45.0	44.6	43.0	43.1	43.3	44.0	34.5
Boone	53.5	52.8	51.9	51.4	49.5	47.2	51.0	53.1
Hamilton	67.3	70.1	67.9	67.5	65.4	61.7	66.7	63.1
Hendricks	67.3	67.4	65.0	63.1	60.9	58.7	63.7	59.2
Henry	66.0	69.6	68.0	67.3	66.3	63.1	66.7	61.7
Johnson	45.0	45.8	43.5	42.7	41.9	40.7	43.3	40.2
Montgomery	49.7	49.2	48.8	49.0	48.3	47.5	48.8	38.2
Morgan	56.5	56.9	55.7	54.3	52.6	51.1	54.5	39.4
Vermillion	59.2	59.5	59.1	57.0	55.4	52.6	57.1	51.4
Nine-county mean	56.6	57.4	56.0	55.0	53.7	51.8	55.1	
Standard deviation	9.1	9.9	9.6	9.5	9.0	8.0	9.1	

Table 7.5. Coefficients for the Regression of Normal Vote Percent Republican on Percent Republican (*Guide* sample)

Election year	Intercept Constant	Slope B	Pearson's r
Normal vote 1870	15.6	.87	.95
Normal vote 1872	13.2	.93	.93
Normal vote 1874	13.8	.89	.92
Normal vote 1876	13.7	.87	.91
Normal vote 1878	15.3	.81	.89
Normal vote 1880	18.6	.70	.87

lican party attachments given in the *Guide* sample. The slopes are direct and positive and fitted by high correlations as well. The decay in slope that is evident as we move from 1870 to 1880 is fully consistent with conceptions of compositional change within these counties over the decade, eroding the goodness of fit of the sample proportions as the distance in time increases from the 1870 base. By 1880, the surrogate normal-vote estimator is likely to be a better one for each county than the 1870 *Guide* proportions. But the two are so highly congruent and consistent that the

Election Dynamics and Party Allegiance, 1868-1880

Table 7.6. Mean Estimated Normal Vote and Standard Deviation, over All Counties, by Election Year, 1870–80

	1870	1872	1874	1876	1878	1880	Decade Average
Mean Normal vote Republican	50.4	50.9	50.2	49.2	48.6	47.0	49.4
Standard deviation	9.5	9.7	9.1	9.4	9.1	9.0	9.2

surrogate estimators, which cycle forward with each succeeding election, may be considered a simple refinement on the aggregation of party attachments in these nine counties for 1870 and lend themselves directly to an extension of the normal vote to all counties in Indiana by the same estimating process.

Table 7.6 presents the means and standard deviations for the Republican normal vote, estimated over all counties for each election year during the 1870s. The final column summarizes these different estimates as an average for the decade. In true part-to-whole fashion, the successive normal-vote estimates are all highly intercorrelated, and each election-year normal-vote estimate also correlates at better than .95 with the average decade normal vote as well. Thus, these normal vote estimates over all counties form a very stable distribution throughout the 1870s.

The geographic meaning of these estimates over a map of the state is shown in figure 7.3, which indicates the Democratic and Republican spheres of influence within Indiana by contrasting shading. Counties standing more than three-quarters of one standard deviation above or below the average-decade mean Republican percentage are further darkened as a way of indicating the "core" Democratic and Republican areas. The map makes visible the north-south geographic bias of party strength within the state, on which V. O. Key and others have commented.[15] What we know, however, is that this geographic bias was not due to southern origins among voters in the 1870s but to Democratic influence when these counties were first established. Thus, there were few Republican counties south of Indianapolis (Marion

157

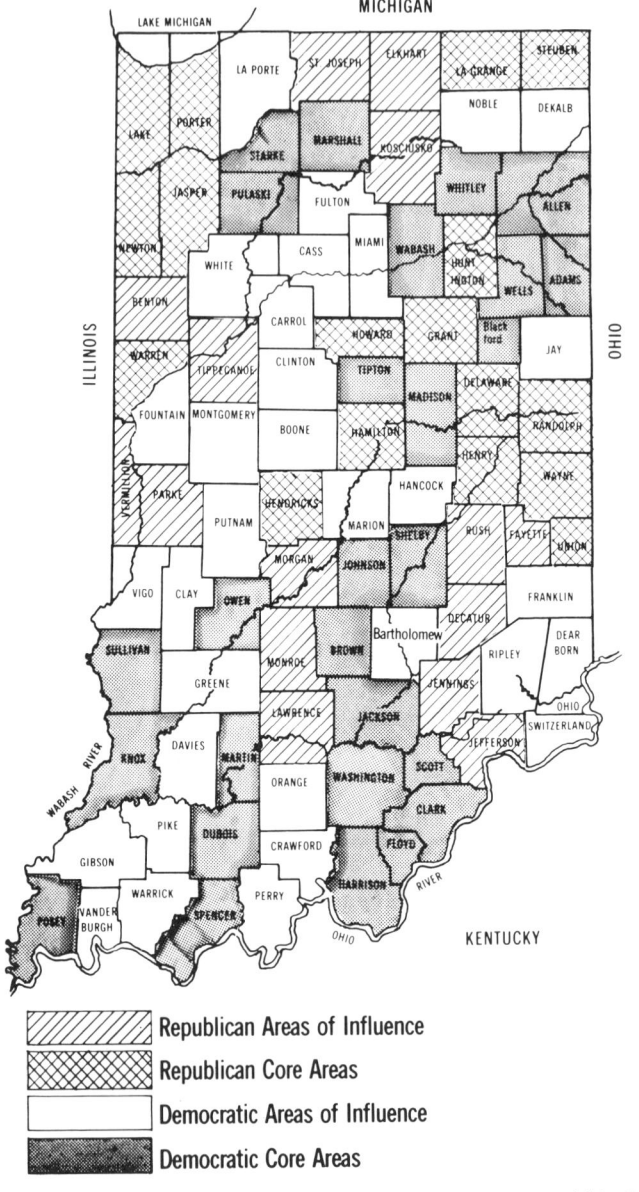

Fig. 7.3 Democratic and Republican spheres of influence within Indiana during the 1870s

County) and no core Republican ones. Most of the core Republican counties spanned the central and northern portions of the state, but with some notable Democratic intrusions into both the central Tipton Till region and the northern Moraine and Lakes area. Thus, core Democratic counties, in contrast to Republican ones, were much more widely dispersed.

The normal-vote estimator establishes a baseline in the expected partisan division of the vote for all Indiana counties in the absence of partisan tides and shifts in turnout that caused defection toward one or another of the parties during the 1870s. As such, it measures the standing strength of the parties across all counties of the state and summarizes the normal relationship between social composition and party support exclusive of the candidates, issues, and events of particular campaigns during the decade. It therefore imputes a very specific meaning to the notion of change, for "change" is measured from the estimated normal-vote baseline and not from a previous election. Measured from a previous election, voting change is the net partisan "swing" and includes the relaxation of defection and of shifts associated with turnout or other factors in the first election, confusing this relaxation of prior tides with, and adding it to, the new movements among voters in the second election.[16] The normal-vote baseline for Indiana cuts this net swing into election-specific net change, so that we can see clearly the impact of party allegiance on voting results and can also see in which particular elections departures were most severe from the division expected on the basis of underlying party attachments. It also allows us to see whether and to what extent the voting results at particular elections moved in correlation with turnout, with third-party activity, or with bases of social composition across counties, independent of their correlation with the normal vote, normal turnout, or third-party support.

Because the *People's Guide* counties were slightly biased along several dimensions of composition when compared to all counties, our next step is to establish the standing relation between social composition across all counties and underlying party attachment in them as estimated by the expected normal vote. Table 7.7 contains seventeen measures of county composition

Chapter Seven

Table 7.7. Means, Standard Deviations, and Correlation Coefficients for Measures of County Social Composition in 1870, All Counties

1870 Measure of Composition	1870 Mean	Standard Deviation	Pearson's r with Av. Decade Normal Vote
% lg. farms	52.3	11.9	.29
Av. val. farms	$3,940	$1,623	.44
Av. assessed property	$1,657	$581	.34
Av. val. fm. prds.	$785	$319	.30
Av. mfg. capital	$3,464	$2,607	−.02
Av. val. mfg. prds.	$7,420	$4,842	−.11
Pop. density p/sq. mi.	11.2	6.6	.04
% Indiana-born	63.4	9.8	−.21
% bdr.-south-born	6.3	3.6	−.12
% North.-born	16.7	11.0	.20
% foreign-born	7.3	6.3	−.16
Ir./for. ratio	26.5	17.2	.25
Ger./for. ratio	45.8	18.9	−.31
% pietistic orgs.	56.7	13.3	.28
% liturgical orgs.	12.0	10.5	−.34
% rural	83.3	14.6	.00
% church seats	61.1	25.9	.00

that were drawn from the 1870 aggregate census returns, together with their means and standard deviations, and shows their correlation with the average decade normal vote, taken over all counties. From the internal structure of our sample nine-county electorate, we should expect the correlation coefficients to be moderate at best, as indeed they are. None reach the level of .50. As at the individual level, where party allegiance did not stand as a simple recoding of class, religion, ethnicity, or any other background characteristic among voters, so at the aggregate level the geographical spread of partisanship across all Hoosier counties during the 1870s was not a simple function of county social composition either.

To understand the meaning of the normal-vote estimator across counties it is important to consider the distinctive patterns of covariation. First, the normal vote Republican was higher where the average value of farms was high ($r = .44$) and similarly increased with increases in assessed county property values ($r =$

.34), farm size (r=.29), and the value of farm products (r=.30). These are the Carleton-type relationships. But we now know that the strong Republican support across these counties of high farm wealth came from the small rural towns, not the farms. Second, the normal vote Republican was lower (and the normal vote Democratic was higher) where the percentage of liturgical organizations (Lutheran and Roman Catholic) was high (r= -.34), and was higher where the percentage of pietistic organizations was high (r= .28). These are the ethnocultural type of relationships. Third, the relative incidence of different birth origins was related to the normal Republican levels. Where the number of Germans among the foreign-born was high, the normal vote Republican declined (r =-.31); it rose with the number of Irish-born, in accord with the different settlement patterns of these two groups. Finally, the normal vote Republican increased where the northern-born were strong (r= .20) and declined where the proportion born in Indiana was high (r= -.21). Thus, several factors of county social composition were related to levels in the normal vote Republican; and compared to average decade turnout (see pp. 124-26), these partisan levels were tuned to quite different factors.

While several possible causal orderings of these county social factors might be proposed, I do not intend to pursue such a line of inquiry. The causes that led to alignments of social and political composition lay in the pre-1870s past, and will not affect analysis of elections during the 1870s once the normal vote itself is taken into account. The impact of each of these factors relative to the others, and their combined relationship to the normal vote Republican, however, is important for establishing the baseline in social composition from which change in specific elections might be measured. I shall use two ways of assessing this combined impact, one by way of step-wise multiple correlation and the other by standard multiple regression.

Step-wise multiple correlation is analagous to the AID procedure used previously, but for ratio level variables such as the county measures provide. It builds a structure of independent variables that successively account for variation in the dependent variable. Table 7.8 shows the step-wise multiple correlation between county social composition and the average decade normal

Chapter Seven

Table 7.8. Multiple Regression and Correlation (Stepwise) of the Average Decade Normal Vote Republican and the Average Decade Turnout on Measures of County Composition, 1870

Compositional Measure	Multiple R	R Squared	R-sq. Change
Average Decade Normal Vote Republican			
1. Average value farms	.44	.20	.20
2. % Liturgical orgs.	.50	.26	.06
3. % Indiana-born	.56	.31	.05
4. % Rural	.57	.33	.02
5. % Pietistic orgs.	.58	.34	.01
Average Decade Turnout			
1. % Indiana-born	.48	.23	.23
2. % Rural	.56	.31	.08
3. % Pietistic orgs.	.59	.34	.03
4. Irish/Foreign ratio	.61	.37	.03
5. German/Foreign ratio	.63	.39	.02

vote Republican on the one hand, and average decade turnout on the other, to a depth of five variables, each of which accounts for more than 1 percent of this normal baseline variation. Both structures yield multiple correlations near the .60 level, accounting for approximately 35 to 40 percent of variation between counties on these measures of normal partisanship and participation. As multiple correlations, these may be seen as moderate to high. And even though county measures tend to average out the underlying "noise," they are nonetheless impressive testimony indicating that social composition made a difference across all counties for the normal vote and average turnout levels. But they also indicate that both partisanship and participation each had a substantial impact of their own, quite beyond the range of such social factors, even averaged within counties and combined across them. Social composition was far from determining either normal partisan levels or average turnout across counties.

The multiple regression procedure must be approached with greater caution, for it provides a way to assess the relative impact of several independent variables, given the impact of each of the others. In particular, it requires that the independent variables not be highly colinear, as variables related at the level of .80 or .90 certainly are.[17] Table 7.9 reproduces the intercorrelation matrix of

Table 7.9. Correlation Matrix of County Composition and Average Decade Normal Vote Republican

	1	2	3	4	5	6	7	8	9	10	11	12	13	14	15	16
1. % large farms																
2.* Av. val. farms	.63															
3. Av. assessed prop.	.66	.67														
4. Av. value fm. prds.	.59	.79	.60													
5. Av. mfg. capital	−.08	.20	.16	−.04												
6. Av. value mfg. prds.	−.08	.15	.13	−.04	.92											
7.* % rural	.04	−.25	−.19	−.07	−.82	−.81										
8. Pop. density	−.09	.30	.14	.07	.75	.71	−.81									
9.* % Indiana-born	.13	−.22	.03	−.01	−.32	−.24	.30	−.19								
10.* % Bdr.-south	.06	−.02	.19	.08	.08	.15	−.08	.18	.59							
11. % Northern-born	−.16	.12	−.18	−.07	−.05	−.13	.09	−.12	−.78	−.74						
12.* %Foreign-born	−.15	−.04	−.11	−.08	.50	.46	−.54	.39	−.49	−.24	−.05					
13. Irish/for. ratio	.37	.44	.43	.45	−.07	−.07	−.02	.01	.29	.39	−.20	−.45				
14.* German/for. ratio	−.31	−.32	−.35	−.29	.12	.12	−.10	.14	−.10	−.19	−.06	.51	−.79			
15. % Liturgical orgs.	−.32	−.25	−.37	−.19	.10	.09	−.06	.04	−.32	−.32	.16	.54	−.47	.49		
16.* % Pietistic orgs.	.20	.10	.24	.05	−.11	−.08	.15	−.13	.22	.21	−.15	−.33	.25	−.25	−.62	
17.* % church seats	.29	.18	.14	.25	−.16	−.15	.15	−.07	.33	.17	−.21	−.23	.22	−.10	−.10	−.14

*Selected as an independent variable from the larger set.

Table 7.10. Standardized Beta Coefficients for the Regression of Each Normal Vote Estimator on Measures of County Social Composition

			Measures of County Social Composition					
	Av. val. farms	% pietistic	% Indiana	% foreign	Ratio Ger./for.	% bdr.-so.	% rural	% rel. inv.	Multiple R
Average decade normal vote	.32	.25	−.24	−.12	−.13	−.07	.04	.02	.58
1870 normal vote	.34	.27	−.27	−.09	−.07	−.04	.04	.05	.56
1872 normal vote	.32	.26	−.24	−.09	−.11	−.05	.02	.03	.56
1874 normal vote	.29	.26	−.24	−.10	−.13	−.08	.04	.03	.56
1876 normal vote	.31	.23	−.22	−.13	−.15	−.10	.04	.00	.58
1878 normal vote	.32	.22	−.23	−.14	−.15	−.09	.03	−.01	.58
1880 normal vote	.32	.22	−.23	−.13	−.16	−.09	.04	.00	.59

the seventeen variables measured for 1870. Most of these were highly colinear with the same compositional factors measured in 1880. Only one set, therefore, is required. But several of these variables, even measured only in 1870, were also highly intercorrelated and colinear. I have marked by triangles and circles all values exceeding .60 as those most highly colinear, and have drawn a subset of eight from the seventeen as relatively independent of one another (indicated by an asterisk in the table). These eight, of course, may be understood not only in their mutual context but also in the full context of the remaining variables as well.[18]

The results of this analysis, which uses eight relatively independent measures of composition, are presented in table 7.10, by each election year for which the normal vote was estimated. These eight factors (or their colinear alternatives, or the same factors measured in 1880) sustain a multiple correlation of about .57, approximately the same level as determined by step-wise multiple correlation. The important coefficients, however, are located in the body of this table. They are standardized beta coefficients (so-called beta-weights) that indicate the impact of each compositional factor exclusive of (or net) the influence of the others, all in directly comparable units of standard deviations.[19]

The results are highly consistent across all election years. Not only are all signs in the same direction over the decade (except for one low value), but even the relative magnitudes are highly congruent. It is as if these values were derived from six sample estimates of the same underlying set of relationships, summarized quite fully in the average decade Republican normal vote.

Standardized beta coefficients may be interpreted quite readily. For an increase of one standard deviation in average farm values, the normal vote Republican increased .32 (or 32 percent) of one standard deviation (and the normal vote Democratic similarly decreased), relative to the impact of all other variables. But an increase of one standard deviation in the rural percentage led only to .04 (or 4 percent) of one standard deviation increase in the normal vote. Thus, the magnitude of these coefficients indicates their effect on the normal vote relative to all others that were included, and their sign indicates the direction of their impact.

The relationships shown in this table are important not because

Chapter Seven

they measured voting change in Indiana during the 1870s but because they defined the *standing relations* of social composition to partisan levels across all Indiana counties—relations which were either sustained or altered by the short-term tides peculiar to each election of the decade. They show the normal-vote baseline in terms of social composition across counties, where all of the distributions have been standardized.

A similar analysis can also be applied to electoral participation as measured by voter turnout. The normal vote itself, of course, was formed to take into account the highs and lows of turnout. Nonetheless, some important differences between low-stimulus elections (averaged over three off-year elections for secretary of state) and high-stimulus elections (averaged over three elections for governor) were present during the 1870s. Table 7.11 divides turnout into these low- and high-stimulus types and makes clear that turnout was tuned differently to social composition than was the normal partisan division, and varied most notably in one particular between off-year and on-year conditions. In low-stimulus off-year elections, when primarily the core electorate was present for the vote, areas of pietistic strength had lower levels of turnout, indicating that the depression issues of the 1870s were not especially salient in these areas. But off-year turnout was high where the Indiana-born were concentrated, in strongly Democratic areas of longer settlement and political maturity. It was also high where counties were more rural than urban, in keeping with our prior hypothesis that rural areas would be responsive to a widespread agricultural depression. Aside from these three factors, other dimensions of county social composition had little effect on turnout in the off years.

Indiana's on-year elections provided a relatively full mobilization of voters across the entire electorate, with general turnout averages in the 90 percent range. Yet, one set of areas failed to respond to this mobilization. A high negative beta coefficient for areas of foreign-born strength indicates how difficult it was to mobilize participation in this group of counties. Where European-born persons were numerous, turnout tended to remain at levels much nearer the off-year levels, and did not follow the more general surge of participation, quite in keeping with the hypothesis

Table 7.11. Standardized Beta Coefficients for the Regression of Turnout Levels on Measures of County Social Composition

				Measures of County Social Composition				
	Av. val. farms	% piet.	% Ind.	% rural	% for.	Ratio Ger./for.	% rel. inv.	% bdr.-so.	Multiple R
Average off-year turnout	.12	−.19	.32	.32	.06	.05	.12	.16	.60
Average on-year turnout	.02	−.19	.16	.23	−.43	.07	.06	.04	.65
Average decade turnout	.09	−.21	.28	.30	−.15	.06	.11	.12	.62

Chapter Seven

of participation barriers that was advanced from the nine-county sample. Thus, high electoral mobilization during the 1870s depended on the Indiana-born percentage and the rural percentage, with both the extent of pietistic organization and the foreign-born percentage associated with lower levels of turnout. Needless to say, the average decade turnout over both low- and high-stimulus elections was associated with these factors of social composition at about average magnitudes.

Having extended the normal-vote estimators from the nine counties of our sample to all counties of Indiana, we can now view the impact of long-term party attachments for each national election during the decade. In table 7.12, the expected Republican normal vote has been related to each succeeding state or national election. The square of the Pearsonian correlation coefficient indicates the proportion of election variation across all counties that was a direct function of long-term party attachment, and the residual indicates the impact of short-term events particular to each election.

As fully expected, the major component of the voting results in every election of this decade was long-term attachment to the major parties among voters within Indiana's counties. At its lowest levels, in the congressional campaigns of 1874 and 1878, this long-term partisan component alone accounted for better than 60 percent of the variation in the election results. At its highest level, in the presidential campaign of 1876, long-term party allegiance accounted for better than 95 percent of the variation in the election outcome. These coefficients are indeed impressive and across this series of elections underscore dramatically that electoral change must be assessed *after* underlying party attachments have been taken into account, even when estimated on county-level aggregates. More interestingly, the normal-vote model points quite clearly to those elections that exhibited the greatest change. For most presidential elections of this decade, very little variation in county election results remain to be explained apart from underlying attachments, rarely more than 10 percent, once the normal vote is taken into account. Even the presence of the National Greenback party in 1876 and 1880, on which attention

Election Dynamics and Party Allegiance, 1868-1880

Table 7.12. A Partition of County Election Outcomes, by Percent Republican, into Long- and Short-term Components, All Counties, 1870–80

Election and Office	Pearson's r	Variation Explained by the Long-term Component of the vote r^2	Residual Due to Short-term Change $(1-r^2)$
1870 congressional	.89	.78	.22
1870 secretary of state	.95	.91	.09
1872 congressional	.97	.94	.06
1872 gubernatorial	.98	.95	.05
1872 presidential	.95	.89	.11
1874 congressional	.80[a]	.64	.36
1874 secretary of state	.93	.86	.14
1876 congressional	.95	.90	.10
1876 gubernatorial	.97	.94	.06
1876 presidential	.98	.96	.04
1878 congressional	.78[b]	.62	.38
1878 secretary of state	.88	.78	.22
1880 congressional	.95	.90	.10
1880 gubernatorial	.96	.91	.09
1880 presidential	.96	.92	.08

[a] No Republican candidate ran in Martin County. The Independent candidate received 20.5 percent of the vote, and this was assigned as the Republican vote in this county.

[b] In the twelfth congressional district, the Republican fusion candidate was counted as the Republican. In the seventh district, the Democratic fusion candidate was counted as the Democrat.

has so often focused, hardly disturbed at all the continuing impact of these party attachments on the county vote.[20]

The meaning of these results can be summarized in a simple schematic diagram of the normal-vote model viewed across all counties, as shown in figure 7.4. This diagram depicts each election result across these counties as the effect of the two primary components, one the impact of long-term party attachment (giving inertia and stability to election outcomes by its weight of major partisans), and the other the impact of short-term issues and events (causing shifts from the expected results if

Chapter Seven

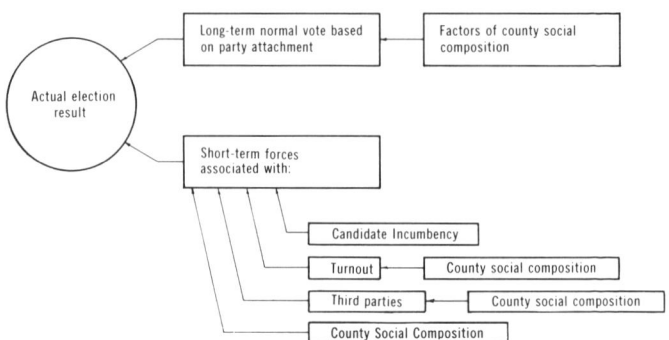

Fig. 7.4 A diagrammatic model of electoral forces using the two-component partition of the vote

voting were only an effect of aggregating the categories of underlying attachments). The diagram, in turn, shows that each of the two primary components was associated with, or mediated the impact of, other factors. Because long-term party attachments in Indiana were related to social cleavages within counties of the state, they mediated the direct effects of county differences in social composition. In formal terms, long-term party allegiance (aggregated as a normal vote) was an intervening variable, powerful in its distinction from, but nonetheless related to, other forms of county social composition. Short-term change on the other hand, was a result of events peculiar to each election, aside from these long-term attachments, and was associated with such political conditions as candidate incumbency, turnout variation, and the presence of third parties. Both turnout and third-party support were themselves associated with social composition and mediated their effects directly. Finally, exclusive of the normal vote, turnout variation from average levels, and third party support, short-term change was itself associated with how counties varied in their social composition.

Table 7.13 summarizes this very simple model by attributing a portion of the total variation in the vote across all counties to long-term party allegiance on the one hand and to the several measures associated with short-term tides on the other hand. These two components of the vote sum to the total explained variation for each election. The remaining variation is assigned to

Table 7.13. The Proportion of County-level Partisan Variation Due to the Long- and Short-term Components of the Vote, National Elections, 1868–80

Factors Accounting for Variation	Presidential Elections				Congressional Elections				
	1868	1872	1876	1880	1870	1872	1874	1876	1878	1880
The long-term component										
Normal vote estimator	.98	.89	.96	.92	.79	.94	.64	.90	.60	.90
Short-term factors										
Turnout	.00	.00	.00	.00	.04	.00	.02	.00	.02	.00
Third parties	.00	.00	.01	.04	.00	.00	.04	.02	.15	.05
Social composition	.00	.04	.01	.01	.04	.01	.04	.02	.06	.01
Total explained variation	.98	.93	.98	.97	.87	.95	.74	.93	.83	.96
Unmeasured factors	.02	.07	.02	.03	.13	.05	.26	.07	.17	.04
Total variation	1.00	1.00	1.00	1.00	1.00	1.00	1.00	1.00	1.00	1.00

Chapter Seven

unmeasured influences affecting each result. In essence, long-term attachments to the two major parties anchored the partisan division of the vote in the electorate, measured by the normal-vote estimator. From the perspective of this anchoring of the vote in underlying party attachments, the presidential election of 1868 was a nearly perfect baseline campaign leading into the 1870s, undisrupted by any short-term shifts due to turnout, third parties, or factors of social composition. In 1872, when Grant ran as the Republican incumbent against Greeley under the Liberal Republican banner, the impact of long-term partisanship was modified by short-term change due to voter shifts associated with differences in county social composition and special features of the campaign, like Grant's incumbency and the Democrats' change in party name, that were unmeasured in the model. Every election during the decade can be summarized in similar terms, measuring for each the proportion of the variation in election results across all counties that was due to each kind or set of factors. From these results, it is clear that aside from the influence summarized by turnout change and third-party strength, factors of social composition alone had relatively small impact in altering election results. Always, the political factors were most important among those that could be measured.

Over the span of the decade, how shall we evaluate the application of this normal-vote model? One way is to observe the variation accounted for by each of the components. Viewed in this way, across the spectrum of national elections during the 1870s long-term attachments to the two major parties were clearly the most important and powerful factors affecting voting results. If partisanship was not treated as a separate component, it would easily be confused with short-term sources of change. In effect, we see clearly that the expected two-party vote, based on underlying attachments, must first be held constant in order to measure the origins of defections and voting shifts that are the essential meaning of change in particular elections. When this division of results into long- and short-term components is done for Indiana during the 1870s, a very clear pattern emerges: voting results departed least from the underlying two-party division, based on party allegiance, in the presidential years (for both presidential and on-year congressional elections), and departed most in the off-year congressional elections of 1874 and 1878. In these same off-year elections, unmeasured conditions of short-term change were more important than any single measured ingredient of the short-term component. These short-term tides, taken together as shifts in turnout, as sources of strength for third-party activity, as voting change associated with county social composition, and as unmeasured factors of change, were all at their height in 1878, the supreme moment of Greenback voting among Hoosiers.

A second way to evaluate this application of the normal-vote model is to recall the voter dynamics on which it was built. In particular, the normal-vote model posited that, as general turnout declined from high presidential levels to lower levels for off-year congressional elections, the Independents and weak partisans would tend to leave the active electorate at a faster rate than partisans strongly attached to the two major parties, across all groups in the electorate. The straightforward deduction was that the off-year electorate would "shrink" to its basic core of strong partisans, and that therefore off-year election results would reflect this fact by a higher correlation with the normal vote than with the on-year presidential election results (other things being equal). These ordinary expectations, however, are quite in opposition to what the variance-accounting coefficients show for Indiana during the 1870s. For these coefficients show that both the presidential and the on-year congressional elections were more closely tuned to the underlying division of strength between the two parties while, as general turnout declined to off-year levels, the electorate was *more,* rather than less, volatile with respect to short-term change from the normal vote. The "reversal" of standard expectations, most dramatic in 1874 and 1878, is precisely of a piece with the puzzle that the voting behavior of rural farmers has posed. And it points quite clearly to the "special conditions" that Converse also specified to account for these reversals.[21] Thus, a second and more fascinating way to evaluate the model is in terms of the expectations it provides for differences in the correlation between the normal vote and particular elections seen as a time-series.

What were the special conditions leading to reversals in the

Chapter Seven

standard pattern of correlations with the normal vote, and did these conditions obtain in Indiana during the 1870s? One condition was that among voters there had to be a gradient for the intake of political information in partial correlation with the strength of party allegiance, where it is understood that those voters at the lowest intake levels will shift least toward the party favored at the moment, while those at higher intake levels will shift the most. A second condition was that strong cues about party positions or candidates had to be present to disturb the normal connection between party allegiance and the vote. A third condition was that turnout had to vary across those sectors of the electorate most affected by the short-term issues. In effect, these conditions all direct attention to the two most inertial categories of voters in an electorate, and the modification of the floating-voter hypothesis. For the two sectors of an electorate that were least likely to shift under this modification were the strong partisans on the one hand, and voters of low political information and involvement on the other.

From all traditional accounts of Indiana during the 1870s, Independent candidates and the Greenback party from 1876 through 1880 arose just because strong issues and events, brought to a focus by the depression, had an impact on voters that altered their partisan assessments.[22] Without a description of the underlying dynamics, such a statement remains a trivial one. What the traditional accounts have failed to tell us is anything about the motivations of farmers as political actors and, in particular, how their attachments to the major parties showed a balance of power that we have taken to indicate weak rather than strong partisan attachments. In addition, we have not known previously that all voters, both townsmen and farmers, showed a gradient of involvement with secondary social institutions (such as the churches provided), suggesting immediately that voters at higher involvement-levels (as among more educated voters today) were more likely to monitor new information and make the translation between issues and their political responses than those at low involvement-levels. Putting these two orders of findings together, we can now see the major features of two categories among Indiana voters who tended to anchor the partisan vote: strong partisans coming from sectors of the electorate other than the farming community on the one hand, and rural voters who were low on institutional involvement (using religious institutions as an index) coming from both the towns and the farms on the other hand. In demographic terms, these two categories of voters were the most inertial ones with respect to their voting behavior, if twentieth-century relationships also held true for Indiana a century ago. Under this condition the basic "swing" group, therefore, was the majority of farmers, who were not strong partisans but who were sufficiently involved with a secondary group-life to monitor and act on new political information channeled to them through the churches, the granges, and the Greenback party itself. The Greenback movement, of course, was not a confined one but spread geographically from a few counties that ran independent candidates in 1874 to sixty-one counties that ran Greenback candidates in the congressional elections of 1876, to the seventy-three counties that ran them in 1878. This was itself a diffusion process, again pointing to the flow of information and the need to make a political translation. These orders of facts are fully in keeping with the reversal in correlation coefficients between the on-year and off-year elections in Indiana during the 1870s, and aside from depression conditions—which affected all voters—begin to indicate why the response of farmers appeared so explosive.

Thus, the second way to evaluate the application of the normal-vote model is in terms of the underlying dynamics that must be posited in order to account for the observed correlations with actual voting results over time. The observed reversal of expectations about these correlations requires more than the floating-voter hypothesis alone provides. It requires in the electorate not only strong partisans as anchoring members (who were not generally Indiana's farmers) but also an anchoring of the vote among voters of low information (some of whom were Indiana's farmers). The depression issues of the 1870s brought their sharpest response from Indiana's farmers, not because they were either highly class-conscious or harder hit by the depression than other voters, nor because they were split between pietistic and liturgical churches, but because as political actors farmers were

Chapter Seven

not strong partisans. Depression conditions kept Indiana's rural turnout rates high even in the off-years, so that farmers of both independent and weak party allegiance remained in the active electorate. With local candidates running as Independents or under the Greenback banner, the off-year congressional vote showed a volatility perhaps as large as any before the 1890s. This result amounts to a reversal of any simple expectations under the normal vote but is comprehended quite fully by its refinement in terms of weak partisanship among farmers, a gradient of information and involvement that channeled partisan cues among both farmers and townsmen, and the flow of organizational and political cues among all voters across Indiana's counties and over these depression-decade elections.

Conclusion

The historical dynamics of Indiana's elections rested primarily on party allegiance as it was distributed within subgroups of the electorate. Indiana itself was composed of several subelectorates, defined by lines of cleavage along widely recognized social dimensions: wealth and status; regional, ethnic, and religious lines; farm and town categories of voters; and counties of residence. Other dimensions, such as age and the timing of settlement, were also important but received little explicit attention in this analysis. These different lines of cleavage, when treated systematically among a sample of individual voters, framed the different subelectorates among which party support varied. No one way of decomposing this electorate into its parts was alone sufficient to capture the dynamics of voting behavior, though among them the relation between partisanship within counties and the aggregate vote across them was strong. This served as the baseline against which departures in the vote at particular elections could be measured.

Strong revisionist interpretations have minimized party support along economic lines in the larger Midwest, yet there was in Indiana substantial variation in party support that followed levels of occupational status. This variation was not based on farm wealth, as Carleton asserted, but on occupational identities

Conclusion

within the different work and residence domains. Research solely focused on geographic aggregates that are heterogeneous with respect to farm and nonfarm occupations minimizes the importance of occupational status because these lines of status can be seen clearly only by distinguishing persons working on the farms and off them and by grouping together persons from separate occupations at comparable status levels. Having made these distinctions among voters within our sample of nine counties, we found that party support varied by occupational status in quite dramatic ways, a finding quite sufficient to revitalize some elements of the older economic interpretation.

Equally important, the ethnocultural view of partisan polarization rests on implicit assumptions about denominational orderings and the extent to which nineteenth-century mass populations were tied to specific religious groups. In Indiana, polarization in party support by denominational group membership, even with the assumption of a (Republican) ordering to the denominations, was hardly greater than that based on occupational status. And when all voters (including those considering themselves "Protestants" and those without religious attachment) were included in the analysis, polarization was less. Constructs like the pietistic-liturgical continuum have arisen in part because aggregate rather than individual data have provided the primary vehicle for analysis, and because areas characterized by their homogeneity in ethnoreligious terms were specially selected for comparison. Nonetheless, religious institutions were major channels of party involvement and political information in the Indiana population, as levels of religious involvement among both native and foreign-born Hoosiers clearly show. But by selecting polar instances of high ethnoreligious concentration among townships and counties, ethnoreligious values have been overstressed as fundamental to the midwestern political context in the late nineteenth century and have been given a shape and meaning they did not inherently possess.

In Indiana during the 1870s the major political parties were themselves relatively distinct and separate interest groups, not tied in any simple or direct fashion to other nonpolitical social

Conclusion

divisions. Easily misconstrued, the relative independence of parties-in-the-electorate from other social groupings has been argued forcefully from Max Weber to Joseph Schumpeter to V. O. Key, Jr., and in recent survey research has led to an increased concern with voting dynamics themselves as grounded in distributions of party allegiance. If party support in Indiana was no simple function of social, economic, or ethnoreligious subgroups, then involvement with the party system itself and the distribution of allegiance to the parties must be viewed as intervening characteristics of subgroups that constrained their voting behavior in patterned ways. I have posited such patterns from current survey research and have sought to derive their implications for aggregate results of voting over time, given the internal structure of Indiana's electorate. Thus, I have argued that native-born farmers in Indiana were a special subcategory of the electorate who were less involved with the major-party system than their rural, small-town counterparts, and that their way of life did not lead to strong commitments toward one or another of the major parties. Further, like their small-town counterparts, these same farmers varied in their party involvement, measured on a religious axis, and were in that degree susceptible to the flow of political information. Our expectation, then, was that farmers, as weak partisans, would be more responsive, or "explosive," with respect to short-term partisan tides during the 1870s, and more dramatically so in off-year congressional elections than in the on-year presidential ones. This expectation was confirmed by the use of county electorates, with voting change measured from a baseline that estimated underlying party attachment as the expected normal vote. With rural turnout running high, and farmers moving into independent and Greenback party support, departures from the expected vote could be understood largely as a function of these "explosive" partisan voting dynamics and the flow of political information across rural areas. This finding certainly fuels the fire of older economic arguments by specifying the political conditions of the electorate that determined subgroup responsiveness to depression conditions. The responsiveness of farmers was more volatile, not because they were harder

Conclusion

hit by the depression of the 1870s but because as political actors they were less constrained along strong party lines. This lack of constraint, I believe, is a major piece in the puzzle that explosive farm protest movements have posed.

Appendix A

Voter Transitions between Parties for Indiana's National Elections, 1868-1880

Electoral analysis may take several complementary forms. In the final chapter we established a model of Indiana's election dynamics rooted in the construct of a normal vote for all Hoosier counties, from which departures in the actual vote may be measured. It may be helpful also to establish a second model as well, one that takes as its baseline not the expected vote but the actual vote in the prior election of its kind, and to estimate for the state as a whole the transition between parties among voters from the prior to the succeeding election at the same level of office, in comparable on years and off years. These two models together provide a dynamic view of the whole electorate during the decade.

First, then, we must establish the voter transition model.[1] Consider table A1, which represents the vote in one county between two successive elections. The value in the far right column for the first row represents the Republican proportion of the vote in the first election, and the value in the second row is the Democratic proportion. Precisely parallel proportions for the second election in the pair are shown for the Republicans at the bottom row of the first column and for the Democrats at the bottom row of the second column. The swing in the vote, therefore, would be 5 percent for this county, decreasing the Republican vote and increasing the Democratic vote by that amount between these two elections. These marginal proportions are known for all counties, of course, and for the state as a whole. What is unknown, however, is the proportion within each of the four cells forming the body of the table, that are here taken to sum to one at the right and that therefore indicate

Appendix A

Table A.1. Exhibit of the Transition between the First and Second Election of a Pair

		Second Election Rep.	Second Election Dem.	Sum Row Proportions	First Election Result
First Election	Rep.	P_{11}	P_{12}	1.00	(.60)
	Dem.	P_{21}	P_{22}	1.00	(.40)
Second Election Result		(.55)	(.45)		(1.00)

the transition among parties for voters from the first to the second election. That is, P_{11} is a value that indicates the proportion of those who voted Republican in the first election who subsequently voted Republican in the second, and P_{12} is the proportion who shifted to a Democratic vote. The cells for P_{21} and P_{22} indicate precisely the same transitions for prior Democratic voters.

In brief, this table presents the ecological problem: from net county marginals that measure the swing in the vote between elections we do not know the gross turnover among voters within each county. This is why W. S. Robinson rightly reported that ecological correlations (on aggregate units such as counties) are no sure guide to the behavior of individuals.[2]

While the problem of inferring gross turnover among voters within each county remains totally intractable at present, the same is not true for the state as a whole, given the swings at the county level. If, rather than asking about voter transitions county-by-county, we ask instead about voter transitions within the whole state, then at least one estimating technique has been developed as a partial solution to the ecological problem.[3] This technique, known as ecological regression, requires that certain assumptions be met, chiefly that voter transitions are relatively constant across the state (or that the expected value of these transitions is constant, subject only to random error), and that the county marginals form a linear scatter with strong correlation. Only the linear relationship and correlation, which are necessary but not sufficient conditions for stable estimates, are observable, while the transition probabilities are themselves the quantities to be estimated.[4] In practice, when these probabilities are neither constant nor subject simply to random error, the probability estimates for the transition between parties may fall outside

Appendix A

Table A.2. Correlation Coefficients between Successive Elections by Office, Election Year, and Party, All Counties, 1868–80

Elections	% Republican	% Democrat	% Greenback
Presidential			
1868–72	.95	.95	—
1872–76	.95	.96	—
1876–80	.97	.97	.43
Congressional (on-year)			
1868–72	.97	.97	—
1872–76	.92	.86	—
1876–80	.92	.89	.43 (.56)*
Congressional (off-year)			
1870–74	.76	.76	—
1874–78	.63	.62	—
Congressional (all years)			
1868–70	.89	.89	—
1870–72	.90	.90	—
1872–74	.80	.80	—
1874–76	.73	.75	—
1876–78	.80	.75	.32 (.78)*
1878–80	.83	.77	.20 (.68)*

*The figure in parenthesis is based only on counties returning a Greenback vote in both elections.

the permissible probability range, taking values greater than 1 or less than 0. Such estimates, like those within the permissible range, are not thereby biased (since the procedure produces unbiased estimators), but they do indicate that key assumptions, such as constant transition, are not met by the data. I mention this fact because, when the procedure is used on these Indiana data, values outside this fixed probability range will be encountered. This invalidates neither the estimators nor the procedure but points to unmet assumptions about the underlying behavior. Because the technique is important in revealing new, otherwise unrecoverable information, I have used it in spite of this problem.

Table A2 shows the correlation between successive pairs of presidential, on-year congressional, and off-year congressional elections from 1868 to 1880. All presidential elections were related by a coefficient at or exceeding .95, indicating very little geographic shifting in partisan levels over Indiana's counties. Similarly, from one on-year congressional election to the next the net partisan swing in the vote was small, with coefficients still exceeding .92 for Republicans and .89 for Democrats.

Appendix A

But the two pairs of off-year elections dropped noticeably below these magnitudes, and the full set of congressional election pairs for both major parties suggests that this drop in the correlation began with the 1872-74 sequence and continued to 1878-80.

The interelection correlations are *net* measures of partisan stability and change. They do not indicate the extent of partisan shifts in the electorate from one election to the next. But this turnover can be estimated for the state as a whole from the county-level data, using ecological regression. These regression estimates result in a series of tables giving the transition probabilities between each pair of successive elections. These tables decompose net change across counties into measures of the gross change within the state, indicating the proportion of voters who voted a second time for the same party and the proportion who shifted their vote toward the opposition. These transition tables cannot indicate where, across the counties, shifts and defections occurred. But by examining these tables together with measures of the short-term change from the normal vote, we are able to observe closely both the transition of voters between elections and the basis in county alignments of departures from the normal vote in each election.

The presidential election of 1868, by all of our measures, was a baseline election. Ulysses S. Grant won 51.5 percent of Indiana's two-party vote. No factors affected this election other than the normal vote itself. The aggregate vote across congressional districts was even closer, with a difference of less than 1 percent separating the parties. Again, only the normal vote affected the election result. Four years later, Grant ran as the incumbent president, opposed by Horace Greeley under the Liberal Republican banner. The Republicans, under Grant, received 53 percent of the vote, a major victory for the party that was not matched at congressional levels.

Table A3 shows voter transitions between the 1868 and 1872 presidential elections and indicates that shifts by prior Democratic voters toward the Republicans outweighed those by prior Republicans moving in the Democratic direction, on the order of 9 percent to 5. In both cases, some portion of these shifts were a return to the home party of those voters who had departed from their normal allegiance in 1868, a movement which we cannot measure. The effects of new defections in 1872, however, appear as county-level departures from the normal vote baseline, and they had a small association with county social composition, on the order of 4 percent of the total election variation. This small variation was associated with a slight increase in Republican voting in areas of northern-born strength and a slight decrease in Democratic voting in

Appendix A

Table A.3. Regression Estimates of Voter Transition Probabilities between Parties for National Elections in Indiana, 1868-72

	Presidential 1872					Congressional 1872				
1868	Rep.	Dem.		% 1868 result	1868	Rep.	Dem.		% 1868 result
Rep.	.95	.05	1.00	(51.5)	Rep.	.94	.06	1.00	(49.5)
Dem.	.09	.91	1.00	(48.5)	Dem.	.06	.94	1.00	(50.5)
% 1872 result	(53.2)	(46.8)		(100.0)	% 1872 result	(50.1)	(49.9)		(100.0)

Stepwise Regression					
1872 presidential vote			1872 congressional vote		
Measure	Variance	Standardized beta	Measure	Variance	Standardized beta
Normal vote	.89	.92	Normal vote	.94	.95
% north.-born	.02	.09	% liturg. orgs.	—	-.08
Ger./For. Ratio	.01	-.16	Av. val. frms.	—	-.11
Ir./For. Ratio	.01	-.11	% turnout	— (.01)	.07
Pop. density	—	-.15	% Ind.-born	—	-.09
% rural	—	-.12	% lg. frms.	—	.07
Total explained variance	.93		Total explained variance	.95	

Irish and German-born areas of concentration. Turnout was not a factor in the election, nor was a third party present. Thus, in all major respects, the result was largely a restatement of the normal vote.

Table A3 also shows that the on-year congressional elections involved voter transitions that were equally balanced between the two parties. With little underlying disturbance, about 1 percent of county-level variation in 1872 could be attributed to immediate defections in the congressional vote that were associated with factors of social composition. These were so slight as to barely register any change at all. Thus, unlike Grant's 53 percent total, the aggregate congressional returns once again differed by less than 1 percent between the major parties.

Table A4 shows voter transitions between the off-year congressional elections of 1870 and 1874, in which Republican shifts added more voters to the prior, narrow Democratic margin of 1870. The 1870 congressional elections had departed from the normal vote in ways systematically associated with short-term levels of turnout and county social composi-

Appendix A

Table A.4. Regression Estimates of Voter Transition Probabilities between Parties, Congress, 1870–74

		Congressional 1874			
	1870	Rep.	Dem.		% 1870 result
	Rep.	.82	.18	1.00	(49.5)
	Dem.	.15	.85	1.00	(50.5)
	% 1874 result	(48.1)	(51.9)		(100.0)

Stepwise Regression

1870 congressional vote			1874 congressional vote		
Measure	Variance	Standardized beta	Measure	Variance	Standardized beta
Normal vote	.79	.77	Normal vote	.64	.75
% turnout	.04	−.19	Third-party vote	.04	−.20
% north.-born	.01	.15	% turnout	.02	−.14
% liturg. orgs.	.01	−.08	% north.-born	.01	.28
Av. val. prop.	.01	.11	% bdr.-south	.02	.23
% rural	.01	.09	Av. val. frms.	.01	−.09
Total explained variance	.87		Total explained variance	.74	

tion. About 4 percent of variation in the 1870 vote was due to Democratic gains that were registered in areas of higher turnout. Another 4 percent of the variation was due to minor shifts for both major parties that were associated with county social composition. Republicans gained slightly in their usually strong areas of northern-born strength and wealthier farms, as well as in areas that were more rural than urban in composition. Democrats added more voters to their total in the more liturgical areas. Thus, although turnout benefitted the Democrats, each party tended to gain additional voters in its own areas of prior strength. But 13 percent of the variation in 1870 was not captured by any of our measures and may indicate the extent to which independents in all areas added further "noise" to the election result.

Because only a few congressional districts were contested by independent candidates in 1874, our transition table does not include them. The variance-accounting procedure over the counties indicates, however, that 4 percent of variation in the 1874 congressional elections was due to these

Appendix A

independent candidacies. Following in the wake of depression and initial farm organization by the Grange, these Independent candidacies cut into Republican support. Similarly, where turnout was high, additional Republican losses were sustained, accounting for another 2 percent of county-level election variation. Another 4 percent can be attributed to defections across the major parties associated with county social composition. Democrats lost voters to the Republicans in areas of northern-born strength and in areas of settlement by persons born in the border-south, while Democrats gained Republican defectors in the wealthier farming areas. Thus, measurable short-term factors in 1874 tended to cut against the grain of prior party strength.

The congressional elections of 1874 were also the first ones following the redrawing of congressional district boundaries. While I have not sought to measure the effects of this change, it no doubt contributed to further election variation, coupled with the first pangs of depression and initial Grange excitement. Fully 26 percent of the variation in the 1874 congressional vote was unaccounted for either by the normal vote, third-party action, turnout, or factors of social composition.

By 1876 the National Greenback party had been formed. In the October congressional elections, sixty-one counties slated these third-party candidates. These county elections were taken by observers as barometers of the coming presidential campaign that followed by one month. Table A5 estimates the transition of voters from the 1872 to the 1876 congressional election, including shifts to the Greenback party. Both 1872 and 1876 were high turnout elections, turnout even increasing slightly at the latter date. And in 1872 the party division had been exceedingly close. Republican shifts to the Greenback party in 1876 outnumbered Democratic shifts on the order of 5 percent to 2, but most voters stayed with the two major parties in this presidential election year. Turnout had no effect on the result. Two percent of county-to-county variation resulted from net Republican losses to the insurgent Greenback party, and defections associated with social composition (almost unmeasurable) accounted for another 2 percent of the variation. Given the close competition between the parties, these minor shifts and the Greenback intrusion on Republican strength were enough to provide a small Democratic plurality in the state-wide vote.

Table A5 also shows that the 1876 presidential election closely paralleled its October predecessor. While Republican shifts from 1872 appear larger and Democratic ones nonexistent, the 1872 base from which these transitions were estimated was itself unusually Republican. It is likely, therefore, that some portion of the shift to the Greenback

Table A.5. Regression Estimates of Voter Transition Probabilities between Parties for National Elections, 1872–76

	Presidential 1876					Congressional 1876			
1872	Rep.	Dem.	Gb.		% 1872 result	Rep.	Dem.	Gb.	% 1872 result
Rep.	.91	.04	.05	1.00	(53.2)	.94	.01	.05	(50.1)
Dem.	.00*	1.00**	.00	1.00	(46.8)	.01	.97	.02	(49.9)
% 1876 result	(48.3)	(49.5)	(2.2)		(100.0)	(47.4)	(49.2)	(3.5)	(100.0)

Stepwise Regression

1876 presidential vote			1876 congressional vote		
Measure	Variance	Standardized beta	Measure	Variance	Standardized beta
Normal vote	.96	.96	Normal vote	.90	.96
% Greenback	.01	−.09	% Greenback	.02	−.15
% turnout	—	.03	% turnout	—	−.03
Av. val. frms.	— (.01)	.04	% Pietistic orgs.	— (.01)	−.04
% bdr.-south	—	−.03	Av. val. fm. prds.	—	.08
% church seats	—	.02	Av. val. prop.	—	−.04
Total explained variance	.98		Total explained variance	.93	

*Actual entry was −.01, rounded up, to fit the probability range.
**Actual entry was 1.01, rounded down, to fit the probability range.

Appendix A

Table A.6. Regression Estimates of Voter Transition Probabilities between Parties, Congress, 1874–78

	Congressional 1878				% 1874 result
1874	Rep.	Dem.	Gb.		
Rep.	.74	.11	.15	1.00	(48.1)
Dem.	.16	.82	.02	1.00	(51.9)
% 1878 result	(44.6)	(47.8)	(7.6)		(100.0)

Stepwise regression 1878 congressional

Measure	Variance	Standardized beta
Normal vote	.60	.88
% Greenback	.15	−.46
% turnout	.02	.22
% foreign-born	.04	.14
% rural	.01	−.24
Pop. density	.01	−.15
Total explained variance	.82	

party attributed to prior Republican voters resulted from Democratic defections to the Republicans in 1872. Observed from the normal vote baseline, the presidential election of 1876 approached that of 1868 in its division strictly along partisan lines. Barely 1 percent of the total variation was due to Republican losses in areas of Greenback strength, though coupled with unmeasured variation this was enough to give the Democrats a very narrow victory.

While Grange social organization among farmers hit its peak in 1875 or 1876, its political reverberations were felt well into 1878. Rural turnout was high in 1874, and it remained high in 1878, compared to other sources of turnout variation. Without leadership on the ticket from national presidential candidates, or even from major state candidates, congressional contests depended on local support. Party lines were broken most fully in 1878, as shown in table A6 by the transition of voters from 1874 to 1878.

The retention rate by the major parties of their previous voters was

Appendix A

lower between this pair than between any other elections of the decade. Lower retention was due in part, of course, to the very volatility of 1874 itself. Higher than normal rural turnout rates in both elections meant that weak partisan voters and those independent of the major parties were present in rural areas on both occasions. Further, rather than with a few independent candidates in scattered congressional districts, the 1878 contests were fought with Greenback candidates in seventy-three counties. This transition table, therefore, shows the maximum of voter shifts between the parties.

Without question, the 1878 congressional elections were the most different from the normal vote of all elections during the decade. The gross change from 1874 is captured equally well by net change due to county-by-county variation in 1878 alone. Fully 15 percent of county variation in the partisan vote was due to Greenback intrusions that reduced Republican levels of strength. Measured by standardized beta coefficients, where the Greenback vote increased by one standard deviation, Republican levels dropped nearly half of one standard deviation, and they dropped again nearly a quarter of one standard deviation further in the most rural areas. Further declines were registered in urban areas of high population density. Only in the context of all of these other factors did the Republican vote show a positive association with turnout and areas of foreign-born strength. While these net losses affected the Republicans most directly, the Greenback vote cut into both parties and resulted in the final aggregate Democratic victory of the decade by 1 percent of the two-party division.

The effects of the Greenback party continued to be felt in 1880, even as the vote across counties returned toward its normal baseline. Voter transitions between 1876 and 1880 are shown in table A7. Republicans who had defected in 1876 increasingly returned to their home party base, and shifts to the Greenback party were more evenly split between prior voters for the two major parties. In both the October congressional and the November presidential elections, Greenback intrusions accounted for about 5 percent of the total variation across counties. Fully 90 percent of the variation in the vote was due to basic party lines. No other short-term factors had any measurable impact on either result. The Republican party was on the road to recovery and managed victory in both 1880 contests by margins of less than half of 1 percent in the two-party vote.

During the 1870s, Indiana was a highly competitive electoral arena. With the exception of Grant's victory in 1872, every election, on-year or off, was won by a margin of victory that most survey organizations would probably term "too close to call." Systematic short-term voting shifts

Table A.7. Regression Estimates of Voter Transition Probabilities between Parties for National Elections 1876–80

	Presidential 1880					Congressional 1880			
1876	Rep.	Dem.	Gb.		% 1876 result	Rep.	Dem.	Gb.	% 1876 result
Rep.	.99	.00	.01	1.00	(48.3)	.95	.03	.02	1.00 (47.4)
Dem.	.02	.95	.03	1.00	(49.5)	.06	.91	.03	1.00 (49.2)
Gb.	.06	.37	.57	1.00	(2.2)	.14	.53	.33	1.00 (3.5)
% 1880 result	(49.3)	(47.9)	(2.8)		(100.0)	(48.9)	(47.9)	(3.2)	(100.0)

Stepwise Regression

1880 presidential vote			1880 congressional vote		
Measure	Variance	Standardized beta	Measure	Variance	Standardized beta
Normal vote	.92	.98	Normal vote	.90	.96
% Greenback	.04	–.20	% Greenback	.05	–.20
% rural	.01	–.06	% rural	.01	–.08
% liturg. orgs.	—	.04	% north.-born	—	
% church seats	—	.04	% liturg. orgs.	—	
% turnout		–.03	% church seats	—	
Total explained variance	.97		Total explained variance	.96	

Appendix A

were largely unassociated with county social composition, other than as they were mediated by turnout or third-party activity. Political events and political responses were the order of the decade as measured by the vote. In presidential years normal, underlying party attachments went largely undisturbed; the National Greenback party, though it may well have cost the Republicans a presidential victory in 1876, was at best a minor disruptive influence both then and in 1880.

It was the off-year congressional elections that were least like the normal vote. Lower off-year turnout, which under usual circumstances would be expected to reflect most closely the core strength of the major parties, instead led to much greater partisan volatility, of the kind that would be expected as independents and weak partisans entered the active electorate in large numbers, unconstrained by a national ticket and seeking rural reform. In 1878, Indiana's farmers had their day.

Appendix B

Designing a Sample from Incomplete Historical Lists

Historical lists generally provide an incomplete enumeration of the population which a researcher wants to investigate. For instance, in historical studies of occupational, geographic, or residential mobility only a portion of the individuals included in one record, such as the U.S. Census, can be successfully traced to a subsequent census, to a business directory, to a tax record, or to some similar list.[1] This kind of partial tracing, or partial record linkage, results in an incomplete enumeration of the original population because not all members can be linked.[2] Again, in studies of banking and studies of aggregates, information of interest such as bank deposits or political party affiliation may be given only for an incomplete enumeration, while some other list—lacking the information of interest—fully enumerates the relevant population.[3] In these cases the questions arise: how do the members observed in an incomplete enumeration relate to the population of interest? In what ways are the observed members a biased subset of that population? How severe are the biases? Can they be made known? Can the biases be taken into account when making inferences to the population of interest?

A partial solution for answers to these questions is proposed for the general case where incomplete historical lists are available that contain vital information of interest, and where a second controlling list enumerates the population and provides additional information about it, though not that of primary concern. The solution is based on known sampling techniques, using information provided by the controlling list to define the biases of the incomplete historical lists. The biases are

Appendix B

derived as a set of strata within which members from the incomplete lists can be reweighted to accord with their probable appearance in the original population.

Two independent sources provided the individual-level data for this study, the *People's Guide* directories for nine Indiana counties and the U.S. Census manuscript returns. It was clear initially that the *People's Guides* published in 1874, were incomplete lists of each county's population; to sample these lists directly would have involved severe and unknown biases. Therefore, the 1870 U.S. Census manuscript returns for these counties were taken as the controlling lists that defined the voting-age citizens in each of them. The census returns, of course, were only approximations to complete lists, for it is known that an undercount was made in thirteen southern states and it is possible that similar errors of coverage also obtained in Indiana.[4] But while corrections for under-enumeration can be made in aggregate totals, the enumerated individuals must stand as the historically accessible population of record. In comparison to the *People's Guides* the census returns can be taken as the complete lists. The 1870 census provides, by name, additional information about individuals complementary to that recorded in the *Guides*: (1) whether the family head, (2) age, (3) race, (4) occupation, (5) value of real estate owned, (6) value of personal estate owned, (7) state or country of birth, (8) whether parents were foreign born, (9) whether literate, (10) whether disabled, and (11) whether the individual was a voting-age male citizen.[5]

These two major sources, then, provide a basis on which data for the population of interest can be generated—taking the 1870 manuscript census returns of voting-age male citizens for each county as lists of the whole population of interest with its social characteristics, and taking the entries in the *People's Guides* of 1874 as probably biased, incomplete historical lists of these same county populations. Note should be made that the primary dependent variable, political party affiliation, occurs only in the *Guide* lists, while a possible index to social class, such as wealth, obtains only in the census. Somehow the variables from these two sources must be brought together over the same set of members in such a way that inference to the original population becomes possible, with a minimum of bias, given the subset of members who are observed.

Since each source enumerates individuals by name, and in the *People's Guides* those names are ordered alphabetically within townships, the tracing of names from the manuscript census to the *People's Guide* provides a feasible, if tiresome, tactic for linkage.[6] Such linkage means that the information from the two sources can be brought to bear on the

Appendix B

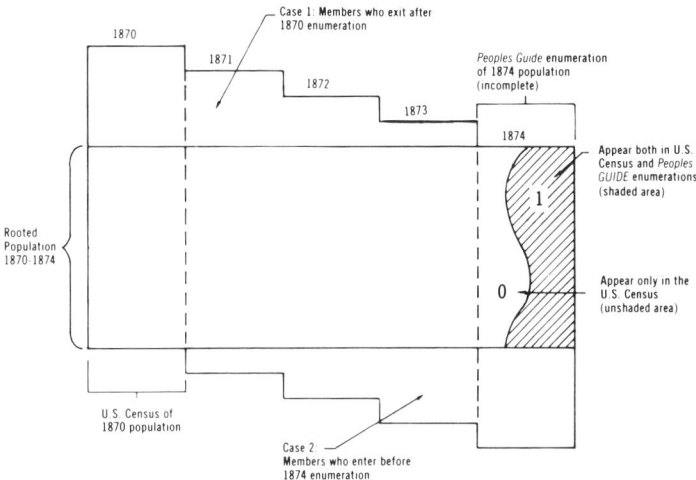

Fig. B1 Schematic diagram relating 1870 to 1874 population

same set of members whenever the tracing from the census to the *Guide*s is successful. This can be shown diagrammatically in figure B1.

The diagram highlights two cases where the tracing and linkage of individuals between the two sources is impossible within a given county. Case 1 refers to members leaving the geographic area after the first enumeration and before the second. Such members would only appear in the U.S. Census lists. Case 2 refers to members entering the area after the first but before the second enumeration. Such members could only appear in the *People's Guide*s. Still a third case could be mentioned, of those who entered and left between enumerations. They would appear in neither list. Births, deaths, and geographic movement would account for these cases that could not be traced, resulting in possible bias. This fact, however, provides its options. Since the span of time between the two enumerations is relatively brief, it is possible to assume that such bias, though present, will be small enough to be safely ignored. Or, it is equally possible, and perhaps simpler, to redefine the universe of interest to include only those voting-age citizens present during the four-year interval: that is, concern can be focused solely on the "rooted" population. As given in figure B1 the rooted population includes all members resident and potentially traceable within each county between 1870 and 1874.

If we redefine the population to include only the nonmobile members,

Appendix B

there then remains only one important source for bias—namely, the incompleteness of the *People's Guides*. As the shaded portion of the diagram indicates, a subset of the rooted population will not appear in the *People's Guides* lists. The failure of such incomplete lists to enumerate all members of the population results in what can be termed "source bias." To this source bias our proposed solution applies, where the controlling lists provide additional information.

In the case at hand it is possible to define the social characteristics recorded in the original U.S. Census lists on both the successfully traced and the untraced members. The census information pertains to the whole rooted population, whether its members are linked to the *People's Guides* lists or not. Thus, if bias is due to those social characteristics which we have for the whole population, it is potentially knowable and, if known, might be taken into account. It is the process and procedures for taking such source bias into account that must be a major burden of designing samples from incomplete historical lists, where a controlling list is available. The proposed solution, however, is partial in two senses. First, it is dependent on the extent of additional information available in the controlling lists; second, that information must have some relation to the sources of bias which are to be taken into account. But at least the second of these two criteria, if not the first, is no different from that involved in any explanatory task, except that bias itself becomes the explanatory object.

The problem of sampling arises when the set of units to be studied has been defined, when that set contains U elements, and when for several reasons such as cost, time, energy, and the availability of members only a smaller subset of u elements can be observed. Sampling is the problem of selecting the u out of U elements so that "the sample shall somehow be a universe in miniature."[7] While the sample provides a way of obtaining units of observation for research, interest does not center on the sample as such but on the universe. We want to infer from the sample to the population.

Leslie Kish suggests a way of characterizing sampling design in general: "Sample design has two aspects: a *selection process*, the rules and operations by which some members of the population are included in the sample; and an *estimation process* (or estimator) for computing the sample statistics, which are sample estimates of population values."[8] Beyond these two aspects, but part of the overall design, are the research objectives themselves as well as the mechanical procedures of coding, recoding, and otherwise preparing the data. These additional aspects enter consideration at many points. But here the concern is primarily

Appendix B

with the two components of the sampling design proper, the selection process and the estimation process.

Given two sources which overlap on a few characteristics, one possible selection process involves choosing two independent random samples, one from each source. Then the two sample distributions can be compared on the characteristics which both enumerate as a test for bias. If each source represents a population whose members have the same distributions of characteristics, then no difference would be expected between the two samples on the variables which both enumerate. If they differed, however, then one of them would be taken to represent the "true" distributions and the other the biased ones. This type of direct sampling procedure would provide a basis for *evaluating* the *People's Guide* lists for bias on a three-variable base, using occupation, age, and place of birth—which both sources contain. Once bias was known, however, there would remain no way, directly to take it into account. Therefore this selection process was rejected as inadequate to the problem.

The sampling design process actually employed to fit the problem comes under the various titles of two-phase sampling, double sampling, or multiphase sampling. The United Nations definition of the procedure may be used to indicate its salient characteristics:

> It is sometimes convenient and economical to collect certain items of information on the whole of the units of a sample and other items of information on only some of these units, these latter units being so chosen as to constitute a sub-sample of the units of the original sample. This may be termed two-phase sampling. Information collected at the second or sub-sampling phase may be collected at a later time, and in this event, information obtained on all the units of the first-phase sample may be utilized, if this appears advantageous, in the selection of the second-phase sample. Further phases may be added as required....
>
> An important application of multi-phase sampling is the use of the information obtained at the first-phase as supplementary information to provide more accurate estimates (by the method of regression or ratio), of the means, totals, etc., of variates obtained only in the second phase.[9]

Two ends have been in view with the use of a two-phase sampling design: (1) that the information in the U.S. Census become supplemental to that given in the *Guide*s; and (2) that a means be provided by which possible biases of the *People's Guide*s entries might be assessed

Appendix B

and taken into account in the estimating process. In consequence, the following six steps were employed:
1. A large, initial, simple random sample has been taken from the U.S. Census for each county. This first step provides a basic random sample of the census-defined population of voting-age citizens, stratified by the counties, which is self-weighting for the computation of estimating statistics. This sample will be referred to as the "Census Sample." From it alone can be derived county-level statistics for the voting-age aggregate which are not available in published reports.
2. Members of the census sample were traced within townships, where possible, to the *People's Guide*s. Step two provides a random subsample of the potentially traceable population common to both the census and the *People's Guide*s. This sample will be referred to as the "traced subsample." Because students and paupers, as well as "blacks," all of whom were listed in the U.S. Census rarely appeared in the *Guide* tracings, these members were eliminated from the nine-county sample. The full census sample, then, includes the white population, excluding students and paupers, with a final size of 3,318 members. The traced subsample of the rooted population has a final size of 1,216 members. In chapter 3 above, table 3.1 indicates the original allocation of sample members among the nine counties, the number successfully traced, the county weight, and the rate of tracing.

Figure B2 may clarify the relation between the traced subsample and the rooted population of interest. This population can be conceived as comprising two major segments. The first segment (A) includes those members appearing in the census but not in the *Guide* lists. The second segment (B) includes those members who appear in *both* the census and the *Guide*. Together, segments A and B make up the whole population of interest. Now a random sample taken from the whole population will include members from both partitions A and B, as is true for the census sample. This sample, in turn, will comprise two subsamples, a and b, each a random draw from the relevant population segment. But given either subsample, an inference from that subsample *to the whole population* would be subject to bias. The tracing procedure has just this effect: it yields a random sample of the potentially traceable members, which is just one segment of the population of interest. Consequently, sample estimators of population characteristics that are based on the traced subsample alone are subject to bias. And the extent of the potential bias is partly a function of the size of the segment for which the characteristic of interest is unknown.

In symbolic terms the point can be codified succinctly in a formula for

Appendix B

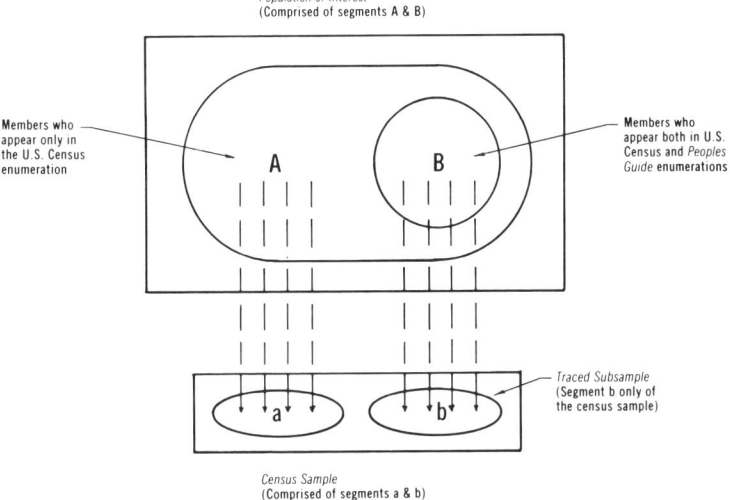

Fig. B2 Schematic diagram of population segments and their related samples

finding the mean, using the following notational meaning.[10] Let $\overline{Y}$ equal the mean for the population, and let W_1 and W_2 represent the relative weights of the two population segments such that $W_1 + W_2 = 1$, where W_2 is the size of the population segment for which no information is obtained. In turn let $\overline{Y}_1$ and $\overline{Y}_2$ represent the respective means of each population segment. Then the mean of the whole population can be expressed as the sum of the weighted means of the two population segments: $\overline{Y} = W_1 \overline{Y}_1 + W_2 \overline{Y}_2$. When an estimate is based only on the known segment the bias is equivalent to the difference between $E(\bar{y}_1)$, the expected value of the mean of the sample drawn from that segment, and the true mean:

$$E(\bar{y}_1) - \overline{Y} =$$
$$\overline{Y}_1 - \overline{Y} = \overline{Y}_1 - (W_1 \overline{Y}_1 + W_2 \overline{Y}_2) =$$
$$\overline{Y}_1(1 - W_1) - W_2 \overline{Y}_2 = \overline{Y}_1(W_2) - W_2 \overline{Y}_2 =$$
$$W_2(\overline{Y}_1 - \overline{Y}_2) = \text{Bias}$$

By step two, then, we obtain a subsample of members traced to the *People's Guide*s which is equivalent to a sample drawn from only one of

Appendix B

two population domains. And since the rate of successful tracing ranges between about 30 and 40 percent it is possible that significant bias could result.

3. A purchase on the probable bias can be obtained by appropriate stratification of the census sample in terms of the multiple social variables which the U.S. Census provides for both the traced and the untraced members. Persons in some social strata of the population are likely to appear in the *People's Guide* more often than persons in other strata. If such strata could be defined for the whole census sample, between which varying appearance in the traced subsample occurred, then the major sources of bias could be recognized and controlled by subsequent weighting. This fact suggests taking inclusion in the *People's Guide* as a dichotomous dependent variable which can be determined for all members of the census sample, and trying to account for it on the basis of variables provided in the census. To this end a computer program known as Automatic Interaction Detection, or AID for short, has been employed, which in effect answers the question, "What are the salient characteristics tor an individual to possess if he is to appear in the traced subsample with a given degree of probability?"[11]

For any individual who appears both in the census sample and in the traced subsample a "1" is assigned; for any individual who appears only in the census sample a "0" is assigned. This variable is defined on all members of the census sample, not just the successfully traced members (again, see figure B1). The AID program explains "statistically" this kind of dichotomous variable, or a ratio variable, in much the same manner as does the correlation ratio, only iteratively. The correlation ratio is a measure of strength of relationship for the combination of a ratio and nominal variable, and can serve to introduce the AID computing procedure.[12]

The correlation ratio employs a set of nominal classes (such as occupational groupings) as predictor (or independent) variables, and measures their relationship to a ratio or dichotomous dependent variable (such as amounts of income, or upper-income versus lower-income classifications). Given a population's income distribution, for instance, the expected value of income for a member chosen at random is the mean. However, if information about the occupational grouping is added, the prediction may be improved by considering the chosen member's value to be the mean of his occupational class. If income is in fact related to occupational class (which seems likely), then values for members of each occupational class should deviate more or less uniformly from the population mean. In turn the mean of each class will also deviate markedly from the population mean even though variation of income

Appendix B

values will remain within the occupational classes. In effect, the total variation in income is partitioned into that portion which can be accounted for by the occupational classes and that portion which cannot be so accounted for, since it remains as variation within the classes. Put more formally, the total variation of the dependent variable can be measured by the total sum of squared deviations about the mean (which is the variance), which can then be partitioned into two components: the first component (or between sum of squares) measures the variation between the class means and the total mean: the second component (or within sum of squares) measures the variation in values within the classes about the means of those classes. Hence, the total sum of squares is equal to the between sum of squares plus the within sum of squares: TSS = BSS + WSS. In this form the percentage of the variation explained by the classification can be expressed by the between sum of squares as a ratio to the total sum of squares.

The Automatic Interaction Detection program uses this variance-accounting method in an iterative fashion, which results in the construction of a tree diagram like that presented in figure B3. Given a parent group (the census sample) and a measure on a dependent variable (such as the dichotomy defining the bias for appearance in the traced subsample), the program searches among predictor variables (census-defined social characteristics) for that one which will partition the parent group into two subgroups by maximizing the between sum of squares. This is represented in the diagram by the first division into subgroups A

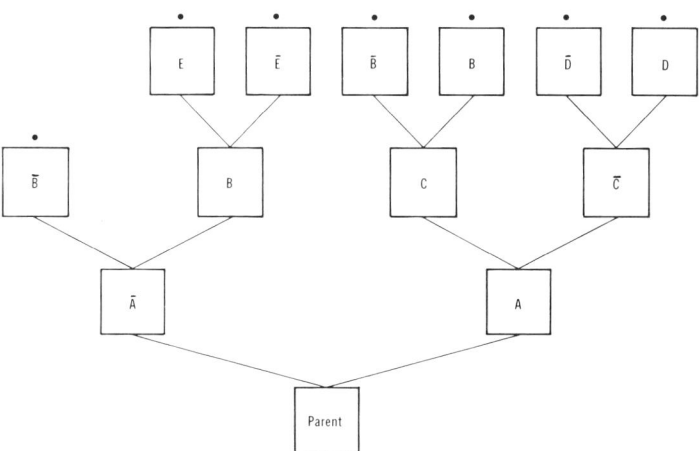

Fig. B3 An example of the AID tree diagram and splitting process

Appendix B

and not-A. Each subgroup in turn may then be viewed as a new parent group subject to further divisions by the same process. These divisions form a splitting process that need not be symmetrical across the cells (or branches) of the resulting tree, as indicated by the repetition in different branches of the B and not-B variable. William A. Belson has termed this kind of splitting process one of "matching and prediction on the principle of biological classification," since it does not follow that a second division based on subgroup A will be the same as the second division for subgroup not-A.[13] After the splitting process has ended, a series of final groups can be defined into which all members have been sorted (marked by dots in the diagram). By this procedure, then, the members of each final group share in common those census-defined characteristics on which the preceding divisions have been based. And these are divisions which have maximized the between sum of squares as a means of accounting for the variation in the dependent variable. Since the dependent variable in this application is the dichotomy which defines the bias, the final groups generated by the AID procedure maximally account for the differential appearance of members in the traced subsample.

4. The final groups defined by the AID routine have been taken as strata within each county, and the traced members from the *People's Guide* in each such stratum have been *assumed* to be a simple random sample from it. At this point we have entered the second phase of the two-phase sampling design.[14]

Since the proportion of elements falling into each stratum from the original census sample provides an estimate of the relative size of that stratum in the original population, that proportion constitutes the stratum weight. These weights are, in turn, attached to subsample estimators (such as the mean) based on the traced members within each stratum. Since the number of original census sample elements falling into each stratum is subject to random variation, the weighting, which takes into account the major sources of bias, adds to the total variance of any estimators developed from this sampling design. This weighting has been included in the formulas for estimators given below. The combination of steps three and four, then, have been used to remove the major sources of bias from the traced subsample for the calculation of estimators. This final sample will be referred to as the "weighted *Guide* subsample," or more simply, as the "*Guide* subsample."

5. The calculation of estimators for the *Guide* subsample, such as means or totals and their variances and standard errors, must be accomplished stratum by stratum within each county. The estimators are weighted at the stratum level, and then summed to the county level,

Appendix B

where they may be summed again to the level of the total sample. The formula for the estimate of the mean, suggested by Kish, is given by:

$$\sum_{g}^{G} W_g \bar{y}_g = \sum_{g}^{G} W_g \sum_{h}^{H_g} w_{gh} \bar{y}_{gh}.$$

For the mean estimator, given above, the following notational meaning obtains: G refers to the number of counties, so that g goes from 1 to G; H_g indicates the number of strata in the gth county in the sample, so that h goes from 1 to H_g; W_g refers to the weight of the gth county (based on its population size); and w_{gh} refers to the estimated weight from the census sample from the hth stratum in the gth county. A weighted *Guide* subsample mean estimator, then, is simply the sum of the weighted stratum means within each county, weighted and summed over all counties.

The estimate of the variance becomes slightly more complex, and can be given by

$$\sum_{g}^{G} W_g^2 \text{var}(\bar{y}_g) = \sum_{g}^{G} W_g^2 \left[\sum_{h}^{H_g} w_{gh}^2 \frac{s_{gh}^2}{n_{gh}} + \frac{1}{n_g} \sum_{h}^{H_g} w_{gh} (\bar{y}_{gh} - \bar{y}_g)^2 \right],$$

with the following notational additions: s_{gh} refers to the traced subsample estimate of the standard error within the hth stratum of the gth county; n_{gh} refers to the number of traced elements in that stratum, and n_g refers to the number of elements traced in the gth county. The second term within the brackets represents the approximate increase in the variance for the second phase over ordinary stratified random sampling.[15]

6. While the rather complex formulas given above become necessary for the calculation of variances, a more direct route is available for computing simple proportions based on the *Guide* subsample, using an inflation factor for each member of each stratum. This procedure brings each stratum, artificially, to the size of the first phase sample. It restores the self-weighting features of the initial stratified random sample with the bias controlled according to the post-stratification of the first phase. However, this inflated n cannot be used for tests of significance nor can the variance be derived directly from the data based on the inflation factors. While computed proportions will correspond to those given for the mean above (step 5), the actual number of cases on which they are based must be noted from the actual subsample n itself. The combination of steps 5 and 6, however, does allow the data to be fully manipulated as a sample. The use of the inflation factor (step 6) permits

Appendix B

standard cross-classifications for weighted data, in which percentage estimators can be compared for subgroups. Where necessary or desirable those estimators could be bounded with confidence limits based on the variance (by step 5) or its root, the standard error. Thus, the basic statistical tests and measures of association can be performed on the data by this design, and the basic criteria for a probability sample are met.

Meeting these criteria does not mean that all bias has been removed, but only that it has been minimized on the basis of available information. This can be illustrated for the case at hand by asking about the extent to which the proposed design was successful. Does the *Guide* subsample, which provides the partisan data, adequately represent the originally sampled census population?

As a means of answering this question and evaluating the *Guide* subsample, a series of goodness-of-fit tests can be presented. In the model of activity for these tests it is assumed that the distribution of population characteristics would remain relatively constant from 1870 to 1874 and, therefore, that the original census sample can provide criterion distributions for characteristics observed on the *Guide* subsample alone. The correspondence between the criterion and the actual distributions of the *Guide* subsample distributions can then be evaluated by the chi-square test for goodness of fit.[16] Four variables from the original census list will suffice to illustrate the procedure, dealing respectively with wealth-standing, occupational groups, places of birth, and age distributions. From these an evaluation of the *Guide* subsample can be made.

First, consider the variable of wealth-standing. In making the goodness-of-fit test the actual wealth values were first grouped into five categories as a function of the mean wealth among census sample members. To accomplish the goodness-of-fit test the proportion of members in each of these categories in the census sample provided the model. These proportions were multiplied by the number of members in the *Guide* subsample (1,216) to yield the *expected number* of members in each wealth group. The *Guide* subsample itself was then used to determine the actual (weighted) proportions in each wealth category, which proportions were also multiplied by the number in the subsample (1,216) to yield the observed number in each category. The absolute difference in numbers between the expected and the observed frequencies was squared and divided by the expected number in each category in accord with standard chi-square procedures. The resulting wealth category values were then summed to give the total value of chi-square, which can be compared

Appendix B

Table B.1 Chi-square Test for Goodness of Fit, Personal Wealth Stratification

Stratum	Census	Guide	Expected f	Observed f	Absolute Diff.	Difference Squared	Contribution to chi-square
Upper	12.1	13.4	147.1	162.9	15.8	249.64	1.70
U-M	15.6	16.0	189.7	194.6	4.9	24.01	.13
Middle	17.5	19.0	213.3	231.0	17.7	331.29	1.55
L-M	26.9	27.5	326.1	334.4	8.3	68.89	.21
Lower	27.9	24.1	339.8	293.1	46.7	2180.89	6.42
Totals	100.0	100.0	1216.0	1216.0		chi-square =	10.01

NOTE: Totals may not sum out due to rounding.

to possible values on the theoretical chi-square distribution. This theoretical distribution allows the probability to be ascertained that the observed value of chi-square would result by chance at least 5 percent of the time even if there were no difference between the expected and the observed stratum distributions. For the wealth stratification variable the critical value for chi-square, with four degrees of freedom, is 9.488. Values this large or larger would not result by chance more than 5 percent of the time, and smaller values would support the assumption that the weighted *Guide* subsample represented an unbiased sample of the population with regard to this variable. Table B1 presents these calculations for stratification on personal wealth.

In this test the value of chi-square for personal wealth stratification (10.01) falls just above the critical value. On a strict interpretation the assumption that the *Guide* subsample represents the same population distribution as the census sample would have to be rejected at the .05 level. The subsample, on this variable, remains biased. The point of the calculation, however, may be viewed in another way. By close examination of table B1 it becomes clear that the major contribution to the value of chi-square arises at specific points in the distribution and most emphatically at a single stratum, the lowest one. Members for whom no personal wealth was reported in the census are significantly underrepresented in the weighted *Guide* subsample, while those in strata above that one tend to be overrepresented. Hence, from the calculation of the chi-square statistic it is possible to know not only that bias continues but also something of its relative location and direction.

The same procedure can be followed on each succeeding variable that allows for comparison between the census sample and the *Guide*

Appendix B

Table B.2. Chi-Square Test for Goodness of Fit: Occupational Stratification

Stratum	% Census	% Guide	Expected f	Observed f	Absolute Difference	Difference Squared	Chi-square Contribution
High farm	11.2	11.5	136.2	139.8	3.6	12.96	.10
Mid farm	9.6	9.1	116.7	110.7	6.0	36.00	.31
Low farm	13.2	14.2	160.5	172.7	12.2	148.84	.93
Non-prop. farm	17.5	18.8	212.8	228.6	15.8	249.64	1.17
Farm labor	12.6	12.5	153.2	152.00	1.2	1.44	.01
Mercantile	6.1	6.5	74.2	79.0	4.8	23.04	.31
Professional	2.9	2.8	35.3	34.1	1.2	1.44	.03
Gen. trades	3.4	3.6	41.3	43.8	2.5	6.25	.15
Bldg. trades	5.8	6.5	70.5	79.0	8.5	72.25	1.02
Metal-wood trades	6.0	7.0	73.0	85.1	12.1	146.41	2.01
Nonfarm labor	7.5	4.7	92.4	57.2	35.2	1239.04	13.41
Missing data	4.1	2.7	49.9	32.8	17.1	292.41	5.86
Totals	100.0	100.0	1216.1	1214.8		chi-square =	25.31

NOTE: Totals may not sum out due to rounding.

subsample. Occupations were classified into eleven "families" with a residual category for missing data on this variable. Table B2 presents the appropriate data, for which the critical value is 19.67, with eleven degrees of freedom. As the table makes clear, chi-square has a value of 25.31, so that again on this variable the strict assumption of representativeness cannot be held. By looking within the table, however, it is possible to locate those strata providing the largest contributions to this value. In two strata it is noticeably high, that of "missing data" and among the "nonfarm laborers," both of which are underrepresented in the *Guide* subsample. The category of nonfarm laborers, especially, provides the critical contribution and indicates another source of persisting bias comparable to the nonpropertied of the wealth distribution. Otherwise, the remaining occupational categories provide an extremely close fit to the original census sample.

What about regional places of birth? The state of Indiana by mid- and late-nineteenth century was located at the intersection of the larger subregions of the United States. And the regional birthplaces of the

Appendix B

Table B.3. Chi-square Test for Goodness of Fit: Places of Birth

Source	Census	Guide	Expected f	Observed f	Absolute Difference	Difference squared	Chi-square Contribution
Indiana	41.2	44.2	501.0	537.5	36.5	1,332.25	2.66
Ohio	14.3	13.8	173.9	167.8	6.1	37.21	.21
Penna.	4.1	4.5	49.9	54.7	4.8	23.04	.46
(North)	3.3	3.7	40.1	45.0	4.9	24.01	.60
Kentucky	12.3	11.7	149.6	142.3	7.3	53.29	.36
N. Car.	8.5	8.6	103.4	104.6	1.2	1.44	.01
Virginia	5.1	4.8	62.0	58.4	3.6	12.96	.21
(South)	4.1	3.4	49.9	41.3	8.6	73.96	1.48
Eng.-Sp.	3.6	2.2	43.8	26.8	17.0	289.00	6.60
Non-Eng.	3.3	3.2	40.1	38.9	1.2	1.44	.04
Totals	100.0	100.0	1,213.7	1,217.3		chi-square =	12.63

NOTE: Totals may not sum out due to rounding.

non-Indiana-born reflect this fact, including a small contingent of members born in Europe. In the test for goodness-of-fit the major states serving as sources of migrants to Indiana were retained as separate categories along with Indiana itself, while the states contributing smaller numbers were combined into general "northern" and "southern" categories. The foreign-born, while small in number, were established in the two categories of English- and non-English-speaking foreign. This yielded ten categories of origin as displayed in table B3, giving a critical value for chi-square of 16.92 with nine degrees of freedom. Taking the census sample proportions as the model once again, an observed value for chi-square of 12.63 is obtained. Since that value falls within the critical limit, it suggests that the two distributions adequately represent the same population. However, it may be noted that the major sources of continuing bias can be observed within the table, where the English-speaking foreign-born (largely British and Irish) are underrepresented while the native-born of Indiana itself are overrepresented.

Finally, an age component to bias may be considered. Using a base of ten-year age-gradings, with a final category for those over sixty, table B4 can be represented. With four degrees of freedom, the critical value for chi-square becomes 5.99. The observed value of 2.94 is within the critical limit at the .05 probability level. It can be noted, however, that the age

Appendix B

Table B.4. Chi-square Test for Goodness of Fit: Age-Cohort Distribution

Age Cohort	p Census	p Guide	Expected f	Observed f	Absolute Difference	Difference Squared	Chi-square Contribution
21–30	36.0	35.1	437.8	426.8	11.0	121.00	.28
31–40	26.8	28.4	325.9	345.3	19.4	376.36	1.15
41–50	15.8	15.3	192.1	186.1	6.0	36.00	.18
51–60	12.3	12.8	149.6	155.7	6.1	37.21	.25
61 over	9.2	8.3	111.9	100.9	11.0	121.00	1.08
Totals	100.0	100.0	1,217.3	1,214.8		chi-square =	2.94

NOTE: Totals may not sum out due to rounding.

range between thirty-one and forty is slightly overrepresented, a cohort just in the prime of the population's life cycle. The underrepresentation of the oldest cohort would seem to reflect the attrition of death.

In sum, for the case at hand, it is now possible to say that bias continues in the weighted *Guide* subsample on at least two variables of interest, those dealing with the distribution of wealth and those dealing with occupational families. In each case, however, as well as in the two falling within the critical limits, it was possible to identify the location and direction of the bias. On the wealth distribution it was the category of persons lacking wealth which was underrepresented; among occupational families underrepresentation occurred for the nonfarm laborers, though they together with the farm laborers held the lowest average personal wealth. A deviation toward underrepresentation also occurred for the English-speaking foreign-born, while overrepresentation was present for the Indiana-born and the age cohort in the prime of the life cycle. These sources and directions of continuing bias suggest just a set of characteristics for members having a high potentiality for geographic mobility. They appear to be characteristics of persons *not* tied to the local culture by notable personal wealth, a locally required skill, nor are they constrained from moving by an alien language barrier. The continuing bias, then, appears to arise from the slight underrepresentation of members least rooted in the local community. And this should not be surprising. While the traced subsample involves the "rooted" members of the population between 1870 and 1874, it has been reweighted according to the 1870 distribution of characteristics, which includes the least-rooted population segments as well. And these least "rooted" members have not been fully accounted for in the weighted

Appendix B

Guide subsample, though from the goodness-of-fit tests they have been nearly so.

The conceptual strategy that has now been presented and empirically evaluated is a general one which can be modified to cover other data sets. It meets a common condition in historical research. This situation is one where a presumably complete listing of a population can be obtained and where some basic variables are present for each member. The U.S. Census is the typical expression of such lists, even with their known coverage errors. However, the research interest focuses on variables of information which are present on other lists covering the same population but which do not give a complete enumeration of its members. The strategy in this situation is to use the information from the (presumably) full list to stratify the population in order to obtain representative members from each stratum who also appear on lists giving the information of interest. These latter members are then weighted according to the size of the population stratum in which they appear. The special AID routine employed to determine the strata for each county in the present case has a very desirable property; it maximizes the difference between the strata directly in terms of the differential appearance between lists, and does so in terms of multiple social (or other) characteristics for members on the complete list.

The extent to which bias can be taken into account by a strategy like this one is dependent partly on the size of the population not represented on the incomplete list and partly on the social characteristics initially known for all members. The finding of continuing bias in the present case suggests not only the coverage difference between the two lists but also that the variables on which the poststratification procedure had to be based were only partially related to the actual sources of bias. That partial relation, however, provided a relatively powerful basis on which to control for and take into account such biases, as a means by which they might be evaluated. In general, the resulting data will never be perfect, in the sense of a simple random sample from the population of interest. But for historical analysis the design presented yields the "best" data for representing a past population because that data can be manipulated as a probability sample which meets the basic requirement of providing "a universe in miniature" with biases known and taken into account.

Appendix C

The Federal Census of 1870 and Measurement of Error on Age

Roy Ekland, Timothy W. Sullivan, Tamara Tieman, and Julienne Wood

The application of rigorous research designs to the study of historical problems has followed advances in data processing. Historians now seek techniques that compensate for incomplete data in one source, that adjust for biases of subsampling between two or more sources, and that evaluate each source for reliability.

The attack on these problems has not been pressed equally on all fronts. In particular, the problems of measurement error, as distinct from sampling error, have received very little systematic attention from historians.[1] Consisting of errors in coverage and content, measurement error occurs both at the time the data were initially generated and through the process of research itself. It results from the original misreporting of information, from mistakes in the original transcription, from mistakes made by the historian in secondary transcription, and from clerical errors in coding, keypunching, and recoding. Measurement error, then, is in part a question of source reliability.

Lacking control over the creation of their data, historians often assume that the original measurement error at the source was small, or at least randomly distributed, and that it therefore exerts minimal influence on substantive results. Their attention has largely focused on minimizing errors of secondary transcription and on the remaining processes over which rather direct control can be exercised.[2] Most measurement error at the source, of course, must go undetected. Only in cases where two or more sources purportedly provide the same informa-

Appendix C

tion can the error be assessed. A comparison of age data recorded in the *People's Guide* directories of 1874 to the age data recorded in the federal manuscript census returns of 1870 allows us to make this assessment for at least one variable within this study, using the original sources themselves.[3]

The census data were drawn as a simple random sample of 3,318 voting-age males in 1870, for nine counties that served as strata. By linking on name, place of birth, and township of residence, a 1,216 member subset of the same voting-age citizens was traced to the 1874 *People's Guide*s, commercially prepared directories compiled for nine rural central Indiana counties. In addition to the linking variables, the two original sources also shared two other variables, occupation and age. These two variables differ, of course, in their logical status with respect to change over time. Logically, occupation may change by any number of social processes, while age must change as a direct function of time itself. Different reports of occupation, therefore, may be due to actual changes in jobs, but differences in reports of age *must* be due to measurement error. It is age, then, that we must consider for possible measurement error.

The two sources differed in how they reported age. The census-takers were instructed to report age "in years," while the *Guide* reported "the year of birth," from which age may be computed. As reports, these two versions of age are not equivalent, for the first is a report that must be recalculated continually by the individual with the passage of time, while the second is a piece of information that, once known by the individual, remains fixed over time. By hypothesis, then, the report of age obtained by census-takers presents much greater opportunity for misreporting, and thereby for measurement error, than does the comparable report for year of birth given in the *Guide*s.

Assuming that linkage between these two sources was highly reliable and that the same individuals had actually appeared in the two separate sources, we nonetheless found that discrepancies in age, as reported in the census and calculated for the *Guide*s, occurred in 219 of the 1,184 cases where both sources provided age information. In other words, age as listed in the 1870 census (plus four years) matched age as calculated from the *Guide*s of 1874 only for 965 voters.[4]

The frequency of these discrepancies exceeded our expectations. We therefore decided to ask whether age discrepancies between the two sources were randomly distributed. While the mean discrepancy in age, calculated for the same base year, was small (-0.62), the mean *absolute* discrepancy approached four years (3.82). The small mean difference

Appendix C

Table C.1. Age Discrepancies between the Census Report and the *Guide* Report, by Census Age-Cohorts

	Age Cohorts					
	0–20	21–30	31–40	41–50	51–60	61–99
Age mismatch	50.0	15.4	22.2	19.8	16.0	14.3	(18.5)
	(5)	(44)	(74)	(48)	(31)	(17)	(219)
Age match	50.0	84.6	77.8	80.2	84.0	85.7	(81.5)
	(5)	(241)	(259)	(195)	(163)	(102)	(965)
% Total	100.0	100.0	100.0	100.0	100.0	100.0	

The critical value for chi-square at the .05 level is 11.070. The actual value was 19.912. Therefore, these differences by age cohorts were significant. Numbers in parentheses are the number of unweighted cases.

(near the zero-point) suggested a near-random distribution, but, as a classification into age cohorts showed, the mean difference obscured the tendency for age errors to concentrate in particular cohorts. Table C1 groups ages by ten-year intervals and compares within each cohort voters whose ages matched between the two sources and those whose ages did not match. It shows that thirty-one- to forty-year-olds had the highest percentage of error by discrepancies on age. The magnitude of discrepancies and the behavior of these discrepancies within age cohorts raised questions about the correlation between age discrepancies and other variables.

If measurement error on age was random, it would have only random relationships to other variables. To test this assumption, the *Guide* sample was divided into two groups, the 219 cases (set A) which were discrepant on age between the two sources and the 965 cases (set B) whose ages matched in both sources. Comparisons were then made between these two sets on three wealth variables and four other nominal variables—religious attachment, party attachment, place of residence, and literacy—as well as on the age cohorts themselves. Under conditions of perfect independence, where measurement error would produce only random effects, percentages within any category of these other variables should closely approximate the breakdown of the total sample into age-match (81.5 percent) and age-mismatch (18.5 percent) categories.

On three of the eight variables—age, residence, and religious attachment—the distributions of sets A and B showed no difference. No residence category or religious denomination was overrepresented in one of these two sets. On age itself, the difference in mean age between set A (40.51 years) and set B (41.74 years) also showed no difference, by a

Appendix C

Table C.2. Age Discrepancies by Categories of Party Attachment (in percentages)

	Party Attachment Categories				
	Rep.	Dem.	NA	Other	
Age mismatch	17.4	22.3	17.5	8.6	(18.5)
	(106)	(86)	(21)	(6)	(219)
Age match	82.6	77.7	82.5	91.4	(81.5)
	(503)	(299)	(99)	(64)	(965)
% Total	100.0	100.0	100.0	100.0	

Differences by chi-square were significant at the .05 level.

two-tailed test of significance (using the .05 level).[5] All of these results pointed toward the random effects of age-discrepant measurement errors.

But the assumption of random effects became questionable in considering the other variables. In the case of party attachments, for instance, table C2 shows that Democrats tended to be overrepresented in set A (age mismatch) and third-party members underrepresented. By a chi-square test, the assumption of independence can be rejected. However, the strength of association between age discrepancies and party attachments was very weak, with values for lambda and the tau statistics approaching zero.

A comparison by categories of literacy was even more striking. Illiterates, as might be expected, were dramatically overrepresented among the 219 mismatched age comparisons. And the percentage of illiterates for whom age was mismatched between the two sources reached almost twice that expected under conditions of complete independence (31.2 percent of illiterates were discrepant between the two reports of age). Accordingly, the chi-square test was well above the significance level.

For the three wealth variables, the comparison of mean wealth between sets A and B further confirmed that age discrepancies between the two sources were related to other variables. For, across all wealth measures, the means of the two sets differed significantly. Mean total wealth for set A (age mismatch) was $1,392 less than mean total wealth for set B. While less extreme, the differences in means for personal wealth and real estate wealth were still more than $500, and, by t-tests, these differences in means were all significant, as shown in table C3.

A breakdown in the wealth variables by gradients ranging from high wealth to no wealth located the wealth levels associated with measure-

Appendix C

Table C.3. Mean Wealth between Age-discrepant and Age-match Categories

	Set A (Age mismatch)		Set B (Age match)		
	Mean	St. Dev.	Mean	St. Dev.	t-test
Real estate	$3,174	$5,393	$4,279	$7,899	2.514
Personal	$762	$1,017	$1,284	$2,271	5.192
Total estate	$3,937	$5,964	$5,329	$4,810	3.074

All figures are unweighted, rounded to the nearest dollar.
The significance value for the two-tailed difference of means test at the .05 level is 1.06.

ment error on age. As table C4 shows, the frequency of age discrepancies between the two sources was generally greater in the lower strata than in the higher.[6] It thus became clear that the misreporting of age between the two sources was related to literacy and wealth and, perhaps through them, to party attachments as well.

The traced sample, of course, was not used in its original form but was weighted to remove the sampling bias induced by tracing only a subset of the larger census sample.[7] Although weighting largely corrected for sampling bias, it was unclear what effect weighting had on the measurement error associated with age discrepancies between the two sources. Accordingly, a second series of tables was constructed employing the same eight variables but modified by the weighting system. Chi-square values were computed as before on each of the variables with respect to age discrepancies, and the contribution to chi-square for each cell of the eight tables was recorded.

Weighting had little effect on age discrepancies within religious-affiliation categories or residence strata, and on neither variable did the chi-square value surpass the level of significance. Age discrepancies within categories of party attachment and literacy both had significant chi-square values in their unweighted version, which increased with weighting. Similarly, the contribution to chi-square over age cohorts showed that the weighting system increased the prominence of the thirty-one- to forty-year-old cohort in set A, nearly tripling its contribution to chi-square. Differential increases in the value of chi-square were also observed for two of the three wealth variables.[8] All of these results are shown in table C5.

Although the process of weighting largely compensated for sampling bias, it greatly exaggerated the age discrepancies between the two sources that resulted from measurement error in the originals. It should

Appendix C

Table C.4. Age Discrepancies by Gradients of Wealth (in percentages)

	High	H.-Mid.	Mid.	L.-Mid.	None	
			Real Estate Wealth			
Age mismatch	15.3	13.9	16.8	24.3	21.4	(18.5)
	(48)	(28)	(19)	(42)	(82)	(219)
Age match	84.7	86.1	83.2	75.7	78.6	(81.5)
	(265)	(173)	(94)	(131)	(302)	(965)
% Total	100.0	100.0	100.0	100.0	100.0	
			Personal Estate Wealth			
Age mismatch	13.5	14.5	22.5	20.2	23.2	(18.5)
	(30)	(41)	(51)	(52)	(44)	(219)
Age match	86.5	85.5	77.5	79.8	76.8	(81.5)
	(192)	(241)	(176)	(210)	(146)	(965)
% Total	100.0	100.0	100.0	100.0	100.0	
			Total Estate Wealth			
Age mismatch	14.2	15.7	18.6	21.2	24.2	(18.5)
	(42)	(36)	(26)	(75)	(40)	(219)
Age match	85.8	84.3	81.4	78.8	75.8	(81.5)
	(253)	(194)	(114)	(279)	(125)	(965)
% Total	100.0	100.0	100.0	100.0	100.0	

In each section differences by chi-square were significant at the .05 level.

Table C.5. Comparison of Chi-square Values for Unweighted and Weighted Tables by Age Discrepancies

| | Values of chi-square | | |
	Unweighted	Weighted	.05 Critical
Age cohorts	19.912	32.160	11.070
Literacy	8.425	10.533	3.841
Real estate strata	10.010	15.045	9.488
Personal estate strata	11.731	12.241	9.488
Total estate strata	10.390	9.672	9.488

be noted that this error would remain even if the complete population of voters, rather than a sample, had been taken. Measurement error is not dependent on sampling but on the sources themselves. Weighting, however, increased its effects. Figure C1 attempts to clarify this relationship. The unweighted *Guide* sample was overrepresented by higher wealth strata, among other variables. Among age discrepancies, however, the lower wealth strata were overrepresented. In correcting for

Appendix C

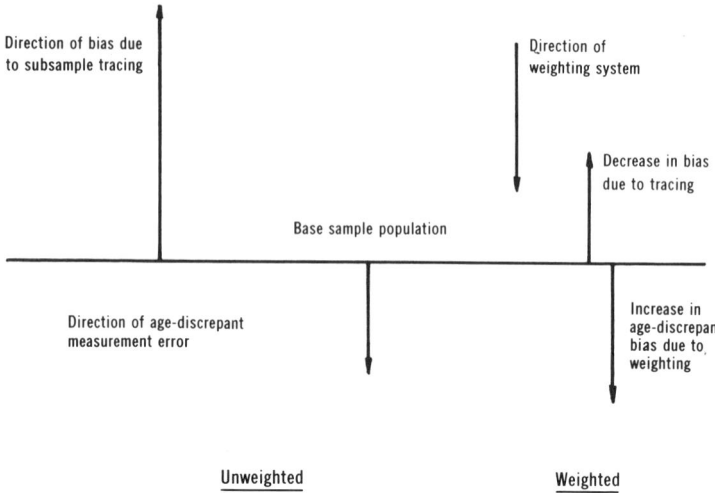

Fig. C1 Schematic graph of the relation between sampling bias and measurement error on age

the sampling bias, the weighting system redistributed the frequencies in the wealth strata, forcing downward the mean wealth of the entire traced sample, as was intended. This redistribution caused further overrepresentation of the lower wealth strata within set A, the category of voters for whom the two sources provided different reports of age. A similar effect resulted with respect to literacy and party attachment.

It has not been our purpose here to evaluate whether the census or the *Guide*s provided the better report of age, although given the differing logical status of the two kinds of reports, it seems likely that the census report offered greater opportunity for error. Rather our intent has been to show that measurement error does occur in the sources that historians must, of necessity, use. Certainly, for studying the mass population of the past, the census manuscripts are among the most important sources. But in these sources, as in all others, measurement error occurs even on so simple an item of information as age, perhaps because it was reported "in years" rather than by date of birth.

The overrepresentation of the poor and illiterate among those whose age reports were discrepant between the two sources we have examined probably occurred for reasons similar to those responsible for the underrepresentation of the poor and illiterate in census returns and city or county directories. That similarity, however, should not confuse two

Appendix C

distinct methodological problems. A correction for sampling bias can compensate for the nonrepresentativeness of a particular source, if ancillary information is used. But correcting for over- and underrepresentation does not necessarily correct for bias associated with measurement error, the diagnosis of which requires the comparison of one source with another (and perhaps even these two with a third) on particular variables in order to observe and, perhaps, resolve discrepancies. Therefore, the diagnosis of measurement error, and the degree to which it is associated with other variables, depends on procedures independent of the sampling design itself and, if evaluated at all, must be evaluated by methods of source comparison.

Notes

INTRODUCTION

1. *The People's Guide: A Business, Political and Religious Directory* (Indianapolis: Cline and McHaffie, 1874).

2. For a description of early survey research on voting behavior, see Peter H. Rossi, "Four Landmarks of Voting Research," *American Voting Behavior*, ed. by Eugene Burdick and Arthur J. Brodbeck (Glencoe, Ill.: The Free Press, 1959), pp. 5-54. For a brief introduction to survey samples, see U.S. Bureau of the Census, *Supplemental Courses for Case Studies in Surveys and Censuses, Sampling Lectures*, ISP Supplemental Course Series, no. 1 (Washington, D.C., 1968).

3. The basic social and political history of Indiana during the 1870s is Emma Lou Thornbrough's comprehensive *Indiana in the Civil War Era, 1850-1880*, vol. 3, *The History of Indiana* (Indianapolis: Indiana Historical Bureau and Indiana Historical Society, 1965).

CHAPTER ONE

1. Solon J. Buck, *The Granger Movement: A Study of Agricultural Organizations and Its Political, Economic and Social Manifestations, 1870-1880* (Cambridge: Harvard University Press, 1913); John D. Hicks, *The Populist Revolt* (Minneapolis: University of Minnesota Press, 1931); Fred E. Haynes, *Third Party Movements Since the Civil War* (Iowa City: The State Historical Society, 1916).

2. For reviews see Allan G. Bogue, "United States: The 'New' Political History," *Journal of Contemporary History* 3 (January 1968): 5-27; Robert P. Swierenga, "Ethnocultural Political Analysis: A New Approach to American Ethnic Studies," *Journal of American Studies* 5 (April 1971): 66-79.

Notes to Chapter One

3. John J. Stucker and Jerrold G. Rusk, "Legal-Institutional Factors and Voting Participation: An Historical Analysis" (paper delivered at the Midwest Political Science Association meeting, Chicago, 1973).
4. Buck, *Granger Movement,* p. 7.
5. Ibid., p. 14.
6. Ibid., pp. 16-19.
7. Ibid., p. 308. The agrarian interpretation of economic conditions has been challenged at several points. See, for example, Allan G. Bogue, *Money at Interest: The Farm Mortgage on the Middle Border* (Lincoln: University of Nebraska Press, 1969), pp. 262-76.
8. Hicks, *The Populist Revolt.*
9. Ibid., pp. 103-4.
10. Stanley B. Parsons, *The Populist Context: Rural versus Urban Power on a Great Plains Frontier* (Westport, Conn.: Greenwood Press, 1973).
11. Thornbrough, *Indiana in the Civil War Era,* 3:274-317; William G. Carleton, "The Money Question in Indiana Politics, 1865-1890," *Indiana Magazine of History* 42 (June 1946): 107-50.
12. Lee Benson, *The Concept of Jacksonian Democracy: New York as a Test Case* (New York: Atheneum, 1966); Samuel P. Hays, "The Social Analysis of American Political History, 1880-1920," *Political Science Quarterly* 80 (1965): 373-94; idem, "Political Parties and the Community-Society Continuum," in William Nisbet Chambers and Walter Dean Burnham, *The American Party Systems: Stages of Political Development,* pp. 152-81. For the contributions of Benson and Hays to the revisionist position, see Bogue, "The 'New' Political History," pp. 46-47.
13. Paul Kleppner, *The Cross of Culture: Social Analysis of Midwestern Politics, 1850-1900* (New York: The Free Press, 1970); Richard J. Jensen, *The Winning of the Midwest: Social and Political Conflict, 1888-96* (Chicago: University of Chicago Press, 1971).
14. Lee Benson, "An Approach to the Scientific Study of Past Public Opinion," *Public Opinion Quarterly* 21 (Winter 1967-68): 522-67; Hays, "Political Parties," stresses the interaction of elites and their local support.
15. Hays, "Social Analysis," pp. 386-87.
16. See Jensen, *Winning of the Midwest,* pp. 60-62, 302-3, 309-15, for use of individual data. While hard statistical work went into Jensen's study, his presentation largely ignored formal measurement in favor of a narrative style. Kleppner employed a strategy of "disaggregation," moving successively from national to regional, state, county, and township levels, using typical wards and townships to make comparative inferences. See his discussion of midwestern voting cycles, *Cross of Culture,* pp. 8-17.
17. Kleppner, *Cross of Culture,* pp. 69-76; Jensen, *Winning of the Midwest,* pp. 62-68.

Notes to Chapter One

18. Kleppner, *Cross of Culture,* p. 75.
19. Ibid., pp. 337-38; Jensen, *Winning of the Midwest,* pp. 278-96.
20. William G. Carleton, "Why Was the Democratic Party in Indiana a Radical Party, 1865-1890?" *Indiana Magazine of History* 42 (September 1946): 207-28.
21. Others have also done so, as for example, Frederick C. Luebke, *Immigrants and Politics: The Germans of Nebraska, 1880-1900* (Lincoln: University of Nebraska Press, 1969); Ronald P. Formisano, *The Birth of Mass Political Parties: Michigan, 1827-1861* (Princeton: Princeton University Press, 1971); Samuel T. McSeveney, *The Politics of Depression: Political Behavior in the Northeast, 1893-1896* (New York: Oxford University Press, 1972).
22. Angus Campbell, Philip E. Converse, Warren E. Miller, and Donald E. Stokes, *The American Voter* (1960; reprint ed., Chicago: University of Chicago Press, 1977), p. 121.
23. Ibid., pp. 89-115.
24. W. Dean Burnham, "The Changing Shape of the American Political Universe," *American Political Science Review* 59 (March 1965): 7-22. A more fully developed version of Burnham's work appeared as *Critical Elections and the Mainsprings of American Politics* (New York: W. W. Norton, 1970).
25. Burnham, *Critical Elections.*
26. Burnham, "Changing Shape," pp. 9-10.
27. Ibid., p. 10.
28. Jensen, *Winning of the Midwest,* p. 307.
29. Campbell et al., *American Voter,* pp. 475-81, 493-98.
30. Burnham, "Changing Shape," pp. 16-17.
31. Philip E. Converse, "Change in the American Electorate," in *The Human Meaning of Social Change,* ed. by Angus Campbell and Philip E. Converse (New York: Russell Sage, 1972), pp. 263-337. See the reply to Converse by W. Dean Burnham, "Theory and Voting Research: Some Reflections on Converse's 'Change in the American Electorate,'" *American Political Science Review* 68 (September 1974): 1002-23, and Converse's reply in the same issue, pp. 1024-27.
32. Jerrold G. Rusk, "The Effect of the Australian Ballot Reform on Split-ticket Voting, 1876-1908" (Ph.D. dissertation, The University of Michigan, 1967).
33. Jerrold G. Rusk, "The Effect of the Australian Ballot Reform on Split-ticket Voting, 1876-1908," *American Political Science Review* 64 (December 1970), pp. 1220-38, and his exchange with Burnham, *American Political Science Review* 65 (December 1971), pp. 1149-51.
34. Converse, "Change in the American Electorate," pp. 30-33. Cf. Joseph P. Harris, *Registration of Voters in the United States* (Washington, D.C.: Brookings Institution, 1929).
35. Converse, "Change in the American Electorate," pp. 35-48. Howard W. Allen discounts Converse's argument on rural fraud after a

Notes to Chapter Two

thorough review of qualitative sources. See his "Vote Fraud and the Validity of Election Data" (manuscript).

CHAPTER TWO

1. Thornbrough, *Indiana in the Civil War Era,* 3:536-41; Stephen S. Visher, "Distribution of Birthplaces of Indianians in 1870," *Indiana Magazine of History* 26 (1930): 126-42.
2. Quoted from Eugene H. Roseboom, *A Short History of Presidential Elections* (New York: Macmillan, 1967), pp. 101-2.
3. The division of the vote is graphed from Svend Petersen, *A Statistical History of the American Presidential Elections* (New York: Frederick Ungar, 1968).
4. V. O. Key, Jr., "A Theory of Critical Elections," *Journal of Politics* 17 (February 1955): 3-18; reprinted in *Electoral Change and Stability in American Political History,* ed. by Jerome M. Clubb and Howard W. Allen (New York: The Free Press, 1971), pp. 26-44. See also, in the same volume, Charles Sellers, "The Equilibrium Cycle in Two-party Politics," pp. 149-77; Gerald Pomper, "Classification of Presidential Elections," pp. 179-213; and Angus Campbell, "A Classification of the Presidential Elections," pp. 105-21.
5. V. O. Key, Jr., and Frank Munger, "Social Determinism and Electoral Decision: The Case of Indiana," in *American Voting Behavior,* pp. 281-99.
6. This state-level pattern masks, however, underlying swings between counties, as shown by David Knoke, "American Third Parties as Half-way Houses: The Case of Indiana," *Journal of Politics* (forthcoming), table A, figure A. At the state-level these swings may be a function of turnout shifts, and therefore the mobilization of new voters.
7. Donald E. Stokes, "Party Loyalty and the Likelihood of Deviating Elections," *Journal of Politics* 24 (1962): 689-702. See also Mark Stern, "Measuring Interparty Competition: A Proposal and a Test of a Method," *Journal of Politics* 39 (August 1972): 889-904, and David J. Elkins, "The Measurement of Party Competition," *American Political Science Review,* 68 (June 1974): 682-700.
8. The standard normal curve is a mathematical model with a mean of zero and a standard deviation of 1, where the area under the curve from the mean to either limit is 50 percent of the total area. Empirical, nonstandard, but roughly normal, distributions are fitted to the standard normal curve by a simple transformation, using the empirical standard deviation as a divisor in an equation that takes the difference between the empirical mean and the deviation from that mean which is of interest. The result is a standardized z-score and locates that point on the standard normal curve corresponding to the point of interest on the nonstandard one. The value of z is found by the formula:
$z = \dfrac{X_i - \overline{X}}{S}$, where, in this case,

Notes to Chapter Two

X_i is the equal division point between victory and defeat;
$\overline{X}$ is the mean for the majority party in the two-party division over a time-series of elections; and
S is the standard deviation of the time series
For Indiana, we have $z = \dfrac{50-51.39}{1.83} = -.759$. The area under the normal curve between the mean and -.759 of one standard deviation is .2760. Since half of the normal distribution is tabled, the probability that an election result would fall below the 50 percent Republican level is given by $.5000 - .2760 = .22$.

9. Burnham, "Theory and Voting Research," p. 1011. Competition is as much a function of the variance as of the mean of a distribution.

10. Kleppner, *The Cross of Culture*, pp. 316-38; Jensen, *Winning of the Midwest*, pp. 278-308.

11. Pennsylvania, Ohio, and Indiana each held October elections for state offices prior to the presidential contest in November and were watched as portents of the national results. See Roseboom, *A Short History*, pp. 97-102. Louis H. Bean, *How to Predict Elections* (New York: Knopf, 1948), was concerned to show how particular constituencies follow characteristic patterns.

12. Although Stanley B. Parsons studied the partisan division of Nebraska's vote, he took no notice of the sharp and steady erosion of Republican strength from 1880 through 1896. See his *The Populist Context*, pp. 60-75.

13. Laws governing eligibility to vote varied state by state and over time. John J. Stucker is making an inventory of this variation in order to provide an appropriate base for computing turnout and mobilization. I am indebted to him for these base figures. See Stucker and Rusk, "Legal-Institutional Factors and Voting Participation," pp. 3-9.

14. David Knoke found that Populist support was not related to the prior pattern of party cleavages across Indiana's counties but that its destination clearly favored the Democrats. These results fit a mobilization hypothesis. Knoke's analysis did not, however, take turnout or mobilization into account. See his "American Third Parties."

15. See Angus Campbell, "Surge and Decline: A Study of Electoral Change," *Public Opinion Quarterly* 24 (Fall 1960): 397-418; reprinted in Angus Campbell, Philip E. Converse, Warren E. Miller, and Donald E. Stokes, *Elections and the Political Order* (New York: John Wiley, 1966), pp. 40-62.

16. The Indiana Constitution of 1816, Article 6, Section 1, in Charles Kettleborough, *Constitution Making in Indiana: A Source Book of Constitutional Documents with Historical Introduction and Critical Notes* (Indianapolis: Indiana Historical Commission, 1916) 1:107.

17. The Indiana Constitution of 1851, Article 2, Section 2, in ibid., p. 304.

18. Cited in ibid., p. cvii.

Notes to Chapter Three

19. Ibid., pp. ciii-cxi.
20. Ibid., p. cxi.
21. Ibid., p. cxii.
22. Ibid. For continuing problems associated with the franchise, see Robert La Follette, "The Adoption of the Australian Ballot in Indiana," *Indiana Magazine of History* 24 (June 1928): 105-20.
23. Letter from T. H. Bringhurst, Special Agent, Post Office Department, Logansport, Indiana, to Honorable Daniel P. Pratt, U.S. Senate, Washington, D.C., January 11, 1874. Indiana State Historical Society letter file.
24. Clyde A. Malott, "The Physiography of Indiana," in *Handbook of Indiana Geology*, ed. by W. N. Logan et al. (Indianapolis: Department of Conservation, 1922), pp. 67-124.
25. Logan Esarey, *A History of Indiana from Its Exploration to 1850*, 2 vols. (Fort Wayne: The Hoosier Press, 1924), 1:230-51.
26. George Pence and Nellie C. Armstrong, *Indiana Boundaries: Territory, State, and County* (Indianapolis: Indiana Historical Bureau, 1922), pp. 28 ff.
27. Stephen S. Visher, "The Geography of Indiana," in *Handbook of Indiana Geology*, pp. 35-43; Pence and Armstrong, *Indiana Boundaries*, pp. 57-58.
28. Visher, "Geography of Indiana," p. 41; Thornbrough, *Indiana in the Civil War Era*, 3:322-36.
29. Pence and Armstrong, *Indiana Boundaries*, provide a map of each county, the date founded, and subsequent legislation affecting its boundaries.
30. Thornbrough, *Indiana in the Civil War Era*, 3:536 ff.
31. *The People's Guide* lists Indiana towns having more than 500 persons, pp. 121-24.
32. Knoke, "Third Parties," Table A, makes a similar observation for presidential elections.
33. Philip E. Converse, "Survey Research and the Decoding of Patterns in Ecological Data," *Quantitative Ecological Analysis in the Social Sciences*, ed. by Mattei Dogan and Stein Rokkan (Cambridge: M.I.T. Press, 1969), pp. 459-85.
34. Ibid., p. 475.
35. See Philip E. Converse, "The Concept of a Normal Vote," in Campbell et al., *Elections and the Political Order*, pp. 9-39.

CHAPTER THREE

1. A description of voting practice and ballot reform in Indiana has been given by La Follette, "The Adoption of the Australian Ballot in Indiana," pp. 114-20. Under early voting systems in other states, poll books, which recorded voters and their votes, were often kept. These sources are now widely scattered but may prove increasingly useful as comparative data. See, for example, Edward M. Cook, Jr., "Rhode

Notes to Chapter Three

Island Voters in an Era of Partisan Realignment, 1760-1800," and David Bohmer, "Participation and Partisanship in the First American Party System: The Case of Maryland" (papers presented at the American Historical Association meeting, San Francisco, 1973). John Rosett, Karen Janes, and James Chapin have each discovered sources of individual-level voting or registration data.

2. Volumes are known to exist for Bartholomew, Boone, Hamilton, Hendricks, Henry, Johnson, Marion, Montgomery, Morgan, and Vermillion Counties. Marion County (Indianapolis) was excluded from the analysis so that a rural population alone might be surveyed.

3. U.S. Bureau of the Census, *Supplemental Courses for Case Studies in Surveys and Censuses, Sampling Lectures.*

4. This example of the format used in the *People's Guide*s comes from the volume for Boone County, pp. 140-41.

5. Bates Harrington, *How 'Tis Done: A Thorough Ventilation of the Numerous Schemes Conducted by Wandering Canvassers Together with the Various Advertising Dodges for the Swindling of the Public* (Chicago, 1879). In Harrington's words, "By fair words, plausible argument, and careful playing upon the sympathies and pride of the victim, that agent has ... put his hand into the man's pocket and robbed him in spite of his inward protestations" (pp. 13-14).

6. Ibid., p. 36.

7. Ibid., p. 59.

8. For instance, the following entry occurs in the *Guide* for Johnson county: "Throckmorton, John: West of F. This man refused to give our agent any information concerning himself; so our patrons will have to be content with knowing that there is such a man, and that he lives somewhere W. of F. We only occasionally come in contact with such men, and, as it seems strange to most reasonable men, that anyone should refuse to have his name, date of birth, settlement, etc., placed before his neighbors, we can only give a few reasons why anyone should do so. A man in Crawfordsville, doing a large business in the sales of agricultural implements, utterly refused to give us his name, or any other knowledge concerning himself, because, as he said, 'we would make money out of it.' The science of physiogomy taught us that the real reason for his refusing were hid within his breast years ago. Some refuse from positive ignorance; some because of egotistical selfishness; and others from a morbid and spiteful hatred they have for all public enterprises."

9. Nineteenth-century censuses are described in Carroll D. Wright and William C. Hunt, *The History and Growth of the United States Census, Prepared for the Senate Committee on the Census* (Washington, D.C.: Government Printing Office, 1900). For the description of constitutional relations see p. 158.

10. A full description of this two-phase design is given in Appendix B.

11. Rigorously defined, bias denotes the difference between the ex-

pected value of a sample statistic and its "true" population value. Bias can refer to errors of estimation (the error of an estimator), of selection ("sampling error"), and of observation ("measurement error"). Our chief concern is with selection bias. See Leslie Kish, *Survey Sampling* (New York: John Wiley, 1967), pp. 13-14.

12. See ibid., pp. 440-46, for a description of two-phase sampling. See also Appendix B.

13. See William A. Belson, "Matching and Prediction on the Principle of Biological Classification," *Applied Statistics* 8 (June 1959): 65-75. I used the computer routine developed by John A. Sonquist and James N. Morgan, *The Detection of Interaction Effects,* monograph 35 (Ann Arbor: Institute for Social Research, 1964).

14. I wish to thank Roy Ekland, Timothy W. Sullivan, Tamara Tieman, and Julienne Wood, the authors of Appendix C, for this important work on measurement error, a subject to which those of us working with quantitative data often give too little attention. Their findings are widely applicable to nineteenth-century censuses and suggest the dire need for a systematic assessment of the censuses strictly in terms of the measurement error they contain.

15. The issue of nonresponse has been formulated for contemporary survey operations, but the terms of these operations do not correspond to situations faced by historians. As with measurement error, historians will have to face this issue themselves and develop their own strategies for dealing with it. See Kish, *Survey Sampling,* pp. 532-62.

16. Max Weber, "Class, Status, Party," *From Max Weber: Essays in Sociology,* trans. and ed. by H. H. Gerth and C. Wright Mills (New York: Oxford University Press, 1946), pp. 180-95.

17. George Belknap and Angus Campbell, "Political Party Identification and Attitudes toward Foreign Policy," *Public Opinion Quarterly* 15 (1951): 601-23; Charles Edward Merriam, *The American Party System* (New York: Macmillan, 1922), p. 31, and his table of partisanship, p. 383.

18. Campbell et al., *The American Voter,* p. 121.

19. Angus Campbell, Gerald Gurin, and Warren E. Miller, *The Voter Decides* (Evanston, Ill.: Row, Peterson, 1954), p. 88.

20. The question invariably arises about where those independent of the major parties should be placed on such a scale. Surely some are off the scale altogether, on some orthogonal dimension. This issue is related, in turn, to questions of alienation from the major party polarity as opposed to indifference toward it. Helpful insight may be gained from the formulation given by O. Davis, M. Hinich, and Peter Ordeshook, "An Expository Development of a Mathematical Model of the Electoral Process," *American Political Science Review* 64 (June 1970): 426-48.

21. The scale has been used in both five-point and seven-point versions. See Campbell et al., *American Voter,* p. 124 and p. 139.

22. A further expansion of the meaning of this ordering is contained in

Notes to Chapter Four

my "Indiana Farmers and the Group Basis of the Late Nineteenth Century Political Parties," *Journal of American History* 61 (June 1974): 96-100.

CHAPTER FOUR

1. Robert P. Sharkey, *Money, Class and Party: An Economic Study of Civil War and Reconstruction* (Baltimore: Johns Hopkins Press, 1966); Irwin Unger, *The Greenback Era: A Social and Political History of American Finance* (Princeton, N.J.: Princeton University Press, 1964).

2. Thornbrough, *Indiana in the Civil War Era*, 3:274-317; Esarey, *A History of Indiana*, 2:849-81.

3. William G. Carleton, "The Money Question in Indiana Politics," pp. 107-50; idem, "Why Was the Democratic Party in Indiana a Radical Party?" pp. 207-28.

4. Carleton, "Why Was the Democratic Party in Indiana a Radical Party?" pp. 208-9.

5. Ibid., pp. 224-25.

6. Ibid., p. 226.

7. County-level data for Indiana were supplied by the Inter-University Consortium for Political Research. ICPR bears no responsibility for the use of the data.

8. Data are drawn either from the census sample (3,318 voters) or the *Guide* sample (1,216 voters). See Chapter 3 and Appendix B.

9. Lorenz curves, the Gini Index of Inequality and the Equal-Share Coefficient are described in Hayward R. Alker, Jr., *Mathematics and Politics* (New York: Macmillan, 1965), pp. 29-42.

10. This Lorenz curve falls between one for Philadelphia (1860), which showed much greater inequality, and one for Hamilton, Ontario (1852), which showed less. See Stuart Blumin, "Mobility and Change in Ante-Bellum Philadelphia," p. 209, and Michael B. Katz, "Social Structure in Hamilton, Ontario," p. 212, both in *Nineteenth Century Cities: Essays in the New Urban History*, ed. by Stephan Thernstrom and Richard Sennett (New Haven: Yale University Press, 1969).

11. Milton M. Gordon, *Social Class in American Sociology* (New York: McGraw-Hill, 1963), p. 3.

12. Richard Centers, *The Psychology of Social Classes* (New York: Russell and Russell, 1961), pp. 21-27.

13. The highest stratum comprised members holding more than twice the mean amount of wealth; the next stratum were those with holdings between the mean and the double-share point; voters between the mean and the half-share point were the next stratum down; then those with less than half the mean amount; and finally, the nonpropertied class followed. For the idea of shares of wealth, see Alker, *Mathematics and Politics*, p. 39.

14. See Michael B. Katz, "Occupational Classification in History," *Journal of Interdisciplinary History* 2 (Summer 1973): 63-88.

15. On the use of occupation for stratification see Albert J. Reiss, Jr., *Occupations and Social Status* (New York: The Free Press, 1961); Otis Dudley Duncan, "Social Stratification and Mobility: Problems in the Measurement of Trend," in *Indicators of Social Change*, ed. by Eleanor B. Sheldon and Wilbert E. Moore (New York: Russell Sage, 1968), pp. 675-719.

16. As a variable, occupation is composed of a large number of discrete categories which, like any category system, may be combined in a very large number of ways. Further, two different reports of occupation are available, one from the 1870 census (on 3,318 voters) and one from the *People's Guide* (on the traced subset of 1,216 voters). This partial double report at two points in time raises several questions. First, as a logical matter a voter's occupation may change over the four-year interval separating these two sources. This means that occupation could not serve as a criterion for tracing the same person over time. Second, the partial double report creates the problem of distinguishing "real" change in occupation among the 1,216 traced voters from "nominal" change in the *terms* used to designate the same kind of work. An assessment of a voter's occupational status therefore depended, in part, on the assessment of the occupational labels found in the two sources and on a resolution of discrepancies that were purely nominal.

The strategy of establishing a single cutting-point follows Peter Blau and Otis Dudley Duncan, *The American Occupational Structure* (New York: John Wiley, 1967), pp. 119-21. In effect, the dispersion of values toward the upper tail of the personal wealth distribution, rather than each occupation's central tendency, is measured.

17. Distinctions between functional, rank-order, and occupational family classifications are considered by Katz, "Occupational Classification," pp. 65-67, and Reiss, *Occupations*, pp. 239-49; see also Richard J. Jensen, "The Religious and Occupational Roots of Party Identification: Illinois and Indiana in the 1870s," *Civil War History* 16 (December 1970): 325-43.

CHAPTER FIVE

1. The concept of party systems "freezing" along distinct lines of cleavage is drawn from Seymour Martin Lipset and Stein Rokkan, "Cleavage Structures, Party Systems and Voter Alignments: An Introduction," *Party Systems and Voter Alignments* (New York: The Free Press, 1967), pp. 1-64.

2. Benson, *The Concept of Jacksonian Democracy*, pp. ix-xi, 165-207. It is not altogether clear where Benson stands on the issue of polarization; he seems to suggest that party polarization was a function of ethnocultural differences at the local level but not beyond; see pp. 290-93.

Notes to Chapter Five

3. Kleppner, *The Cross of Culture,* p. 35.
4. Jensen, *The Winning of the Midwest,* p. 58.
5. Kleppner, *Cross of Culture,* p. 71.
6. Ibid., pp. 69-91; Jensen, *Winning of the Midwest,* pp. 58-88.
7. See Visher, "Distribution of Birthplaces," pp. 126-42; idem, "Indiana's Population, 1850-1940, Sources and Dispersal," *Indiana Magazine of History* 38 (1942): 51-59; and Maurice G. Baxter, "Encouragement of Immigration to the Middle West During the Era of the Civil War," *Indiana Magazine of History* 46 (1950): 25-38.
8. Thornbrough, *Indiana In the Civil War Era,* 3:536-55; Visher, "Distribution of Birthplaces," p. 130.
9. The act governing the census of 1850 applied as well in 1870, with the following instruction: "The facts relating to churches may generally be obtained with perfect accuracy from the pastor or clergyman having the same in charge; and, in case of his absence, application should be made to a warden, elder, or trustee." See Wright and Hunt, *The History and Growth of the United States Census,* p. 649.
10. These county-level indices were attempts to gauge the relative importance for each county of the kinds of religious groups that Kleppner and Jensen suggested as relatively pietistic or liturgical. See Kleppner, *Cross of Culture,* p. 70; Jensen, *Winning of the Midwest,* pp. 85-87. See also Formisano, *Birth of Mass Political Parties,* pp. 138-39.
11. On geographic mobility as a short-range step-function process, see Donald J. Bogue and Warren S. Thompson, "Migration and Distance," *American Sociological Review* 14 (April, 1949): 236-44. Also see James C. Malin, *The Grassland of North America: Prolegomena to Its History* (Gloucester, Mass.: Peter Smith, 1967), pp. 278-91.
12. Leaders of the Liberal Republican movement in 1872 received the label of "Mugwumps," denoting "independent influence among reasonable and intelligent voters," in Matthew Josephson, *The Politicos, 1865-1896* (New York: Harcourt, Brace and World, 1938), pp. 159-64, cf. p. 293. J. Rogers Hollingsworth, *The Whirligig of Politics: The Democracy of Cleveland and Bryan* (Chicago: University of Chicago Press, 1963) viewed "Mugwumps" as "bankers, businessmen, lawyers and newspapermen" and more generally as, "urbane, middle-class Protestants" (pp. 79-80). Richard Hofstadter, *The Age of Reform: From Bryan to FDR* (New York: Knopf, 1965), drew them as a distinct type fitted to his status-revolution thesis: "the old gentry, the merchants of long-standing, the small manufacturers, the established professional men, the civic leaders of an earlier era" (pp. 135-40).
13. "The classic 'independent voter' of high interest but low partisanship is a deviant case," was an early phrasing of this hypothesis in Bernard R. Berelson, Paul F. Lazarsfeld, William N. McPhee, *Voting: A Study of Opinion Formation in a Presidential Campaign* (Chicago: University of Chicago Press, 1966), p. 27. See also, Campbell et al., *The American Voter,* pp. 142-45. Robert E. Agger, "Independents and

Party Identifiers: Characteristics and Behavior in 1952," in *American Voting Behavior*, ed. by Burdick and Brodbeck, pp. 308-29, attempted to identify different kinds of independents. Also see Philip E. Converse, "The Nature of Belief Systems in Mass Publics," in *Ideology and Discontent*, ed. by David E. Apter (New York: The Free Press, 1964), pp. 206-61.

14. Carleton, "Why Was the Democratic Party in Indiana A Radical Party," p. 223; V. O. Key, Jr., and Frank Munger, "Social Determinism and Electoral Decision" in *American Voting Behavior*, ed. by Burdick and Brodbeck, p. 283; David Knoke, "American Third Parties."

15. It is always desirable to observe directly the voters of interest, but often this cannot be done because the information no longer exists or is difficult to come by. Voters, therefore, are often studied by the use of some other unit of observation, like the county, and observations that hold across counties are used to infer the behavior of individuals within them. These are instances of the general ecological problem where "the unit of observation is a set of which the unit of interest is a member" (Murray G. Murphey, *Our Knowledge of the Historical Past* [Indianapolis: Bobbs-Merrill, 1973], p. 157 ff).

16. Campbell et al., *The American Voter*, p. 270.

17. Kleppner, *Cross of Culture*, p. 70; Jensen, *Winning of the Midwest*, pp. 85-88; Jensen, "Religious and Occupational Roots of Party Identification," pp. 325-43. See also Formisano, *Birth of Mass Political Parties*, pp. 137-64, and his estimates of partisan distributions, p. 192.

18. Other than political data could be used to validate a pietistic-liturgical continuum, using explicit scaling techniques. For a suggestive approach, see Clyde Coombs, *Theory of Data* (New York: John Wiley, 1964), pp. 454-56.

19. These studies, together with Samuel Lubell, *The Future of American Politics* (New York: Harper, 1956) and V. O. Key's concept of a critical election have all combined to renew interest in the religious and ethnic bases of politics in America's electoral history. See, for example, John L. Shover, "The Emergence of a Two Party System in Republican Philadelphia, 1924-1936," *Journal of American History* 60 (March 1974): 985-1002; the evaluation of Robert P. Swierenga, "Computers and American History: The Impact of the 'New' Generation," *Journal of American History* 60 (March 1974): 1053-55; and David Knoke, "Religious Involvement and Political Behavior: A Log-linear Analysis of White Americans, 1952-1968," *The Sociological Quarterly* 15 (Winter 1974): 51-65.

20. It should be clear that these categories do not measure active involvement within associational groups. Nor do they measure "religious perspectives." See Gerhard Lenski, *The Religious Factor: A Sociological*

Notes to Chapter Six

Study of Religion's Impact on Politics, Economics and Family Life (Garden City, N.Y.: Doubleday, 1961), pp. 22-26.

CHAPTER SIX

1. Thornbrough, *Indiana in the Civil War Era,* 3:362-64; 394-403.
2. [James D. McCabe, Jr.] *History of the Grange Movement, or The Farmer's War against Monopolies,* by Edward Winslow Martin (Chicago: National Publishing Co., 1874), p. 450.
3. *Maps of Indiana Counties in 1876,* reprinted from *Illustrated Historical Atlas of the State of Indiana,* published by Baskin, Forster & Co., Chicago, 1876 (Indianapolis: Indiana Historical Society, 1968). Lowry Nelson, *The Mormon Village: A Pattern of Technique of Land Settlement* (Salt Lake City: University of Utah Press, 1952).
4. Paul Wallace Gates, "Land Policy and Tenancy in the Prairie Counties of Indiana," *Indiana Magazine of History* 35 (March 1939): 1-26; Thornbrough, *Indiana in the Civil War Era,* 3:366-69.
5. Fred A. Shannon, *The Farmer's Last Frontier, Agriculture 1860-1897,* vol. 5, *The Economic History of the United States* (New York: Harper and Row, 1968), pp. 309-48.
6. Ibid., pp. 3-4. McCabe urged an idealized view: "The American farmer is, as a rule, an intelligent, clear-headed, practical man. He is the possessor of, at least, a common school education. A reader of newspapers and a lover of books, he manages to keep himself abreast of the questions of the day, and has definite and intelligent opinions concerning them, which he is able to express vigorously when occasion demands. He is strong-armed as well as strong-minded ..." (*History of the Grange,* p. 286).
7. Thornbrough, *Indiana in the Civil War Era,* 3:396-97.
8. Ibid., pp. 394-96.
9. Ibid., p. 398; J. Wallace Darrow, *Origin and Early History of the Order of Patrons of Husbandry in the United States* (Chatham, N.Y., 1904).
10. Oliver Hudson Kelley, *Origin and Progress of the Order of Patrons of Husbandry in the United States; A History from 1866 to 1873* (Philadelphia: J. A. Wagenseller, 1875).
11. Thornbrough, *Indiana in the Civil War Era,* 3:398.
12. McCabe, *History of the Grange,* pp. 412-15.
13. Thornbrough, *Indiana in the Civil War Era,* 3:399.
14. Ibid., p. 285; 313-17; Carleton, "Money Question," pp. 117-19; Buck, *The Granger Movement,* pp. 80-82.
15. See pp. 58-59.
16. Carleton, "Money Question," pp. 118-24; 137-39; John D. Macall, "Ezra A. Olleman: The Forgotten Man of Greenbackism, 1873-1876," *Indiana Magazine of History,* 65 (September 1969): 173-96.

17. This turnout average was calculated using the off-year vote for secretary of state and the on-year vote for governor in order to minimize the effect of national offices.

18. Campbell, et al., *The American Voter*, pp. 402-40.

19. Ibid., p. 403.

20. Occupational data as well as descriptions of secret organizations, theological societies, and schools from the *People's Guide*s show this diversity township by township.

21. Thornbrough, *Indiana in the Civil War Era*, 3:672-90, discusses the role of newspapers within the intellectual, cultural, and social life of Indianians, a life which depended largely on the rural town structure.

22. See Hammarberg, "Indiana Farmers," pp. 91-115.

23. Sonquist and Morgan, *The Detection of Interaction Effects*. A futher discussion of the AID routine is given in Appendix B.

24. The social factors used as the predictor variables all have been considered as dichotomies. For instance, three levels of real estate wealth become two dichotomous variables by setting voters holding no real estate wealth against all others, and setting those with more than the mean against those with less than the mean. Similarly, four categories for region of birth are treated as dichotomies: the northern-born were set against all others, the Indiana-born against all others, the southern-born against all others, and the foreign-born against all others. Among the religious groups, all Baptists were grouped together, as were Methodists and Wesleyan Methodists. The United Brethren and Universalists were combined with other small denominational groups. And in the light of their similar Democratic norms, Lutherans and Roman Catholics were also grouped. Among occupations, the craft specialties and other occupations were combined, as were professionals and merchants. Finally, age groups were ended at the fifty-years-and-older mark. In total, then, thirty-four dichotomies, formed from the variables developed previously, were used as predictors in the Automatic Interaction Detection multiple correlation routine.

25. The tactic represents a simple extension to three ordered categories of standard recoding for dichotomies and assumes not only that the categories are ordered but also that the distances between categories are equal.

CHAPTER SEVEN

1. Letter from the Marion County Republican Central Committee, November 1, 1876, in the pamphlet file of political material, Indiana State Historical Society.

2. See Thomas C. Cochran, "The Presidential Synthesis in American History," *American Historical Review* 53 (July 1948): 748-59.

3. As an alternative model to that offered in the text, I have also included a second one in Appendix A. These two approaches represent

different, but complementary, mathematical attacks on the continuity and disruption of election-to-election voter dynamics.

4. Converse, "Concept of a Normal Vote," pp. 9–39.

5. Ibid., p. 12.

6. Ibid., p. 15.

7. Ibid., pp. 16-18; 21-23. An election-by-election background for these observations is Campbell, "Surge and Decline: A Study of Electoral Change," pp. 40-62.

8. Converse, "Concept of a Normal Vote" pp. 19-21.

9. Ibid., p. 19 and the methodological note, pp. 34-39, for the specific modifications.

10. Philip E. Converse, "Information Flow and the Stability of Partisan Attitudes," in Campbell et al., *Elections and the Political Order,* pp. 136-57.

11. Ibid., pp. 148-57, for suggestive insights with respect to past levels of political information and involvement.

12. On the flow of information in a mass electorate, see Converse, "The Nature of Belief Systems in Mass Publics," pp. 206-61. With respect to the low level of constraint between basic political orientations and issue perceptions see Donald D. Searing, Joel J. Schwartz, and Alden E. Lind, "The Structuring Principle: Political Socialization and Belief Systems," *American Political Science Review* 67 (June 1973): 415-32.

13. Harvey M. Kabaker, "Estimating the Normal Vote in Congressional Elections," *Midwest Journal of Political Science* (February 1969), pp. 58-83; Nancy H. Zingale, Technical Note in "Partisan Realignment: A Systematic Perspective," by Walter Dean Burnham, Jerome M. Clubb, and William H. Flanigan (paper presented at the Conference on Popular Voting Behavior, Cornell University, June, 1973), pp. 43-46; E. F. Cox, "The Measurement of Party Strength," *Western Political Quarterly* 13 (1960): 1022-42.

14. For example, the normal vote estimator for each county, prior to the 1870 congressional races in Indiana, was constructed as the mean percent Republican (or Democratic) taken over the two off-year congressional races of 1862 and 1866 and the two gubernatorial races of 1864 and 1868. Prior to the 1872 elections, the normal vote estimator for each county was recalculated over the gubernatorial elections of 1864 and 1868 and the off-year congressional election of 1866 and the off-year election for secretary of state in 1870.

15. Key and Munger, "Social Determinism and Electoral Decision" p. 283; David Knoke, "American Third Parties as Half-Way Houses."

16. Considerable care must be exercised to understand what kind of "change" is being measured. What Butler and Stokes termed "straight conversion" in their discussion of British politics is a function of total "swing" rather than of defection from party allegiance as defined here.

Notes to Appendix A

See David Butler and Donald E. Stokes, *Political Change in Britain* (New York: St. Martin's Press, 1971), pp. 152-65. Similarly, in arguing for the role of issues in provoking voting change, V. O. Key, Jr., *The Responsible Electorate* (Cambridge, Mass.: Harvard University Press, 1966), examined specifically only those citizens who changed their vote between elections, rather than the electorate as a whole.

17. Robert A. Gordon, "Issues of Multiple Regression," *American Journal of Sociology* 73 (March 1968): 592-616. When variables are highly colinear, regression coefficients will be unstable because variation attributed to them jointly is not uniquely attributed to either one.

18. Among the eight selected measures of composition, the average value of farms serves as one index of relative county wealth among the intercorrelated set of such measures. Similarly, the percentage of the rural also indexed (inversely) the extent of manufacturing and population density (or urbanism). The percentage born in Indiana and the percentage born in the border-south each stood inversely to the percentage of northern-born and were themselves positively related ($r = .59$) at a level where one of them might well have been excluded. The ratio of Germans to the foreign-born was inverse to the Irish-born ratio, just as the percentage of pietistic church organizations was inverse to the percentage of liturgical ones. Finally, the percentage of seats in churches (to the total population) was included. These eight factors of social composition, while not fully mutually independent, were the least intercorrelated among all measures.

19. Precisely the same result is obtained by expressing all variables in unit normal form, in which case the intercept term, a, in the regression equation, $Y = a + bx + e$, goes to zero.

20. O. B. Carmichael, "The Campaign of 1876 in Indiana," *Indiana Magazine of History* 9 (December 1913): 276-97; Carleton, "Money Question," pp. 126-34, 142-44.

21. Converse, "Information Flow," p. 144.

22. Carleton, "Why Was the Democratic Party in Indiana a Radical Party?" pp. 207-28; Thornbrough, *Indiana in the Civil War Era*, 3:313-17.

Appendix A

1. The model follows Donald E. Stokes, "Cross-level Inference as a Game against Nature," in *Mathematical Applications in Political Science*, vol. 4, ed. Joseph L. Bernd (Charlottesville: University of Virginia Press, 1969), pp. 62-83.

2. W. S. Robinson, "Ecological Correlation and the Behavior of Individuals," *American Sociological Review* 15 (1950): 351-57.

3. Leo A. Goodman, "Ecological Regression and the Behavior of Individuals," *American Sociological Review* 18 (1953): 663-64; idem, "Some Alternatives to Ecological Correlation," *American Journal of*

Notes to Appendix B

Sociology 64 (1959): 610-25. The literature on ecological regression is now extensive. For a review, see Murphey, *Our Knowledge of the Historical Past*, pp. 156-69.

4. Stokes, "Cross-level Inference," pp. 70-73.

APPENDIX B

1. Basic studies which have faced this problem include Merle Curti *The Making of an American Community: A Case Study of Democracy in a Frontier County* (Stanford, Calif.: Stanford University Press, 1959) and Stephan Thernstrom, *Poverty and Progress: Social Mobility in a Nineteenth Century City* (Cambridge: Harvard University Press, 1964). Recent work can be surveyed in *Nineteenth Century Cities*, Stephan Thernstrom and Richard Sennett, eds. (New Haven: Yale University Press, 1969).

2. Record linkage techniques are becoming standardized in both a clerical and computer mode. See Ian Winchester, "The Linkage of Historical Records by Man and Computer: Techniques and Problems," *Journal of Interdisciplinary History,* 1 (Autumn 1970): 107-24.

3. An important article, germane to the present discussion, is James K. Kindahl, "Estimation of Means and Totals from Finite Populations of Unknown Size," *Journal of the American Statistical Association* 57 (March 1962): 61-91. See Melvyn A. Hammarberg, "The Indiana Voter: A Study of Nineteenth Century Rural Bases of Partisanship" (Ph.D. dissertation, University of Pennsylvania, 1970).

4. The underenumeration of the 1870 Census is reported in U. S. Bureau of the Census, *Comparative Occupation Statistics for the United States, 1870-1940*, by Alba M. Edwards (Washington, D. C.: Government Printing Office, 1943), p. 141. On the study of census coverage see Morris H. Hansen, William N. Hurwitz, and Leon Pritzer, "The Accuracy of Census Results," *American Sociological Review* 18 (August 1953): 416-23, and Peter Knights, "A Method for Estimating Census Under-Enumeration," *Historical Methods Newsletter* (December 1969): 5-8. The extensive geographic mobility of individuals out of a given areal unit can be readily noted in Thernstrom, *Poverty and Progress*, pp. 84-90, and Curti, *Making of an American Community*, pp. 65-76.

5. A description of the content, definitions, and instructions for nineteenth-century U.S. Censuses can be obtained in C. D. Wright and W. H. Hunt, *History and Growth of the U.S. Census*. For that of 1870, see pp. 51-58, 154-59.

6. The actual tracing procedure was accomplished completely by hand. For a discussion of tracing criteria and the use of computing techniques to carry out such tracing, see Winchester, "The Linkage of Historical Records."

7. Johan Galtung, *Theory and Methods of Social Research* (New

Notes to Appendix B

York: Columbia University Press, 1964), p. 51. Galtung's volume appears particularly useful for its discussion of social as opposed to psychological measurement problems. In data collection, its use of the data matrix concept seems especially useful.

8. Kish, *Survey Sampling*, p. 4. While hardly a beginning text, Kish provides a lively and practical approach to the more esoteric sampling lore. Along with Kish I also relied on William G. Cochran, *Sampling Techniques* (New York: Wiley, 1963). For a nonmathematical treatment of the major concepts employed in sampling, see Morris J. Slonim, *Sampling in a Nutshell* (New York: Simon and Schuster, 1960).

9. Kish, *Survey Sampling*, p. 440, followed by his discussion of multiphase sampling.

10. Cochran, *Sampling Techniques*, pp. 355-59 provides the discussion of bias from which these expressions were obtained. Bias is also discussed by Kish, *Survey Sampling*, especially on pp. 11-13 and pp. 566-71.

11. For a description of this program consult John A. Sonquist and James N. Morgan, *The Detection of Interaction Effects*. Sonquist and Morgan developed this program at the Survey Research Center, University of Michigan, while the particular version I have employed is a revision into Fortran IV by Eli Marks of the Wharton School, University of Pennsylvania.

12. A discussion of the correlation ratio (Eta^2) as a measure of association may be obtained in Hubert M. Blalock, *Social Statistics* (New York: McGraw-Hill, 1960), pp. 266-67.

13. See Belson, "Matching and Prediction on the Principle of Biological Classification," pp. 65-75. Belson's work in this regard appears parallel to that of Sonquist and Morgan, but does not employ the vigorous variance-accounting scheme. The diagram is drawn from Belson's article, p. 69.

14. The second phase normally assumes a second random draw from among the members of each stratum defined on the basis of information obtained in the first phase, a condition which cannot be met here. Further, if all of the bias were accounted for by the AID procedure the result would be final groups (strata) containing either all traced members (all '1's) or all untraced members (all '0's), which would require the redefinition of the sampled population rather than a reweighting of the sampled members.

15. See Kish, *Survey Sampling*, pp. 445-46, under complex two-phase selections for these formulas.

16. The use of the chi-square test for goodness of fit is readily discussed and illustrated in Robert S. Weiss, *Statistics in Social Research* (New York: Wiley, 1968) pp. 256-65. In these tests on the present data all of the variables used come originally from the census so that classification error between the two lists is not at issue.

Notes to Appendix C

APPENDIX C
1. For definitions and a more complete discussion of measurement error, see Kish, *Survey Sampling,* pp. 509-27.
2. An excellent description of one large historical data-collection project is Theodore Hershberg, "The Philadelphia Social History Project" (Ph.D. dissertation, Stanford University, 1973).
3. These data are available from the Inter-University Consortium for Political Research and are based on Melvyn Hammarberg, "The Indiana Voter."
4. Fifty-three percent of the discrepancies showed a difference of no more than two years, while a three-year interval accounted for 69.4 percent. Twenty-one cases (9.8 percent) resulted from heaping, the tendency of reports of age to cluster more heavily than expected at ages ending in zero or five. Missing data on age reduced the number of cases used in all calculations to 1,184.
5. We used a difference of means test with a pooled estimate of the standard deviation. Because the direction of bias was not predicted, we used a two-tailed test. The equation for the t-test is:

$$t = \frac{\bar{X}_1 - \bar{X}_2}{s_{\bar{X}_1 - \bar{X}_2}},$$

where

$$s_{\bar{X}_1 - \bar{X}_2} = \sqrt{\frac{s_1^2}{N_1} + \frac{s_2^2}{N_2}}.$$

(Adapted from Hubert M. Blalock, Jr., *Social Statistics,* 2d. ed. [McGraw-Hill, 1972], p. 224.)

6. See J. Morgan Kousser, "Ecological Regression and the Analysis of Past Politics, *Journal of Interdisciplinary History* 4 (1973)."
7. See Appendix B above.
8. Weighting the total wealth variable decreased its total chi-square value. Because total wealth was an additive function of real and personal wealth, weighting may have brought the observed cell chi-square values closer to the expected cell frequencies.

Bibliography

Agger, Robert E. "Independents and Party Identifiers: Characteristics and Behavior in 1952." In *American Voting Behavior,* ed. by Eugene Burdick and Arthur J. Brodbeck. Glencoe, Ill.: The Free Press, 1959.

Alker, Hayward R., Jr. *Mathematics and Politics.* New York: Macmillan, 1965.

Baxter, Maurice G. "Encouragement of Immigration to the Middle West During the Era of the Civil War." *Indiana Magazine of History* 46 (1950): 25-38.

Bean, Louis H. *How To Predict Elections,* New York: Knopf, 1948.

Belknap, George, and Angus Campbell. "Political Party Identification and Attitudes Toward Foreign Policy." *Public Opinion Quarterly* 15 (1951): 601-23.

Belson, William A. "Matching and Prediction on the Principle of Biological Classification." *Applied Statistics* 8 (June 1959): 65-75.

Benson, Lee. "An Approach to the Scientific Study of Past Public Opinion." *Public Opinion Quarterly* 21 (Winter 1967-68): 522-67.

——. *The Concept of Jacksonian Democracy: New York As a Test Case.* New York: Atheneum, 1966.

Berelson, Bernard R.; Paul F. Lazarsfeld; and William N. McPhee. *Voting: A Study of Opinion Formation in a Presidential Campaign,* Chicago: University of Chicago Press, 1966.

Blau, Peter, and Otis Dudley Duncan. *The American Occupational Structure.* New York: John Wiley, 1967.

Blumin, Stuart. "Mobility and Change in Ante-Bellum Philadelphia." In *Nineteenth Century Cities: Essays in the New Urban History,* ed. by Stephan Thernstrom and Richard Sennett. New Haven: Yale University Press, 1969.

Bibliography

Bogue, Allan G. *Money at Interest: The Farm Mortgage on the Middle Border.* Lincoln: University of Nebraska Press, 1969.

———. "United States: The 'New' Political History." *Journal of Contemporary History* 3 (January 1968): 5-27.

Bogue, Donald J., and Warren S. Thompson. "Migration and Distance." *American Sociological Review* 14 (April 1949): 236-44.

Bringhurst, T. H. Special Agent, Post Office Department, Logansport, Indiana. Letter to Honorable Daniel P. Pratt, U.S. Senate, Washington, D.C., January 11, 1874. Indiana State Historical Society Letter File.

Buck, Solon Justus. *The Granger Movement: A Study of Agricultural Organization and Its Political, Economic, and Social Manifestations, 1870-1880.* Cambridge: Harvard University Press, 1913.

Burnham, W. Dean. "The Changing Shape of the American Political Universe." *American Political Science Review* 59 (March 1965): 7-22.

———. *Critical Elections and the Mainsprings of American Politics.* New York: W. W. Norton, 1970.

———. "Theory and Voting Research: Some Reflections on Converse's 'Change in the American Electorate'." *American Political Science Review* 68 (September 1974): 1002-1023.

Butler, David, and Donald E. Stokes. *Political Change in Britain.* New York: St. Martin's, college edition, 1971.

Campbell, Angus. "A Classification of the Presidential Elections." Reprinted in *Electoral Change and Stability in American Political History,* ed. by Jerome M. Clubb and Howard W. Allen. New York: The Free Press, 1971.

———. "Surge and Decline: A Study of Electoral Change." *Public Opinion Quarterly* 24 (Fall 1960): 397-418. Reprinted in Campbell, Angus; Philip E. Converse; Warren E. Miller; Donald E. Stokes, *Elections and the Political Order.* New York: John Wiley, 1967.

———, Philip E. Converse; Warren E. Miller; and Donald E. Stokes. *The American Voter.* Reprint. Chicago: University of Chicago Press, 1977.

———, Gerald Gurin, and Warren E. Miller. *The Voter Decides.* Evanston, Ill.: Row, Peterson, 1954.

Carleton, William G. "The Money Question in Indiana Politics, 1865-1890." *Indiana Magazine of History* 42 (June 1946): 107-50.

———. "Why Was the Democratic Party in Indiana a Radical Party, 1865-1890?" *Indiana Magazine of History* 42 (September 1946): 207-28.

Carmichael, O. B. "The Campaign of 1876 in Indiana." *Indiana Magazine of History* 9 (December 1913): 276-97.

Centers, Richard. *The Psychology of Social Classes.* New York: Russell and Russell, 1961.

Cline and McHaffie. *The People's Guide: A Business, Political and*

Bibliography

Religious Directory, Indianapolis, 1874. Separate volumes were published for the following counties: Bartholomew, Boone, Hamilton, Hendricks, Henry, Johnson, Montgomery, Morgan, Vermillion.

Cochran, Thomas C. "The Presidential Synthesis in American History." *American Historical Review* 53 (July 1948): 748-59.

Converse, Philip E. "Change in the American Electorate." In *The Human Meaning of Social Change,* ed. by Angus Campbell and Philip E. Converse. New York: Russell Sage, 1972, pp. 263-337.

———. "The Concept of a Normal Vote." In Angus Campbell et al., *Elections and the Political Order.* New York: John Wiley, 1966, pp. 9-39.

———. "Information Flow and the Stability of Partisan Attitudes." In Angus Campbell et al., *Elections and the Political Order.* New York: John Wiley, 1966, pp. 136-60.

———. "The Nature of Belief Systems in Mass Publics." In *Ideology and Discontent,* ed. by David E. Apter. New York: The Free Press, 1964, pp. 206-56.

———. "Survey Research and the Decoding of Patterns in Ecological Data." In *Quantitative Ecological Analysis in the Social Sciences,* ed. by Mattei Dogan and Stein Rokkan. Cambridge: M.I.T. Press, 1969, pp. 459-85.

Coombs, Clyde. *Theory of Data.* New York: John Wiley, 1964.

Cox, E. F. "The Measurement of Party Strength." *Western Political Quarterly* 13 (1960): 1022-42.

Darrow, J. Wallace. *Origin and Early History of the Order of Patrons of Husbandry in the United States.* Chatham, New York, 1904.

Davis, Otto A.; Melvin J. Hinich; Peter C. Ordeshook. "An Expository Development of a Mathematical Model of the Electoral Process." *American Political Science Review* 64 (June 1970): 426-48.

Duncan, Otis Dudley. "Social Stratification and Mobility: Problems in the Measurement of Trend." *Indicators of Social Change,* ed. by Eleanor B. Sheldon and Wilbert E. Moore. New York: Russell Sage, 1968.

Elkins, David J. "The Measurement of Party Competition." *American Political Science Review* 68 (June 1974): 682-700.

Esarey, Logan. *A History of Indiana from its Exploration to 1850.* 2 vols. Fort Wayne: The Hoosier Press, 1924.

Formisano, Ronald P. *The Birth of Mass Political Parties: Michigan, 1827-1861.* Princeton: Princeton University Press, 1971.

Gates, Paul Wallace. "Land Policy and Tenancy in the Prairie Counties of Indiana." *Indiana Magazine of History* 35 (March 1939): 1-26.

Goodman, Leo A. "Ecological Regression and the Behavior of Individuals." *American Sociological Review* 18 (1953): 663-64.

———. "Some Alternatives to Ecological Correlation." *American Journal of Sociology* 64 (1959): 610-25.

Bibliography

Gordon, Milton M. *Social Class in American Sociology.* New York: McGraw-Hill, 1963.

Gordon, Robert A. "Issues of Multiple Regression." *American Journal of Sociology* 73 (March 1968): 592-616.

Hammarberg, Melvyn. "Designing A Sample from Incomplete Historical Lists." *American Quarterly* 23 (1971): 542-61.

———. "Indiana Farmers and the Group Basis of the Late Nineteenth-Century Political Parties." *Journal of American History* 61 (June 1974): 91-115.

———. "The Indiana Voter: A Study in Nineteenth Century Rural Bases of Partisanship." Ph.D. dissertation, University of Pennsylvania, 1970.

Harrington, Bates. *How 'Tis done: A Thorough Ventilation of the Numerous Schemes Conducted by Wandering Canvassers Together with the Various Advertising Dodges for the Swindling of the Public.* Chicago, 1879.

Harris, Joseph P. *Registration of Voters in the United States.* Washington, D.C.: Brookings Institution, 1929.

Haynes, Fred E. *Third Party Movements Since the Civil War.* Iowa City: State Historical Society, 1916.

Hays, Samuel P. "Political Parties and the Community-Society Continuum." In *American Party Systems,* ed. by William Nisbet Chambers and Walter Dean Burnham. New York: Oxford University Press, 1967, pp. 152-81.

———. "The Social Analysis of American Political History, 1880-1920." *Political Science Quarterly* 80 (1965): 373-94.

Hershberg, Theodore. "The Philadelphia Social History Project." Ph.D. dissertation, Stanford University, 1973.

Hicks, John D. *The Populist Revolt.* Minneapolis: University of Minnesota Press, 1931.

Hofstadter, Richard, *The Age of Reform: From Bryan to FDR.* New York: Knopf, 1965.

Hollingsworth, J. Rogers. *The Whirligig of Politics: The Democracy of Cleveland and Bryan.* Chicago: University of Chicago Press, 1963.

Jensen, Richard J. "The Religious and Occupational Roots of Party Identification: Illinois and Indiana in the 1870s." *Civil War History* 16 (December 1970): 325-43.

———. *The Winning of the Midwest: Social and Political Conflict, 1888-96.* Chicago: University of Chicago Press, 1971.

Josephson, Matthew. *The Politicos, 1865-1896.* New York: Harcourt, Brace and World, 1938.

Kabaker, Harvey M. "Estimating the Normal Vote in Congressional Elections." *Midwest Journal of Political Science,* February 1969, pp. 58-83.

Katz, Michael B. "Occupational Classification in History." *Journal of Interdisciplinary History* 2 (Summer 1973): 63-88.

Bibliography

———. "Social Structure in Hamilton, Ontario." In *Nineteenth Century Cities: Essays in the New Urban History,* ed. by Stephen Thernstrom and Richard Sennett. New Haven: Yale University Press, 1969.

Kelley, Oliver Hudson. *Origin and Progress of the Order of Patrons of Husbandry in the United States; A History from 1866 to 1873.* Philadelphia: J. A. Wagenseller, 1875.

Kettleborough, Charles. *Constitution Making in Indiana: A Source Book of Constitutional Documents with Historical Introduction and Critical Notes.* Vol. I. Indianapolis: Indiana Historical Commission, 1916.

Key, V. O., Jr. *The Responsible Electorate.* Cambridge, Mass.: Harvard University Press, 1966.

———. "A Theory of Critical Elections." *Journal of Politics* 17 (February 1955): 3-18. Reprinted in *Electoral Change and Stability in American Political History,* ed. by Jerome M. Clubb and Howard W. Allen. New York: The Free Press, 1971, pp. 26-44.

———, and Frank Munger. "Social Determinism and Electoral Decision: The Case of Indiana." *American Voting Behavior,* ed. by Eugene Burdick and Arthur J. Brodbeck. Glencoe, Ill.: The Free Press, 1959.

Kish, Leslie, *Survey Sampling.* New York: John Wiley, 1967.

Kleppner, Paul. *The Cross of Culture: Social Analysis of Midwestern Politics, 1850-1900.* New York: The Free Press, 1970.

Knoke, David. "American Third Parties as Half-way Houses: The Case of Indiana." *Journal of Politics* (forthcoming).

———. "Religious Involvement and Political Behavior: A Log-linear Analysis of White Americans, 1952-1968." *The Sociological Quarterly* 15 (Winter 1974): 51-65.

Kousser, J. Morgan. "Ecological Regression and the Analysis of Past Politics." *Journal of Interdisciplinary History* 4 (1973).

LaFollette, Robert. "The Adoption of the Australian Ballot in Indiana." *Indiana Magazine of History* 24 (June 1928): 105-20.

Lenski, Gerhard. *The Religious Factor: A Sociological Study of Religion's Impact on Politics, Economics, and Family Life.* Garden City, N.Y.: Doubleday, 1961.

Lipset, Seymour Martin, and Stein Rokkan. *Party Systems and Voter Alignments,* New York: The Free Press, 1967.

Lubell, Samuel. *The Future of American Politics.* New York, 1956.

Luebke, Frederick C. *Immigrants and Politics: The Germans of Nebraska, 1880-1900.* Lincoln: University of Nebraska Press, 1969.

Macall, John D. "Ezra A. Olleman: The Forgotten Man of Greenbackism, 1873-1876." *Indiana Magazine of History* 65 (September 1969): 173-96.

Malin, James C. *The Grassland of North America: Prolegomena to Its History.* Gloucester, Mass.: Peter Smith, 1967.

Malott, Clyde A. "The Physiography of Indiana." In *Handbook of*

Bibliography

Indiana Geology, W. N. Logan et al. Indianapolis Department of Conservation, 1922, pp. 67-124.

Maps of Indiana Counties in 1876. Indianapolis: Indiana Historical Society, 1968. Reprinted from *Illustrated Historical Atlas of the State of Indiana.* Chicago: Baskin, Forster and Co., 1876.

[McCabe, James D., Jr.] *History of the Grange, or the Farmer's War Against Monopolies* by Edward Winslow Martin. Chicago: National Publishing Co., 1874.

McSeveney, Samuel T. *The Politics of Depression: Political Behavior in the Northeast, 1893-1896.* New York: Oxford University Press, 1972.

Merriam, Charles Edward. *The American Party System.* New York: Macmillan, 1922.

Murphey, Murray G. *Our Knowledge of the Historical Past.* Indianapolis: Bobbs-Merrill, 1973.

Nelson, Lowry, *The Mormon Village: A Pattern and Technique of Land Settlement.* Salt Lake City: University of Utah Press, 1952.

Parsons, Stanley B. *The Populist Context: Rural versus Urban Power on a Great Plains Frontier.* Westport, Conn.: Greenwood Press, 1973.

Pence, George, and Nellie C. Armstrong. *Indiana Boundaries: Territory, State, and County.* Indianapolis: Indiana Historical Bureau, 1922.

Petersen, Svend. *A Statistical History of the American Presidential Elections.* New York: Frederick Ungar, 1968.

Pomper, Gerald. "Classification of Presidential Elections." Reprinted in *Electoral Change and Stability in American Political History,* ed. by Jerome M. Clubb and Howard W. Allen. New York: The Free Press, 1971.

Reiss, Albert J., Jr. *Occupations and Social Status.* New York: The Free Press of Glencoe, 1961.

Robinson, W. S. "Ecological Correlation and the Behavior of Individuals." *American Sociological Review* 11 (1950): 351-57.

Roseboom, Eugene H. *A Short History of Presidential Elections.* New York: Macmillan, 1967.

Rossi, Peter H. "Four Landmarks of Voting Research." In *American Voting Behavior,* ed. by Eugene Burdick and Arthur J. Brodbeck. Glencoe, Ill.: The Free Press, 1959, pp. 5-54.

Rusk, Jerrold G. "The Effect of the Australian Ballot Reform on Split-Ticket Voting, 1876-1908." *American Political Science Review* 64 (December 1970): 1220-38.

Searing, Donald D.; Joel J. Schwarts; and Alden E. Lind. "The Structuring Principle: Political Socialization and Belief Systems." *American Political Science Review* 67 (June 1973): 415-32.

Sellers, Charles. "The Equilibrium Cycle in Two-Party Politics." Reprinted in *Electoral Change and Stability in American Political*

Bibliography

History, ed. by Jerome M. Clubb and Howard W. Allen. New York: The Free Press, 1971, pp. 149-77.
Shannon, Fred A. *The Farmer's Last Frontier; Agriculture 1860-1897*. Vol. 5, *The Economic History of the United States*. New York: Harper and Row, 1968.
Sharkey, Robert P. *Money, Class and Party: An Economic Study of Civil War and Reconstruction*. Baltimore: Johns Hopkins Press, 1966.
Shover, John L. "The Emergence of a Two-Party System in Republican Philadelphia, 1924-1936." *Journal of American History* 60 (March 1974): 985-1002.
Sonquist, John A., and James N. Morgan. *The Detection of Interaction Effects*, monograph 35. Ann Arbor: Institute for Social Research, 1964.
Stern, Mark. "Measuring Interparty Competition: A Proposal and a Test of a Method." *Journal of Politics* 39 (August 1972): 889-904.
Stokes, Donald E. "Cross-Level Inference as a Game against Nature." In *Mathematical Applications in Political Science*, vol. 4, ed. by Joseph L. Bernd. Charlottesville: University of Virginia Press, 1969, pp. 62-83.
———. "Party Loyalty and the Likelihood of Deviating Elections." *Journal of Politics* 24 (1962): 689-702.
Stucker, John J., and Jerrold G. Rusk. "Legal-Institutional Factors and Voting Participation: An Historical Analysis." Paper delivered at the Midwest Political Science Association Meeting, Chicago, 1973.
Swierenga, Robert P. "Computers and American History: The Impact of the 'New' Generation." *Journal of American History* 60 (March 1974): 1053-55.
———. "Ethnocultural Political Analysis: A New Approach to American Ethnic Studies." *Journal of American Studies* 5 (April 1971): 66-79.
Thornbrough, Emma Lou. *Indiana in the Civil War Era, 1850-1880*. Vol. 3, *The History of Indiana*. Indianapolis: Indiana Historical Bureau and Indiana Historical Society, 1965.
Unger, Irwin. *The Greenback Era: A Social and Political History of American Finance*. Princeton: Princeton University Press, 1964.
United States Bureau of the Census, *Supplemental Courses for Case Studies in Surveys and Censuses, Sampling Lectures*, ISP Supplemental Course Series, no. 1. Washington, D.C.: Government Printing Office, 1968.
United States Census Office. *9th Census, 1870. Population Schedules*. National Archives Film, roll nos. 299, 300, 319, 322, 323, 330, 345, 346, 365.
———. *9th Census, 1870, Statistics*. 3 vols. Washington, D.C.: Government Printing Office, 1872.

Bibliography

———. *10th Census, 1880 Statistics of Population*, vol. 1. *Manufactures*, vol. 2. *Productions of Agriculture*, vol. 3. Washington, D.C.: Government Printing Office, 1883.

Visher, Stephen S. "Distribution of Birthplaces of Indianians in 1870." *Indiana Magazine of History* 26 (1930) 126-42.

———. "Indiana's Population, 1850-1940, Sources and Dispersal." *Indiana Magazine of History* 38 (1942): 51-59.

———. "The Geography of Indiana." In *Handbook of Indiana Geology*, by W. N. Logan et al. Indianapolis: Department of Conservation, 1922.

Weber, Max. "Class, Status, Party." In *From Max Weber: Essays in Sociology*, tr. and ed. by H. H. Gerth and C. Wright Mills. New York: Oxford University Press, 1946.

Wright, Carroll D., and William C. Hunt. *The History and Growth of the United States Census, Prepared for the Senate Committee on the Census*. Washington, D.C.: Government Printing Office, 1900.

Zingale, Nancy H. "Technical Note." In "Partisan Realignment: A Systematic Perspective," by Walter Dean Burnham, Jerome M. Clubb, and William H. Flanigan. Paper presented at the Conference on Popular Voting Behavior, Cornell University, June 1973.

Index

Adams, Justus C., 142
Age, 14, 34, 55, 56, 73, 130-31, 177, 207-8, 211-17
Allegiance, party. *See* Party allegiance
American Voter, The, 11
Andreas, Captain A. T., 53-54
Australian ballot, 15, 35
A.I.D. (Automatic Interaction Detection), 134-35, 161, 200-202, 209

Balance of power, 82-83, 88-89, 112, 115, 127-38, 140
Baptist, 97, 107, 136
Belson, William, 202
Benson, Lee, 8, 9, 91
Bias, 55-57, 71, 101, 121, 124, 157, 159, 183, 193-204; goodness of fit tests for, 204-17
British, 207
Buck, Solon, 5-8
Burnham, W. Dean, 12-15, 24

Campbell, Angus, 59
Carleton, William G., 10, 63-64, 71, 82, 88-89, 161, 177
Catholic, Roman, 1, 10, 97, 108-11, 115-16, 136, 161
Census, federal: manuscript returns, 2-3, 55, 75, 97, 193-209, 211-17, 225n9, 235n5
Centers, Richard, 74
Christian (Disciples of Christ), 107
Civil War, 3, 6, 18, 23, 35, 60, 62, 90
Class(es), social: consciousness of, 5-8, 17, 74, 91, 175 (*see also* Status; Wealth); definition of, 73-75
Cleavage, 1, 3, 8, 10-11, 17, 76, 90, 101, 107, 112, 118, 170, 177, 223n14, 228n1. *See also* Polarization
Cline and McHaffie, 52-54, 56, 219n1
Colored Farmers' Alliance, 7
Competition, party, 3, 18-27, 31-32, 35-36; levels of, 19, 23-24, 31-32, 41-42, 46, 50, 142-43; measurement of, 20-24, 41, 223n9. *See also* Partisanship

Index

Congress, 36
Constitution, state, 33-34
Converse, Philip, 14-15, 144-45, 147-48, 154, 173
Cooke, Jay, and Co., 63
Counties: measures of social composition among, 64-73, 92-101, 121, 126; as political units, 2-3, 18-19, 35-36, 41-49, 63, 121, 142-43, 151-52, 154, 157-59, 169, 176, 179, 227n7. See also *People's Guide* counties

Defection, 16, 143, 145, 147, 159, 172, 184-89, 233n16
Democratic-liturgicals, 10
Democratic-ritualists, 10, 109
Depression, 7, 10, 16, 62-63, 67, 82, 120, 141, 143, 150. 166, 174-76, 180, 187
Directories. See *People's Guide* directories

Ecological problem, fallacy, 106, 182-84, 230n15
Education, 14, 149
Elections: dynamics of, 1-4, 10-12, 16, 18, 50, 62, 148-49, 177, 179; legal framework of, 11, 14-17, 33-35; institutional practices of, 14, 16; presidential versus congressional, 27, 31-32, 41-50, 142, 144, 148-50, 153, 155, 172-73, 179. See also Voting
Elite(s), 8-9, 17, 62, 220n14
English-, non-English-speaking, 101, 103-4, 113, 207-8
Ethnoreligious (ethnocultural) attachments, groups, identities, 5, 8-11, 17, 89, 91-92, 97, 107-10, 115-17, 161, 178, 228n2; aggregate measures of, 92-101, 161, 229n10; continuum of, 10-11, 91-92, 97, 108-10, 115-16, 178, 230n18

Europe(an), 90, 92, 97, 101, 103, 115, 126, 128, 166, 207

Farm laborers, 80-81, 129-30, 140
Farmers: as class conscious, 6-8, 16-17, 126, 175; organizations of, 5-7, 118-20; as political actors, 3, 5-9, 16-17, 83, 89, 104, 118-20, 123, 126-34, 138-41, 143, 173-80, 231n6; status of, 80-83
Far West, 7
"Floating" voters, 105, 147-50, 174-75, 229n12, 229n13
Foreign-born, 1, 27, 34, 46, 90, 92-105, 113-17, 121, 123, 126, 128-30, 135, 140, 161, 166, 168, 178, 190, 207-8

Gallup poll, 1
General Assembly, state, 34-36, 38
German, 10, 92, 97-98, 101, 103-5, 115, 121, 123, 161, 185
German Lutheran, 108, 115, 128, 130. See also Lutheran
German Roman Catholic, 128, 130. See also Catholic, Roman
Gini index, 73
Gordon, Milton, 73
Grange, 7, 120-21, 140, 187, 189
Granger, 1, 36, 58, 121
Grant, President U. S., 172, 184, 190
Greeley, Horace, 172, 184
Greenback, 1, 5, 9, 118, 120-21, 123-24, 126, 142, 150, 173-75

Harrington, Bates, 53-54
Harris, Joseph P., 15
Hays, Samuel, 9
Hendricks, Thomas A., 35
Hicks, John, 7-8

Illinois, 18, 24-25, 31, 53-54, 101
Independents, 1, 9, 12, 60, 76,

Index

84, 88, 104-7, 112, 115, 128-29, 131-32, 135, 138, 146-48, 150, 153-54, 173-74, 176, 187
Indiana Farmer, 119
Indianapolis, 2, 38-39, 49
Indianapolis Journal, 34
Information (communication), flow of, 104-5, 113, 115, 117, 128, 140-41, 149-50, 174-76, 178, 179, 233n11, 233n12
Involvement, political, 12, 14, 73, 75-76, 79, 90, 101-5, 111-13, 117, 143, 149-50, 174-79
Involvement, religious: aggregate measures of, 98, 124; individual measurement of, 110-12, 230n20; levels of, 112-17, 128, 133-34, 178
Iowa, 9, 24-25, 31, 53, 120
Irish, 10, 92, 97-98, 101, 103, 115, 128, 130, 161, 185, 207

Jackson, President Andrew, 19
Jacksonian period, 91
Jensen, Richard, 8-10, 12-13, 91, 108-9
Jewish, 108

Kabaker, Harvey M., 155
Kansas, 6, 24, 27-28
Kelly, Oliver H., 120
Kentucky, 18, 24, 28, 38, 101
Key, V. O., Jr., 12, 19, 157, 179
Kish, Leslie, 196, 203
Kleppner, Paul, 8-10, 12, 91, 108-9

Leaders, 3, 9, 18, 34, 36, 62-63, 142, 150
Liberal Republicans, 172, 184
Lorenz curve, 73-74
Lutheran, 97, 109, 116, 136, 161

Masonry, 120, 128
Massachusetts, 15

Mean, time-series, 20-27, 32, 41, 43, 45-46, 124, 155, 173
Merriam, Charles E., 59
Methodist, 97, 107, 135
Michigan, 18, 24-25, 31
Midwest, 6-9, 13, 24, 28, 36, 53, 91, 115-16, 177
Minnesota, 24-25, 53
Mississippi Valley, 6
Missouri, 24, 31
Model, 3, 22-23, 43-45, 143, 148, 170, 173, 181, 222n8, 232n3
Morton, Oliver P., 35

National Farmers' Alliance, 7
National Farmers' Alliance and Industrial Union, 7
National Greenback party, 7, 168, 187, 192
National Republican party, 19
Native-born, 1, 27, 90-105, 113-14, 117, 128-29, 178-79, 207
Nebraska, 6-7, 24, 27-28, 31
Negro, 35
New England, 53
New York, 38, 91
Normal vote, 144-66, 168-70, 179, 181, 184-85, 187-92, 233n13, 233n14. *See also* Party allegiance
North Carolina, 101

October elections, 31
Odd Fellows, 128
Ohio, 6, 18, 24-25, 27-28, 101

Parsons, Stanley, 7
Participation: citizen, civic, popular, 1, 12-13, 16-19, 27-31, 36, 124, 162, 166; aggregate effects of, 12-16, 124-26; legal conditions of, 32-35, 55, 224n1. *See also* Turnout
Partisanship: aggregate effects of, 5, 12-16, 43, 143-48, 156-68, 179; county levels of, 43-46, 63,

249

151, 154–57, 166, 223n12; measurement of, 43–49, 152, 157; structure of, 134–40. *See also* Party allegiance
Party allegiance, attachment, identification: aggregate effects of, 2–5, 11–14, 74, 143, 145–47, 152–57, 160, 168, 177 (*see also* Normal vote); dynamic features of, 11, 145–47, 173–77; individual reports of, 3–4, 19, 52–54, 56–58, 61, 144, 151–52, 156, 160, 177; meaning of, 11–12, 16, 19, 59–60; measurement of, 57–60, 121, 127, 140, 145, 152, 154, 226n20; scale, rates of, 76, 79, 81, 83, 87–88, 91, 107, 112–15, 129–34, 151–52; strength of, 59–60, 106, 127, 132, 140, 145; voting anchored in, 12, 143, 148–49, 172, 174–75. *See also* Partisanship
Patrons of Husbandry, 7, 120
Pearsonian correlation, 42, 168
Pennsylvania, 24, 27–28, 101
People's Guide counties, 2–3, 19, 36, 39–50, 64, 68–71, 92–101, 121, 124, 152–53, 155
People's Guide directories, 2–3, 51–56, 59–60, 64, 71, 86, 90, 107, 120, 127, 153
Polarization, 73, 75–79, 82, 84, 89, 91, 105–9, 112, 116, 118, 134, 178, 228n2
Population: coverage of, limits of, 2, 54–55, 193–209, 235n4; growth of, 39–40, 68, 123; voting age, adult, 2, 28, 32–33, 46, 54–56, 194–95
Populist, 5, 7, 9
Pratt, Daniel P., 36
Presbyterians, 109, 110, 116, 140
Prohibition, 9
Protestant(s), 1, 107–14, 116, 135–36, 140, 178

Quaker, 97, 109, 116, 135, 138

Republican-pietists, 10, 109
Railroads, 6, 38–39
Region(s): of birth, 105–7, 131; of Indiana, 36–41
Registration, 15–16, 34–35, 51, 54–55
Regular Baptist, 109
Residence, 86–89, 129, 135, 151
Robinson, W. S., 182
Rusk, Jerrold, 15

Sample: of counties, 4, 36, 41–50, 52, 54, 57, 68, 71, 92–116, 151–53, 155, 160, 168, 178 (see also *People's Guide* counties); of individuals, citizens, voters, 2–3, 17, 50, 52–57, 60, 104, 144, 151, 156, 177, 193–217; probability, random, 36, 52–56, 197–98, 200, 202–3, 211, 219n2, 236n4
Schumpeter, Joseph, 179
South, 6–7, 138
Status, occupational: domains of, classifications of, 64, 78–89, 177–78; measurement of, 80–81, 83, 109, 131–32, 206, 211, 228n16. *See also* Class
Stokes, Donald, 22
Suffrage, legal conditions of, 32–35, 55
Supreme Court, state, 35
Survey, 2, 11–14, 16, 51–56, 59, 97, 105, 144–45, 179, 190, 219n2
"Swing," partisan, 25, 144, 153, 181–82; definition of, 159

Tennessee, 24, 28
Third party, third parties, 5–6, 8–9, 19, 27, 57–59, 63, 76, 120–21, 126, 141–43, 150, 155, 159, 170, 172–73, 185, 187, 192; aggregate measure of strength of, 121–24
Thompson, Captain T. H., 53

Index

Thornbrough, Emma Lou, 8, 10
Tipton Till region, 46, 49, 71, 101, 159
Turnout: aggregate effects of, 5, 12, 124-26, 128, 146-48, 153, 155, 172-74, 185, 199, 222n6; low versus high conditions of, 31, 45-49, 124, 146-48, 153, 155, 166, 168, 173; measurement of, 12-14, 27-32, 45, 146-47, 162, 166, 170, 223n13, 232n17; rates of, levels of, 14, 16, 27-31, 46, 49, 118, 124, 128, 143, 148, 153, 155, 159, 162, 166, 168, 172-73. *See also* Participation

United Brethren, 109
U.S. Census, 193-94, 198, 200, 209

Virginia, 101

Voting: conditions of, 33-35; fraud, 16, 34-35, 221n35; secrecy of, 14-15, 34-35, 51. *See also* Elections; Participation

Washington, D.C., 31, 36
Wealth classes, strata, 62, 64, 73, 75-80, 88, 118; aggregate measures of, 64-71, 78, 82, 86, 88-89, 161; individual measures of, 71-78, 204, 227n13. *See also* Class
Weber, Max, 179
West, 18
Whigs, 19
Wisconsin, 24-25, 31, 53

Zingale, Nancy H., 155

3 6660 00115 8012

324.2 Hammarberg, M.
H224i The Indiana voter